D0810150

WORSHIPPING THE STATE

WORSHIPPING THE STATE

HOW LIBERALISM BECAME OUR STATE RELIGION

BENJAMIN WIKER, PH.D.

Since 1947
REGNERY
PUBLISHING, INC.
An Eagle Publishing Company • Washington, DC

Cataloging-in-Publication data on file with the Library of Congress
ISBN 978-1-62157-029-5

Published in the United States by
Regnery Publishing, Inc.
One Massachusetts Avenue NW
Washington, DC 20001
www.Regnery.com

Manufactured in the United States of America

10 9 8 7 6 5 4 3 2 1

Books are available in quantity for promotional or premium use. Write to Director of Special Sales, Regnery Publishing, Inc., One Massachusetts Avenue NW, Washington, DC 20001, for information on discounts and terms, or call (202) 216-0600.

Distributed to the trade by
Perseus Distribution
250 West 57th Street
New York, NY 10107

"*It is only by believing in God that we can ever criticise the Government. Once abolish…God, and the Government becomes the God. That fact is written all across human history…. The truth is that Irreligion is the opium of the people. Wherever the people do not believe in something beyond the world, they will worship the world. But, above all, they will worship the strongest thing in the world.*"
—**G. K. Chesterton**

CONTENTS

PART I

THE WAR ON CHRISTIANITY

CHAPTER 1

READING
THE SIGNS
OF OUR TIMES

The rotunda of the Wisconsin State Capitol building now hosts an unusual nativity scene during the holiday season. There's the familiar stable backdrop, but with an astronaut floating above in place of an angel and a baby girl in a manger in place of the infant Jesus. Instead of Mary and Joseph, the babe is flanked by Thomas Jefferson and the Roman fertility goddess Venus. Various wise persons also appear— Charles Darwin, Albert Einstein, Mark Twain, and anarchist heroine Emma Goldman.[1]

The manger scene isn't the only Christian symbol that is being repurposed in America today. Language that used to be reserved exclusively for Jesus Christ is now applied in a very different context. "First of all," said actor Jamie Foxx at the 2012 Soul Train Music Awards, "give an honor to God and our lord and savior Barack Obama."[2] Similar things have been said about the president before. Who can forget Chris Matthews's giddy "This is the New Testament....I feel this thrill going up my leg," or Ezra Klein's "He is not the Word made flesh, but the triumph of word over flesh, over color, over despair." And then there's *The Gospel According to Apostle Barack* by Barbara Thompson.

It's bad enough that Christian language and symbols are being taken over for new and startlingly different purposes. But Christian institutions are under threat as well. The Department of Health and Human Services has announced that even religious employers are now required to provide health insurance that covers contraception, sterilization, and abortifacient pills. So Catholic hospitals will have to provide contraception for their employees, and Evangelical colleges will have to pay for abortion pills. In other words, Catholics and Evangelical Christians now have to run their institutions according to a radically different moral view from their own, a morality imposed on them by the secular state—or get out of the business of running schools and hospitals altogether.

There are all too many signs in our times that there is a fierce battle being waged over who will be in control in America. Consider the legal conflicts over crèche scenes and displays of the Ten Commandments, the aggressive evangelization of public school children for the sexual liberationist agenda (under cover of promoting their "reproductive health" and safety from bullying), and the unprecedented usurpation of the authority of religious institutions to set their own policies even on questions of religious doctrine. It's not just a "war on Christmas," that we're seeing play out in America today. It's a war on Christianity.

Christianity is being deliberately pushed out of our culture—so that secular liberalism can be established in its place.

I use the term "establish" quite deliberately. One religion is being actively disestablished, while another is being (in fact, largely has been) established in its place.

But is liberalism really a religion? When the Freedom from Religion Foundation crows about placing that anti-nativity scene in the Wisconsin rotunda, they're clearly attacking Christians, who, according to the FFRF's co-president Dan Barker, think "they own the month of December. We don't agree. No month is free from pagan reverie!" Barker and his allies are not just removing Christianity from the public square; they're actively promoting secularism as its replacement. As it says on the plaque in the Capitol, "At this season of the Winter Solstice, may reason prevail. There are no gods, no devils, no angels, no heaven or hell. There is only our natural world. Religion is but myth and superstition that hardens hearts and enslaves minds."[3] But in what sense is that worldview an actual religion in competition with Christianity?

The Messiah of Liberalism?

There is a clue in the messianic enthusiasm of the language so frequently applied to our president. Barack Obama is the quintessential liberal politician, and apparently he seems a lot like the Messiah to a large number of people. (Possibly even to himself, if we go by the "this was the moment when the rise of the oceans began to slow and the planet began to heal" speech.)

Religious zeal for Obama is so remarkable that several collections of quotations celebrating his alleged Messiah-like qualities appear on the internet.[4] Here's a short sampler (if the reader can bear it).

According to Lawrence Carter, "No one saw him coming, and Christians believe God comes at us from strange angles and places we don't expect, like Jesus being born in a manger."

Mark Morford opined, "Barack Obama isn't really one of us. Not in the normal way, anyway.... Many spiritually advanced people I know (not coweringly religious, mind you, but deeply spiritual) identify Obama as a Lightworker, that rare kind of attuned being who has the ability to lead us not merely to new foreign policies or health care plans or whatnot, but who can actually help usher in *a new way of being on the planet*, of relating and connecting and engaging with this bizarre earthly experiment. These kinds of people actually help us *evolve*. They are philosophers and peacemakers of a very high order, and they speak not just to reason or emotion, but to the soul."

Louis Farrakhan told Nation of Islam devotees, "You are the instruments that God is going to use to bring about universal change, and that is why

Barack has captured the youth. And he has involved young people in a political process that they didn't care anything about. That's a sign. When the Messiah speaks, the youth will hear, and the Messiah is absolutely speaking."[5]

But President Obama isn't the real problem (much less the real Messiah). If he were the only motive force behind the liberal attempt to disestablish and replace Christianity, then those of us who don't want to worship the state would be facing only one powerful man.

The truth is that secular liberalism is a political religion, one that is much, much older than Barack Obama. As we shall see, the push to replace Christianity with a secular liberal religion has already been going on for literally half a millennium. Liberals' outpouring of religious zeal for the president is simply a sign that their five-hundred-year-old ambition to displace Christianity is finally coming to fruition in America.

While Barack Obama is not *the* problem, the messianism that marks his political career is instructive. As we'll see, the kind of religious zealotry that we've recently experienced in American politics has been characteristic of political religions associated with liberalism stretching all the way back to the French Revolution's Religion of Reason. The stream flows through various liberal political movements in the nineteenth century into positivism's Religion of Humanity and humanism, and drains into early twentieth-century Progressivism, to which Obama rightly claims to be heir. Liberal secularism has already become a state religion more than once in world history, and the current attempt to make it our state religion is in complete continuity with that history. All during that long history, it has been at war with the Christianity that its adherents so passionately want to displace.

The Atheists' Frontal Assault

Our contemporary battles are part of that long war. The attacks on Christianity always seem to flare up at Christmas—which, after all, celebrates the very beginning of Christianity.

We've seen the Freedom from Religion Foundation celebrating the placement of an anti-nativity scene at the Wisconsin Capitol. Let's take a close look at other battles that have been fought (and won) by the FFRF. Over the past few years Santa Monica, California, has been the scene for the now all too familiar Christmas battle between those who want to put up a nativity scene and those who most zealously do not want to see Mary and Joseph in a stable looking adoringly at the Christ child in a manger.

For sixty years Santa Monica had the tradition of setting up a series of life-size scenes in Palisades Park depicting key biblical moments such as the Annunciation and the Nativity of Christ.[6] They were not built by the city, but sponsored and built by various local businesses and associations.

Given the limited number of display booths and the large number of businesses and associations vying for the honor of constructing the scenes, the city had a lottery system. FFRF's strategy was to enter the lottery and win the right to display—only they chose to display *anti*-Christian messages. In 2011, the atheists won eighteen of the twenty-one places. So viewers working their way along from booth to booth would come to one with, for example, a sign quoting Thomas Jefferson, "Religions are all alike—founded on fables and mythology," and on the reverse, "Happy Solstice."[7]

Santa Monica has stopped the displays because they couldn't figure out a way to keep the FFRF from entering the lottery without contravening the Supreme Court's reading of the Establishment Clause of the First Amendment. The displays are moving to private turf. (One wonders how long it will be before the FFRF attempts to force Santa Monica itself to change its so-obviously Christian name.)

The Freedom from Religion Foundation is now suing the U.S. Forest Service to have a World War II memorial on a Montana mountain removed—a large statue of Jesus, hands outstretched. The FFRF's reasoning is worth noting: "The U.S. Forest Service has unlawfully misused federal land owned by all of us to further Christianity in general, and Roman Catholicism in particular. This diminishes the civil and political standing

of nonreligious and non-Christian Americans, and shows flagrant governmental preference for religion and Christianity."[8] The Foundation has
already forced Sylvania, Alabama, to remove a Bible verse from its welcome
sign.[9]

And it's not just the FFRF and the well-known ACLU on the assault.
There are plenty of other militantly secularist organizations pitching in to
strip Christianity from every public space. The Military Association of
Atheists and Freethinkers (MAAF) is getting Gideon Bibles out of lodgings
on military bases.[10] The California branch of the American Atheists successfully compelled the Oakland Zoo to remove a Ten Commandments
monument.[11] The ever vigilant Arkansas Society of Freethinkers stepped
in to quash an elementary school field trip to see *A Charlie Brown Christmas*
staged at a nearby church. Quoth Anne Orsi of the ASF, "The problem is
that it's got religious content and it's being performed in a religious venue
and that doesn't just blur the line between church and state—it oversteps
it entirely."[12] Apparently free thinking doesn't include the freedom to think
about the Christmas passage from the Gospel of Luke, as quoted by Linus.

Speaking of nixing classics, a Davis, California, high school recently
brought the axe down on that great—and almost entirely secular—classic,
Charles Dickens's *A Christmas Carol*. The convoluted reasons given by the
administration were as follows: "the overly impacted December schedule,
which led to the original performance dates falling on Hanukkah, concerns
about the inclusiveness of material, and the desire of the district to respect
the cultures of everyone. Another point that was discussed was the power
of words and the impact they can have."[13] That certainly clears things up.

In Tecumbia, Alabama, last year, a primary school was asked that "Silent
Night" be given the boot from their annual Christmas pageant.[14] In a Stockton, California, elementary school, teachers and students were informed
that they couldn't display Santas, Christmas trees, and even poinsettia
plants. A school memo explained that snowflakes and snowmen were
"safe."[15] In 2007 New York City schools were allowed to use the Jewish

menorah and the Muslim star and crescent in the "holiday" displays, but not a Christian nativity scene.[16]

The examples could fill a book. And Christianity isn't being stripped just from public property. Banks yank Christmas trees that might offend customers; employees of mega-stores are told that they may not utter "Merry Christmas."

The Pretense of Neutrality

Are all traces of Christianity being successively and successfully removed from the public sphere so as to leave an empty space, a neutral public square where people of all religions and none can be equally at home? That's the impression you'd get from the decisions that okay menorahs and Muslim crescents, and from the FFRF's language about how the Montana World War II memorial "further[s] Christianity in general, and Roman Catholicism in particular."

It sounds as if the FFRF is concerned about protecting non-Christians, but its real goal is to remove religion as such and replace it with a kind of humanist paganism. Apparent neutrality is a key secular strategy in the war: pose as a protector of other religions against Christianity, and under that pretense use the courts to drive all religion out of the public square so that something else can be put in its place. Secular liberalism is well on its way to establishment as our state religion.

The anti-nativity scene in Wisconsin captures exactly what is going on. It's not just a direct and obvious attack on Christianity, but an attempt to *put something else in its place.* That's what liberal secularists want to do not just with the Wisconsin Capitol rotunda, but with our whole culture. They want to claim the very heart of our culture for their own humanist religion, something FFRF's Dan Barker rightly defined as a new kind of paganism.

It isn't just about removing Christianity from the public square, so as to be fair to everyone who's not Christian. It's really, at heart, a revolution to establish secular liberalism as the defining worldview for our whole society. As we look more and more deeply into what this worldview really is, we'll find ourselves exploring a revived and transformed form of paganism, one that bears more than a little resemblance to what the earliest Christians encountered in the pagan world into which Christ himself was born, the pagan world that tried to destroy Christians as enemies of the state. The war on Christmas has been going on longer than we thought—almost two thousand years. And Christians soon will be enemies of the secular state once again, if the aggressive secularizers achieve the final victory.

The Larger Religious War

The reality of the war on Christianity is easily seen in the direct assault on Christianity by the various atheist (or even explicitly pagan) organizations.

Taking down Ten Commandment plaques, removing religious statues, prohibiting prayers at graduation, eliminating Bible reading in school, denying funding for religious school students even for transportation and other secular purposes—all of this is a now familiar, and has been for some time, running all the way back to the landmark 1947 Supreme Court case, the famous or infamous *Everson v. Board of Education*, in which Justice Hugo Black read Jefferson's "separation of church and state" into the Establishment Clause of the First Amendment. Since *Everson*, the federal government (or secular liberal groups using the federal government) has been bent on driving Christianity out of the public square.

Everson v. Board of Education was followed by a host of judicial decisions that, one after another, allowed the state to remove Christian symbols and practices from public view. In *Engel v. Vitale* (1962) the court decided that a short mandatory daily prayer in public schools violated the Establishment Clause. In *Abington Township School District v. Schempp* (1963), Bible reading in public schools was deemed a violation of the Establishment Clause. In *Lemon v. Kurtzman* (1971) the court declared that public school districts could not reimburse the salaries of private religious school teachers who taught secular material. In *Wallace v. Jaffree* (1985) the court declared that public schools could not even observe a moment of silence. In *County of Allegheny v. ACLU* (1989) the Supreme Court declared that having a nativity scene at the county court house violated the Establishment Clause. In *Lee v. Weisman* (1992) the court declared that no prayers were allowed at public school graduations. In 2003 a federal court declared in *Glassroth v. Moore* that a display of the Ten Commandments in the Alabama state judicial building violated the Establishment Clause, and the Supreme Court declined to hear the case, thereby affirming the decision. And in two separate cases in 2005—*Van Orden v. Perry* and *McCreary County v. ACLU of Kentucky*—the Supreme Court ruled that the Ten Commandments were allowed at the Texas state capitol because there they somehow fit into an overall "secular purpose," but then ruled that they were not allowed in several Kentucky courthouses because in that case they somehow didn't. Meanwhile, state power protects and promotes anti-Christian speech and art—such as the infamous crucifix in urine that won an art award partially funded through the National Endowment for the Arts.

With *Everson* as a precedent, the federal government has acted as an instrument of secularization, that is, of disestablishing Christianity from American culture, *and establishing in its place a different worldview.* That rival worldview is actually a religion in its own right, one that would ideally occupy all the same territory as Christianity, and so inevitably comes into conflict with it. That worldview has a number of names: secular liberalism, liberal secularism, atheism, humanism, and so forth. We've already seen that some secularists openly embrace a return to paganism.

And as we look more closely at the history of this worldview, going back many centuries before *Everson*, we will see that the "Religion of Humanity" (to quote Auguste Comte, one of its founders and most ardent proponents) has at its heart the worship of other things besides God—of nature, of ourselves, of the state. Thus liberalism is more than a political persuasion. It's a religion with its own doctrines about cosmology and morality.

I am aware that this is a controversial claim; it will take the bulk of this book to prove it. But here I'd like to point to some compelling evidence that the secular liberalism that is and has been for some time in the ascendant in the United States today really is bent on replacing Christianity with its own competing beliefs.

The religious nature of liberalism is obscured by liberals' ostensible embrace of neutrality, pluralism, and tolerance. These are the reasons given for the disestablishment of Christianity. But what actually occurs is that "neutrality, pluralism, and tolerance" are inevitably used as instruments for establishing liberal doctrines and dogmas in the place of Christian ones. In no area is this clearer than in regard to morality.

Imposing Secularist Morality

Let's take a closer look at the HHS mandate that insurance cover contraceptives and abortifacient pills. That mandate is contained in regulations that HHS Secretary Kathleen Sebelius issued as part of the implementation of the Patient Protection and Affordable Care Act, more commonly known as Obamacare.

President Obama pushed that act through Congress in his first term with true messianic zeal (and more than casual disregard for legislative procedure). The Obamacare law gave the federal government power to define "health." And for liberalism, "health" includes being able to have sex without consequences, and hence being able to get contraceptives and, in case they fail, backup emergency contraception—in other words, abortifacients.

So according to the HHS mandate, effective August 1, 2012, employers *must* provide contraception, abortifacients, and sterilization as part of their insurance packages, or face the wrath of the federal government. The main target of the HHS mandate was the Catholic Church, which rejects contraception, abortion, and sterilization. The U.S. Catholic bishops reacted with surprising vigor, protesting the move, offering their own legal counteroffensive, and vowing to go to jail rather than allow the government to force them to violate Catholic moral doctrine. Evangelical Christian institutions have sued the administration as well. We are still waiting to learn from the courts whether the mandate will survive constitutional scrutiny.

But note what this bold-as-brass move by the Obama administration is really attempting. Liberals embrace sexual liberation—that is, liberation from shame and guilt, and ultimately from Christian moral doctrines about sexuality. At first, this liberation was sold as "choice." You've seen the T-shirt: "Against abortion? Don't have one." The selling point was that women were being freed from the tyranny of Christians imposing their morality on everyone else through laws against abortion. Everyone would be free to choose according to her own personal morality. But the pretense of neutrality was just that—a pretense. As soon as a "pro-choice" administration acquired the power to do so, it imposed *its own morality* on everyone, requiring even Christian institutions to pay for abortion-inducing pills. The liberal state is requiring that Christians obey liberal moral doctrines, even though that means they must violate their own moral doctrines. Nothing could more clearly illustrate the clash between one set of beliefs and another.

If the HHS mandate is not overturned by the courts, the fines for defying it will push Christian schools and hospitals into bankruptcy. President Obama seems set to drive religious institutions out of business simply for dissenting from his own liberal morality. And to repeat an important point, his administration seems to be undertaking the propagation of that liberal morality with messianic zeal.

Avoiding the *Reductio ad Hitlerum*

Still, as secular religion goes—and especially as it went in the last century—things could be much, much worse. (Or, less optimistically, they could still get much, much worse.) Our modern world has been plagued by what have rightly been called "political religions."[17] We saw appalling examples of state-worship in the last century, with regimes that bent their people's natural religious impulses entirely to political ends. Nazi Germany comes to mind as the most horrific example, with National Socialism becoming the state religion, demanding absolute devotion, and driving the German people to commit unfathomably wicked crimes in obedience to the peculiar Nazi morality.

Barack Obama is no Hitler. He doesn't even come close. But that doesn't mean that we don't have to worry about political religion here in the United States. As we'll see in the chapters ahead, secular religion has taken many forms over the past centuries. And there's plenty of room for things in twenty-first-century America to get pretty bad, without approaching anywhere near to 1930s Germany. The case of Nazi Germany is both too easy to judge and too far removed from us in place and time to be really useful in understanding the problem we face today. We need to avoid what the political philosopher Leo Strauss called the *reductio ad Hitlerum*, the tendency to make Hitler both the standard and sum of evil[18]—with the implication that anything that doesn't obviously parallel or threaten to lead to something done by the Third Reich must not be all that bad.

So we're not going to be looking primarily at Nazi Germany, or Soviet Russia, or even Revolutionary France. Nor will I engage in tiresome name-calling—abused by those on both Left and Right—and declare that liberals are Nazis. Our goal is to look at our own situation, more broadly at modern liberalism, and more particularly at how the liberalism we experience here and now has itself become our political religion.

Going beyond Our Political Debates

This goes beyond party politics, Democrats vs. Republicans. Of course, radical liberalism is more obviously associated with the Left, and insofar as the Left has a firm hold on the Democratic Party, the Democrats will seem to be more to blame for wanting to make liberalism a kind of state religion. Since the Left is prone to be unreligious, if not irreligious, and is also fond of using big government to carry out its big visions, it isn't much of a stretch to accuse liberals in the Democratic Party of substituting an ideology for religion and using state power to establish it with a zeal that can only be called, well, religious.

But if we stay on that level of analysis, then we'll never dig down very deep. We'll never really see how liberalism is becoming, or has in fact already become, our state religion. Liberalism is much older than we think, and is far more deeply entrenched in our institutions, our way of thinking, our words, our very souls. On different levels, and in different ways, it defines both Democrats and Republicans, because to some extent it defines the mindset of nearly everyone today.

That's why winning or losing an election or two won't make a real difference—something that many frustrated citizens show they realize when they mutter, disconsolately, that there's not a dime's worth of difference between Democrats and Republicans. It was this feeling of frustration that kept many voters at home in 2012 and allowed Obama to be reelected, this time without nearly as much enthusiasm even among his previously zealous supporters.

There may in fact be a dime's worth of difference between the two political parties, but a dime is not all that much. Beneath the surface there are deep similarities of outlook and shared opinions arising from liberalism that shape the general visions of *both* parties. Secular liberalism is that deeply ingrained in our contemporary culture. It permeates our society, our assumptions, our educational institutions, our language, our law, our notions of justice—in short, it shares all the same comprehensive space and depth that Christianity had once achieved in Christendom.

But What *Is* Liberalism?

And that brings us to the definition of liberalism itself, because just what is meant by that term is not obvious, given the number of competing definitions and viewpoints.

Modern liberalism is a movement in politics and philosophy that cannot be given a fixed definition apart from the long history of its development. But we can say that the liberals in ascendancy in America today are the intellectual heirs of a way of thinking that from the beginning has been characterized by a desire to be *free from* the burden of Christianity. (*Liber* in Latin means free.) Anti-Christian liberalism is much older than the ACLU and the Freedom from Religion Foundation. It arose about five hundred years ago within an almost entirely Christianized culture. As a rebellion against Christianity, its negative goal defined its positive form: *the desire to remove the church and replace it with the state gave liberalism its structure, beliefs, and goals.*[19] Freedom from Christianity defines the political goal of liberalism. As the liberal state takes over the form and functions of the church, it excludes the actual Christian church from having any presence or influence in the public square.[20] In its most virulent forms it actually persecutes Christians, as if Christianity were a kind of heresy deviating from the liberal religion.

The term "liberal," of course, has been applied to those who aimed at other freedoms—freedom from the power of kings, or from governmental controls, especially of the economy—the view that has been called "classical liberalism."[21] How this notion of liberalism is or is not connected to liberalism as we understand it today is a complex and ambiguous topic, one that we'll address in some detail at the proper place below.

But at this point, for the purposes of beginning our investigation, I want to focus on the kind of liberalism that we know and readily recognize today: antagonistic to Christianity; pushing against every moral boundary defined by the Judeo-Christian tradition; championing freedom from every sexual limit, freedom from any notion of moral propriety, freedom to define marriage at one's whim, freedom to manipulate human reproduction and the human genome, freedom to be obscene and vulgar, freedom from work and moral responsibility, freedom from the past. A typical example would be the Los Angeles school district pushing a pro-LGBT education agenda—under the guise of fighting bullying—that insists the Christian rejection of homosexuality is evil.[22]

Liberals complain about Christians' indoctrination of children with rigid dogmas, but one can't help noticing that liberalism itself is as dogmatic as any religion. Liberals are quite as impatient of dissent as any religious fanatics—and as passionate about indoctrinating young people. And this is nowhere more obvious than in our universities. As we'll see, the takeover of universities has been essential to the cultural victory of liberalism over Christianity, going back at least to the nineteenth century. And today liberalism in its purest and most radical form is found on college and university campuses, where its religious zeal has the greatest scope. As we'll see, the takeover of American universities by secular liberals was central to the historical ascendancy of liberalism in America. But there's also another reason to take a close look at the signs of the times in higher education: we'll get a glimpse of the future. At our college and university campuses, we see what liberalism would do in our larger society if it ever gained complete political power. It's a frightening prospect.

Indoctrination U

In the campus regime of "political correctness," dissenting opinions are simply quashed. All dissent is characterized as a sign of the various evils—racism, patriarchy, religious intolerance, and so forth—from which liberalism supposedly delivers us. On politically correct college campuses, as in Marxist countries, disagreement with the party line is only confirmation that one is irredeemably among the damned.

I saw this firsthand during my graduate school experience earning my Ph.D. at Vanderbilt University. Even mild disagreement with the liberal party line was met with hysterical accusations and verbal attacks. Not arguments, mind you. I was informed by one well-indoctrinated young woman that rationality and logic were instruments of male domination, and that she would have no part of them. She was good to her vow, as were her mentors. It was very clear what one was allowed and not allowed to say, and which moral and political positions were considered clean and unclean, and the unclean were not permitted to speak.

My experience was not unusual. The combination of liberal dogmatism backed up by institutional authority is the rule, not the exception, in academia. And in fact, it has gotten far worse, both on the graduate and even more on the undergraduate level, since I was in school. Today incoming students routinely undergo intensive indoctrination during freshman orientation week, and it continues for the rest of the year, administered in regular doses by heavy-handed propagandists in the administration, on the faculty, and by converted students (especially the RAs who oversee dorm life).

Freshman orientation has become a gate of entry through which only the doctrinally clean can pass safely. The goal of such "orientation" is quite literally "thought reform," as Greg Lukianoff, the author of *Unlearning Liberty*, reports in depressing detail.[23] Pardon me for depressing you with some of that detail.

At the University of Delaware the Office of Residence Life imposed a speech code forbidding "any instance that is perceived by those involved as being racist, sexist, anti-Semitic, homophobic, or otherwise oppressive." Note: it's clear that Christians were *not* among those whom it was a violation to offend. Christians were the ones being implicitly charged with sexism, anti-Semitism, and homophobia. As Lukianoff points out, the goal of the orientation program in which students were indoctrinated into the world-view behind the speech code was "the interior transformation of the beliefs of all seven thousand students in the University of Delaware dormitories on issues as varied as moral philosophy, environmentalism, tolerance, human rights, and social policy, to make those beliefs conform to a specific political agenda." In one of the many excesses of the orientation program, students were forced to engage in a little "exercise," in which they had to "stand along one wall if they supported various social causes, including the right to gay marriage or abortion, and along the other wall if they didn't." Quite obviously this exercise "functioned as a state-sponsored public sham-ing of students with the 'wrong' beliefs."[24] If a Christian dared to say that she opposes gay marriage, she would most definitely be "perceived" as "homophobic" and therefore "oppressive." It would be a violation of the speech code, and sanctions would begin. While the University of Delaware speech code has been modified, Delaware's program has become a model for similar programs at other schools.

Interestingly enough, Lukianoff is a self-declared liberal and atheist, but one who believes in free speech and works tirelessly for it through his Foundation for Individual Rights in Education (FIRE). "If you told me twelve years ago," Lukianoff confides, "that I, a liberal atheist, would devote a sizeable portion of my career to defending Christian groups, I might have been surprised. But almost from my first day at FIRE, I was shocked to realize how badly Christian groups were often treated."[25] On campuses across the nation, persecution is directed at Christians by liberals intent upon imposing uniformity in the name of diversity, complete intolerance in the name of tolerance, liberal absolutism in the name of relativism— and all this with identifiably religious zeal in inculcating liberal beliefs as orthodoxy.

Another popular exercise during campus orientations is to put fresh-persons through "The Tunnel of Oppression," where in a succession of rooms off a main hallway (the tunnel) new students are made to witness mini-dramas meant to cleanse them of the sins of their heterodox views (for example, one skit shows how religious parents hate gay offspring; another, how white people think black women are welfare queens).[26] These displays function as the *exact* equivalent of the above-mentioned nativity scenes at Santa Monica, or for Catholics, the Stations of the Cross. They are dramatic instruments meant to instill a particular religious worldview in those who view them.

The totalitarian manipulations in George Orwell's *1984* come to mind. College bureaucrats are in the forefront of imposing liberalism on campus, as the case of the Association for Student Conduct Administration (ASCA), the lead umbrella group for academic administrators overseeing discipline, demonstrates. ASCA has devised a model program that allows the meddlers from above to persecute infractions that were not previously punishable under university regulations. A student accused of some vaguely defined offense must sit one-on-one with an administrator for four sessions in order to learn to "take accountability" for what he's done. The student must write down what he thinks he's done, but the administrator won't accept the student's account until he gets it "right." The student must draft and redraft his confession until his will is broken and he admits the offense as defined by the administrator. The student, by the way, has to pay for the privilege of these four sessions of humiliation.

Lukianoff exactly captures the spirit of ASCA's model program. "Like the famous scene in *1984* in which Winston is forced to say he sees five fingers when his interrogator is holding up four, you would complete the program only when you described your behavior using the exact (strained and strange) language the program wanted you to use."[27]

The fact that we are dealing with two rival belief systems is evident from the way these liberal orientation programs clash so frequently with Christianity. The same pattern holds in the classroom as well. One Emily Brooker, an Evangelical Christian, was given a mandatory assignment in class in her freshman year at Missouri State University: go out in public and display homosexual behavior, and then write a paper about the experience. In her senior year she was required by a professor, as a class assignment, to write to the state legislature, advocating adoption for gay foster parents. She was subjected to a closed two-and-a-half-hour interrogation by seven professors when she was deemed irredeemably Christian.[28]

University-administered and -approved programs and events are skewed against Christians and Christianity; they promote the liberal religion instead. At a Florida community college the Christian Student Fellowship was banned from showing *The Passion of the Christ* (allegedly because of its R rating), even while the administration smiled upon a production on campus that included a skit with a title too blasphemous for me to include in this book, in which the most solitary of sexual acts (to put it as delicately as I can) was aimed at an image of Jesus. Resident Assistants at the University of Wisconsin were barred from holding private Bible studies in their own rooms, even while other RAs were applauded for putting on the infamously vulgar *Vagina Monologues*. The Christian Legal Association was banned from the University of California and at Vanderbilt, and Christian sororities and fraternities are no longer allowed at San Diego State University.[29]

So on college campuses, where liberalism is most unconstrained, it certainly acts like a religion—specifically, a religion in fierce competition with Christianity for students' hearts and minds. Thus the hostility of campus liberals seems to be aimed directly at Christianity itself, rather than religion in general. Lukianoff has noticed this strange truth: the politically correct are intolerant of anti-Semitism; they are curiously affirmative of Islam; but they are decidedly anti-Christian.[30] They go out of their way not to offend Jews and Muslims. And they go out of their way to offend Christians.

The Return of Paganism and the Worship of the State

There is a deep reason for this specifically anti-Christian antagonism. As we'll be exploring in much more depth in the chapters to follow, liberalism actually defines itself *against* Christianity. That makes the prospect of the ultimate triumph of liberal secularism of great concern to Christians— myself among them. But I hope that readers of other faiths will understand very clearly by the end of this book that they also stand to lose if liberalism is fully established as our state religion. For now, liberals tend to affirm other religions so as to reduce Christianity's hold on the culture, but that will continue only as long as these religions are useful to liberalism, and only insofar as these other religions do not transgress liberalism's creed. When any of these non-Christian religions dares to assert the integrity of its own beliefs on its own terms, it will be brushed aside. So this isn't just a Christian fight.

Yet, it *is* a Christian fight in another, important sense, precisely because liberalism, from its earliest beginnings hundreds of years ago, has defined itself in opposition to Christianity.

So we cannot even understand liberalism until we understand some important things about Christianity. And all of us who don't want to live under a secular liberal regime imposed as a religion—whether we're Christians, Jews, Muslims, or unbelievers like Greg Lukianoff—urgently need to understand liberalism before it is fully and irrevocably established in our culture and our country

The key clues to a real understanding of our current situation lie, in large part, in the history of relations between church and state. Unlike liberalism, Christianity does not aim at the fusion of church and political power. Though it may come as a surprise to readers, the church actually invented the distinction between church and state in the Christian Middle Ages. Outside Christendom (and even in the West before the church hammered out the distinction), political and religious power were fused, as for example in pagan Rome, where the emperor was considered divine. The church rejected this fusion, pulled religion and government apart, and made them distinct in both form and function, thereby giving to the world a great gift.

But modern politics is characterized by nation-states attempting to absorb the powers of the church again, so that they can use religion as an instrument of their political ends. Hence such horrific "political religions" as Nazism and Fascism. But hence also liberalism. All three involve a return to the status quo in pagan societies, where religion was entirely subordinate to the state. In arguing that we need to disestablish liberalism as our state religion, I am not asserting that we need to have a fusion of Christianity and the state, but in fact quite the opposite—for the good of both the state and the church. We need to turn away from the pagan fusion of political and religious power and return to the original Christian arrangement, where there is a real distinction between religious and political power and each has its own defined role.

That brings us to one final point. As we shall see, liberalism began as a return to pagan thought, and an attempt to use pagan thought to dislodge the church from its prominent position. In this, it attempted to reverse history. The church was born amidst the pagan world, and overcame paganism by conversion, thereby creating a Christianized world. In overcoming the pagan world, it threw out what it considered either evil or unsalvageable and offered qualified acceptance of what it found to be salvageable. The founders of liberalism believed that Christianity was a huge historical mistake, and therefore they reached back again to the pagans for help in loosening the Christian hold on the world, and quite often adopted precisely those things in paganism that Christianity had rejected.

That is why the morality of liberalism so greatly resembles that of the pagan world. In a very real sense, liberalism has achieved what it originally sought to do: return the world to paganism. As we'll see in the next chapter, the fact that liberalism is a kind of return to ancient paganism shows itself most clearly in the rejection of Christian morality and the embrace of the old pagan this-worldly hedonism.

Liberalism at its very essence is the return to this world as the highest good, the embrace of the natural and the rejection of the supernatural. Consequently it is a shedding of the moral seriousness that Christianity had imposed by its embrace of the cross, and a return to the far less morally demanding world of ancient paganism.

But liberalism is a *new* kind of paganism. That we must keep firmly in mind. It is one thing to have a kind of innocent embrace of this world *before* one has heard of Christianity; it is quite another to reject life in the next world as defined by Christianity, and everything in this world that might lead to it.

Liberalism rejected the good things in paganism that Christianity had baptized. They had become too closely associated with the Christian worldview. And it embraced everything in paganism that Christianity had rejected—the crass materialism, the cynicism, the nihilism and fatalism, the hedonism.

The presence of these things in our contemporary culture—and their association especially with radical liberalism—is no accident of history. They were all right there at the beginning of liberalism, a half-millennium ago.

But to understand all this, we must go back even further, to the very beginning of Christianity itself, and see how much the ancient pagan moral world resembles our own, the world formed by modern liberalism. That will allow us to see that our present state of degradation has resulted not just from the rejection of Christianity, but also from the reassertion of paganism—and this includes the pagan subordination of religion to the state. The situation of the first Christians will look distressingly familiar to us.

We're in serious crisis. But we won't even be able to see the real danger, much less defend against it effectively, unless we have a thorough understanding of what's actually going on. This book is intended to set us on a path to disestablishing liberalism as our state religion. That will take a lot of work, and we must be thoroughly prepared intellectually (and spiritually). The liberal assault on religion is much older and much deeper than we assume.

PART II

CHRISTIANITY
DESTROYS THE
PAGAN IDOL
OF THE STATE

CHAPTER 2

—

BACK TO THE BEGINNING: THE CHURCH VERSUS PAGAN IMPERIAL ROME

Taking down crucifixes and crosses, forbidding Bible reading and prayer in public schools, removing nativity scenes from public squares, prohibiting Christian organizations from meeting on public property while smiling upon degraded anti-Christian art as "freedom of speech" and even supporting it with federal funding, requiring Christian employers to violate their consciences and pay for abortion-inducing pills—it all adds up to conclusive evidence of extraordinary (and extraordinarily effective) hostility directed by the liberal state against the Christian church. The liberal campaign to remove Christianity from its place at the center of our culture has been quite successful.

But to understand the enmity behind that successful campaign, we need to go back two thousand years.

Government hostility to the church isn't new. It's as old as the church itself. The Roman Empire, the state into which the Christian religion was born, was the first state that tried to snuff Christianity out. The situation

of the church today strangely resembles its original situation. That's the
important parallel we'll be exploring in this chapter.

Render unto Caesar

We all know about the famous "Render unto Caesar" episode recorded
in the Gospels of Matthew (22:15–22), Mark (12:13–17), and Luke (20:20–
26).[1] The Pharisees ask Jesus whether they should pay taxes to Caesar. Jesus
bids them to show him a coin and tell him whose likeness and inscription
are on it, to which they answer "Caesar's." And Jesus replies, "Render therefore to Caesar the things that are Caesar's, and to God the things that are
God's" (Matthew 22:21).

It would seem, taking this passage in isolation, that there was a nascent
distinction between the church and the state already present in the very
earliest Christianity. The things of God are different from the things of
Caesar. Because money is one of the things that belong to Caesar, Christians
should pay taxes.

St. Paul would seem to affirm and extend this distinction by emphasizing civil obedience: "Let every person be subject to the governing authorities," he tells the Roman Christians. "For there is no authority except from
God, and those that exist have been instituted by God. Therefore he who
resists the authorities resists what God has appointed, and those who resist
will incur judgment. For rulers are not a terror to good conduct, but to bad"
(Romans 13:1–3).

Simple enough—only things weren't that simple. At the time when Jesus
spoke the words "Render unto Caesar," the Roman emperor was Tiberius.
Roman emperors since Augustus, who reigned at the time of Christ's birth,
had been considered divine. Tiberius certainly made that claim, and he
made it good through the force of imperial law and imperial propaganda.

One of the great sources of propaganda was coinage.[2] The silver denarius of Tiberius would most likely have been the coin handed to Jesus when
he was asked by the Pharisees whether they should pay taxes to Caesar. Each
emperor liked to strike his own coins. Tiberius's denarius bore the inscription

TI CAESAR DIVI AVG F AVGVSTVS, "Caesar Augustus Tiberius, Son of the Divine Augustus." The "son" of the divinized Augustus was also divine (even though he was actually a step-son of Augustus rather than his natural-born divine offspring).

The reverse of the coin had PONTIF MAXIM for *Pontifex Maximus*, identifying the Roman emperor as high priest of Rome's pagan religion. Imperial and religious power were fused in one man, who was both priest and emperor.

The maintenance of Roman religion had been seen as vital to the well-being of the Roman Republic, and that religion, with the addition of the worship of the emperor, was seen as essential to the health of the empire as well. The most distinguished Romans were appointed by the emperor to the priesthood. Not because of their personal belief, mind you. Many if not most were quite skeptical of the Roman gods, and certainly by the time of the empire none of the prestigious augurs believed in augury. Priesthood was an honored and powerful position considered essential to political order.

At the very pinnacle of the priesthood was the divine emperor. Obviously the Jews living in the Roman Empire were not keen on worshipping a pagan emperor or paying oppressive taxes to the imperial government that had taken over their holy land. That's the context of the Pharisees' question to Jesus, and the double meaning of the coin, expressing both the emperor's divinity (in conflict with the Jews' commandments forbidding worship of other gods and idols) and his political power (which evoked Jewish frustration with the imperial boot on the Promised Land).[3]

The Corruption of the Divine Caesars

But what kind of person was Caesar? Just before Jesus began his public ministry, Tiberius had taken a tyrannical turn for the worst. He fell into the most shameful private sexual debaucheries, being especially fond of "freeborn children" as victims.[4] Tiberius died in 37 AD, not long after the conversion of St. Paul. The equally morally repugnant emperors Caligula and Claudius followed. Meanwhile, the church slowly (and entirely unnoticed as anything but some variant of the "Jewish rites" the Romans detested) was spreading through the Roman Empire.

After the living god Claudius died in 54 AD, Nero became emperor. In Nero, tyrannical passion, the hubris of proclaimed divinity, the corruption of power, and indulgence in "every filthy depraved act, licit or illicit"[5] seemed to reach an imperial nadir. He not only had a passion for "free-born boys" but he also "married" other men and even a boy, sometimes playing the part of the woman in the union and sometimes the man.[6]

When the famous great fire in Rome in 64 AD wreaked its destruction (whether it was caused by Nero, or merely enjoyed by him), Nero blamed the Christians as scapegoats, and made an imperial spectacle of them: they were "torn to piece by dogs, or crucified, or made into torches to be ignited after dark as substitutes for daylight."[7] But that was only the beginning of the persecution.

The Church versus the Degraded Pagan State

In the historical context into which the church was born and began to grow, worship of the emperor was a political act. Failure to worship him was a kind of treason, punishable in the most horrifying ways. So right at the beginning of the church there was a clash between church and the Roman imperium, between the first Christian believers and the exceedingly corrupt pagan theocratic imperial power. There was an essential *antagonism* between the church and the Roman Empire, not a mere distinction of function. In the first century AD it was the church *versus* imperial Rome, not the church *and* imperial Rome.

And it was not only a politico-theological antagonism, but a moral one as well. What kind of obedience could a Christian render unto a Caesar who was so cruel, so sexually depraved, who used Christians as living torches for his amusement?

The essential moral antagonism was not just between Christians and the emperor, but between Christianity and Roman culture in general. The imperial cruelty and sexual degradation of Tiberius, Caligula, and Nero accurately represented what was occurring in Roman culture at large.

We may picture the Romans as austere and virtuous, but this image is based upon the writings of a small number of great Roman moralists such as Cato the Elder, Seneca, and Cicero, and on the good character of later emperors such as Trajan and Marcus Aurelius (who, by the way, also persecuted the Christians). But all their moralizing was aimed at rampant Roman immorality. Hearkening back to the austere early heroes of the Roman Republic was the way that moralists attempted to remind their present-day degraded Rome of its better past.

There were few brakes on sexuality in the Roman Empire at the time of Christ[8]—a fact that is directly related to pagan religion. "In antiquity," historian John Riddle notes, "the evidence suggests, sexual restraint was largely ignored; pagan religion normally did not attempt to regulate sexual activity. Free males could do almost anything sexually, even if they had to resort to slaves, with no moral or societal consequences to themselves."[9]

With sexuality free from religious restraint, the results were predictable. We find that pornographic painting and decoration were common in Roman homes and public places.[10] Prostitution was morally and legally sanctioned, and prostitutes were even integral to some religious festivals.[11] One of the most sacred and omnipresent symbols was the *fascinum* or phallus, embodying fertility, sexual pleasure, power, and magic in one venerated object. Marriage was in bad shape. Divorce was easy, adultery common, and concubinage licit.[12]

By the time of Christ, homosexuality was just as widespread among the Romans as it was among the Greeks—one sign of which is that it was condoned even by the stolid Stoics.[13] The Romans had adopted the pederasty of the Greeks (aimed, generally, at boys between the ages of twelve and eighteen). Slaves, both male and female, were considered property, and that included sexual property. Homosexuality between free adult men was also common. It was not homosexuality as such but the crossing of the line from slave boys and consenting adult males to (sometimes kidnapped) free-born children that affronted the more austere of the Roman moralists.[14] In the notorious career of Nero, as we have seen above, the outrages went as far as the celebration of same-sex marriages.[15]

All of these things occurred in a generally sexually vulgarized culture. Anyone reading such ancient writers as Plautus, Catullus, Ovid, Martial, Juvenal, or Apuleius (without the polite sidestepping of the sexual crudity that is standard in older English translations) will see that our own sexually raw times have their parallel in the ancient world.

And violence was as out of control as sex in the Roman Empire. The destruction of human life for amusement was at the heart of the gladiatorial entertainment at the Roman circus, and the killing of deformed infants was mandated by Roman law.[16] Suicide (or, to use the nearest Roman term, *mors voluntaria*, voluntary death, which is closer to our term euthanasia) was not only accepted but in certain cases honored.[17] Such was the "norm," as historian Ian Dowbiggin notes, until "the ancient Roman definition of good death [that is, euthanasia] was toppled by the revolutionary Christian doctrine upholding the sanctity of life and condemning anything that resembled suicide, assisted suicide, or mercy killing."[18]

It may be hard for us to believe, given the battles we now face in America, but contraception, abortion, and infanticide were not moral issues until Christianity came along. They were simply part of the accepted way of life in Rome—and in the entire ancient world.[19] The condemnation of these and other pagan practices by Christians, as evidenced in the *Didache*, the first-century catechetical manual for pagan converts,[20] must have seemed nothing short of astounding to the pagans.[21]

The original pagan embrace of this world was broken by Christians preaching a kingdom not of this world—and a more severe morality to go with it. In presenting pagans with an eternal kingdom above the Roman Empire and beyond this life, Christianity demoted and relativized both: the empire no longer commanded one's total allegiance, and the embrace of this fallen world was loosened as converts reached beyond this life toward the next.

The Church Overruns the Empire

Of course, there would not have been any antagonism against the church if the church had kept to itself. But it did not, because of the command of Jesus Christ himself, "Go, therefore, make disciples of all the nations; baptize them in the name of the Father and of the Son and of the Holy Spirit, and teach them to observe all the commands I gave you" (Matthew 28:19–20).

Because of this command, Christianity could not be a kind of privatized sect hidden away from the world. Christians immediately began evangelizing the pagan Roman Empire. By 70 AD, less than forty years after the death and resurrection of Jesus, churches had been established in major cities stretching north from Jerusalem all the way around the northern rim of the Mediterranean, including Rome itself, and even some along the northern shores of Africa.[22] By 200 AD, both the number of churches and the geographical reach of Christianity had more or less doubled, there now being churches in every major city.[23]

The rate of conversion to Christianity is nothing short of miraculous. We know that the original number in the church was quite small—the apostles, Jesus's own mother, Mary Magdalene, and just a few others. The best estimate by historians is that by the end of the first century there were still fewer than 10,000 Christians. By 200 AD, there were over 200,000. When Christians were undergoing their harshest persecutions under Diocletian near the end of the third century, they numbered about six million, or nearly 10 percent of the empire's population. Perhaps most important was the population growth of Christians in the city of Rome itself, where they numbered well over half the population by the year 300 AD. The growth in the other major cities of the empire was equally impressive.[24] Churches in all these cities were centers of organization and evangelization. As the church grew, so did its visibility—and its capacity to irritate the empire.

The Roman Empire Strikes Back

Given the dramatic increase in the number of converts between the first and fourth centuries, the church obviously became a very visible counter-weight (including a moral counter-weight) to the Roman imperium. It is not surprising that antagonism increased with the increase of the church. Persecutions, which began under Nero (who ruled from 54–68 AD), also took place under Domitian (89–96 AD), Trajan (98–117 AD),

Marcus Aurelius (161–180 AD), Septimius Severus (193–211), Maximinus (235–238), Decius (249–251 AD), Valerian (253–260 AD), and then peaked in their severity under Diocletian (284–305) and Galerius (305–311). Some of these emperors were as wicked as Nero. Others, such as Trajan and Marcus Aurelius, were austere, dedicated, and morally commendable. But all persecuted the Christians as enemies of Rome.

Christians could have avoided all this—and some did—simply by sacrificing to the emperor and the Roman gods, denouncing Christ, and then retreating into a private and unassuming interior faith that didn't challenge Roman culture. The easy way out had been offered to them from the time of the earliest persecutions, as evidenced in the reign of the emperor Trajan in the early second century AD. We have, for example, the Roman provincial governor Pliny writing to Trajan that he had arrested a number of persons on suspicion of being Christian and then released some who proved willing to offer incense to the emperor and curse Christ.[25]

But faithful Christians would not bow to the state, and so that state could not tolerate Christians. As historian Stephen Benko rightly notes, even as good and mild-mannered an emperor as Trajan "assumed that Christianity automatically and inevitably led to wrongdoing, at least in the sense that refusal to worship the Roman gods harmed the tranquility of the state."[26] While there were wild rumors accusing Christians of sexual libertinism and cannibalism,[27] the main problem was political. There could be nothing more upsetting to the pagan Roman imperium than the absolute Christian rejection of all other gods, including the gods of the empire, even in the face of death.

From the vantage point of the pagan emperors and aristocracy, it appeared that Christians were a swarming hoard that must be destroyed before they entirely overwhelmed the empire. To the Romans, it was the imperium vs. the church, and it was a most serious battle.

Why? For one thing, the empire seemed to be coming apart at the seams in the third century, with continual fighting among rival claimants to be emperor, increasing problems defending the borders, economic collapse and debasing of the currency, and greater and greater control of political power by the military.

Turmoil tends to centralize power and increase it, and the focus on the divinity of the emperor had correspondingly intensified. Increased centralization and more intense worship of the emperor were both meant to stop the empire from disintegration by making the emperor himself the divine representative of political order and increasing his actual bureaucratic-military power, a manifestation of his divine omnipotence. Religious and political power were therefore even more tightly fused.[28]

But Christians wouldn't worship the emperor. And so, as the Christian historian Eusebius tells us, in 303 AD Diocletian ordered "the churches to be razed to the ground and the Scriptures destroyed by fire," and the leaders of the churches to be "coerced by every possible means into offering sacrifice" to the deified emperor and the Roman gods.[29] Only that would signify true subservience to the Roman imperium.

Punishments for those who refused were severe, as the accounts of the time make sickeningly clear.[30] The martyrs would not compromise or retreat to the private sphere. The very word "martyr" means witness—martyrdom was not a private act. In fact, the martyrs' extreme, very public courage, the complete triumph over the fear of death they displayed, amazed many pagan onlookers and brought them into the Christian flock.[31] Even the pagan intellectuals and philosophers (such as Epictetus and Galen) who rejected Christianity were astounded at the Christians' bravery in the face of death.[32]

Christian Orthodoxy versus Pagan Tolerance

Wonder as they might at the martyrs' courage, pagans couldn't understand the Christian insistence on the exclusive truth of their faith. For the most part pagans had a live-and-let-live attitude. As Ramsay MacMullen rightly argues, in the Roman Empire "the unchallenged right of anyone to say or do or believe anything he wanted about any deity he addressed, so long as it was not aggressively hostile to other beliefs, is easily shown in a thousand proofs."[33] That's why most subjects of the empire could sacrifice to the emperor, and then go on about their preferred religious practices without any anxiety. Roman tolerance in matters of religion extended to almost everyone—everyone who was willing to participate in the cult of the emperor. But Christians, as Celsus, a pagan critic of Christianity, pointed out, were different from the members of other religions because they refused to take part in the public religious rites alongside their Christian rites.[34]

What made Christians so stubbornly different? Orthodoxy. The Christians' peculiar insistence that the church alone had the truth grew out of (1) the Jewish radical rejection of other gods as evidenced in Hebrew Scriptures, (2) the Christians' acceptance of the Hebrew Scriptures as fundamentally formative, and (3) most important, the church's affirmation of Jesus Christ as the fulfillment of those Scriptures, the Word, and the Son of God, himself fully divine and fully human, the way, the truth, and the life.

It is impossible to understand the later historical development of the distinction between religion and political power in the West without understanding the church's concern for orthodoxy from the very beginning. It was only because Christians had a definite set of beliefs, as defined by canonical writings and church leaders, that there could be something as distinct as a "church" and not just an amorphous and endlessly diverse mass of loosely associated worshippers of gods and goddesses as one finds in paganism (so loosely organized as not to constitute any kind of a unified threat to the Roman Empire). Orthodoxy brought institutional unity, institutional unity was a challenge to the religious cult of the emperor that supported his political authority, and so orthodoxy brought on persecution. Christians' adamant concern for orthodoxy prevented them from paying any homage to any god other than the one true God, and so they were persecuted by Rome.[35]

We can easily imagine with what joy, what amazement, Christians in the second decade of the fourth century greeted the news that the pagan Roman emperor himself, Constantine, had converted to Christianity. They thanked

God for this miracle and saw the conversion of the emperor as a fruit of their obedience to Christ's command to make disciples of all the nations—including the leaders of those nations trying to exterminate Christianity. Now, Christians would no longer be hunted enemies of the state. We'll explore the great change that Constantine's conversion brought in a subsequent chapter. Let's finish out this one with reflections on some important parallels between the situation of Christians in ancient Rome and in our own society.

Parallels to Our Situation

Christians today find themselves in a largely secularized society that looks a lot like the pagan Roman society into which Christianity was originally born. Given our cultural acceptance of easy sexuality, easy divorce, homosexuality, homosexual marriage, contraception, abortion, infanticide, euthanasia, pornography, extremely violent and extremely vulgar entertainment, and so on, it is as if Christianity is being erased from history, and things are being turned back to the cultural status quo of two thousand years ago. Perhaps it's no accident that Christians today have that same persecuted feeling as they did way back in ancient Rome. The disestablishment of Christianity in our culture (including its moral disestablishment) would seem to bring us right back to the beginnings of Christianity.

The supremely tolerant religious approach of the Roman pagans also sounds familiar to our ears—*worship whatever or whomever you want; just don't bother anyone else.* The imperium amended this to *as long as you worship and obey the state, any lesser god or goddess is of no consequence.* Perhaps that is why modern liberalism, as a kind of return to ancient paganism, is so tolerant of non-Christian religions, especially those without any well-defined core doctrines, even while it cannot tolerate Christianity, with its concern for doctrinal orthodoxy.

As I've noted, the conflict between the church and the ancient pagan imperium was at least partly explained by the unity of the church, which was grounded in the Christians' adamant insistence on orthodoxy (in much the same way as the Law was the source of unity for the Jews, setting them apart from all nations). The pagan religions had no such unity, and were therefore no real threat to the state. But the church's highly organized, unified association, which was spread throughout the empire's cities, constituted a parallel source of social order and a threat to the imperium. In regard to the church as a stubbornly independent social and moral authority, I can do no better than to offer the words of the historian J. H. W. G. Liebeschuetz:

> The Church could never be simply the religious department of the *respublica*, as the old religion had been. The Church had its own officers, the clergy, who were absolutely distinct from the officers of the state. It accepted the authority of sacred writings and of traditions which were not part of Graeco-Roman civilization....The weekly services, sermons, the discipline of penance, and religious instruction offered the clergy means of indoctrination which had no precedent.[36]

The church therefore acted as an "intermediate institution"—to use our modern term, associated with Edmund Burke and Alexis de Tocqueville—buffering individuals from the state and giving them a source of social organization outside its control. That made the church dangerous, the Romans perceived, as a beachhead for any potential political rebellion.

Political philosophers from Aristotle to Burke and Tocqueville have noted that such intermediate institutions are hated by tyrants, by totalitarians, by despots, by all-encompassing state-planners, and of course by emperors because loyalty to such institutions is a source of organized political antagonism.[37] The Christian churches were not the only source of a parallel social order in the Roman Empire. Other intermediate institutions were well known in ancient Greece and Rome, where the name for them was *hetaeria* (from the Greek *hetairos*, a companion) or *collegium* (from the Latin *collega*, a colleague).As with the churches, these other institutions constituted a kind of buffer existing between Rome and the individual, and one that potentially diverted ultimate loyalty from the imperium and could easily become a source of insurrection.[38] But there is no doubt that Rome viewed the Christian church, unified as it was by orthodoxy, as a unique and fast-growing threat, and that the persecutions were in no small part, an attempt by Rome to eliminate the threat of this greatest intermediate institution.[39]

And ultimately Christianity did in fact displace the Roman Empire, entirely justifying all these suspicions. The persecutors of the church were right to believe that, for the pagan state to continue, the church had to be destroyed. And today the church is once again a buffer between the state and the individual that must be eliminated—if liberalism is to assert total political control.

To these points must be added one that may, perhaps, startle us in these days when believers appeal to "freedom of religion" in the face of state encroachments. The primary concern of Christians in the Roman Empire was not religious liberty but religious *truth*. There is nothing so clear from the New Testament and the plethora of Christian writings in the first three centuries as that Christians believed that *the* truth had been revealed to them, and it was their responsibility to take that truth and make it boldly known to all the nations. They didn't suffer the most horrible martyrdoms so that Isis, Bacchus, or Jupiter could be safely adored by their respective cults. They died for Christ—the way, the truth, and the life.

And it was precisely this claim to have the truth that irked the Romans, and made them suspicious of Christians. As Benko remarks, "The Romans believed that when Christians claimed exclusive possession of divine knowledge, they were capable of anything....An irreconcilable difference existed between pagans and Christians on this issue. The pagan took the position that matters pertaining to the divine mystery were obscure and so should be left open to debate. The Christian, however, was convinced that he was in possession of the truth, because Jesus Christ embodied the ultimate revelation about God."[40] That revelation came from God, the God above all nations, who judges all nations. The church was the keeper of that revelation—of the truth that came from a source outside of and above Rome.

And so we see another parallel to our own time. If liberalism is to reassert total political control today, then it cannot allow this revelation to be true. It must rule that claim outside the bounds of permissible public discourse. Or, perhaps more effectively, it must reduce it from a claim about truth to a harmless myth, or brand it with the ignominious label "intolerant," or failing all that, simply assert that all truth claims are relative (a kind of scorched-earth policy). Liberalism has in fact made use of all these strategies.

CHAPTER 3

HOW THE BIBLE KEPT THE CHURCH FROM BECOMING A DEPARTMENT OF THE STATE

W e've been to pagan Rome and seen the essential antagonism of the Roman state to the Christian church. We've also seen that this ancient antagonism between the imperium and the church bears a strange resemblance to our situation today, when liberalism is using state power to remove Christianity from its culturally central place. And we've noted that there's more than a little similarity between the moral situation in pagan ancient Rome and the moral positions pushed by liberalism today.

But we won't really understand where we are today if we simply compare ancient Rome with modern America and Europe. We can't leap over the time in between. We've got to see what secular liberalism is rejecting—because it defines itself by what it opposes. First and foremost, liberalism rejects the Christianization of culture that took place as pagan Europe was evangelized. But it also rejects the church's invention of the distinction between the church and state, which went along with that evangelization.

That last point is an important and counter-intuitive one. We moderns are not the inventors of the separation of church and state. It was an achievement of the ancient and medieval church. The Christianization of the empire did not entail the fusion of church and political power (as we may believe), but their separation. The church rejected the pagan identification of religion and political power, the use of religion as a prop and servant of the state. The church insisted that it must be independent of the state for two very good reasons: so that the church would not corrupt itself by becoming worldly, and so that the state would not corrupt the church by bending the Christian religion to serve political ends. Liberalism seeks a kind of return to the pagan condition in which the church, rather than being independent, is subservient to and defined by this-worldly political goals.

How the Church Invented
the Distinction between Church and State

We'll investigate how liberalism collapsed the church-state distinction in later chapters, but we first need to see how and why the church came up with the distinction between church and state to begin with. As we'll see, the issue would come to a point with Emperor Constantine's conversion.

Why? It's easy to conceive of the church as a distinct institution when the state is out to destroy it. Prior to Constantine, in the age of the martyrs, Christians were (following St. Paul's admonitions) respectful of the state even while they refused to bow down to the emperor or condone his moral corruption. So for example Speratus of Scillium (near Carthage in Africa) famously gave witness: "I can never recognize a deified emperor on this earth; I serve the God whom the human eye has never seen nor can ever see."[1] He was martyred in 180 AD. Justin Martyr, beheaded in 165, informed the emperor Antoninus Pius that, as Christ had told them to render to Caesar his due, he could not worship the emperor since that was not his due, "but in all other things we gladly serve you, acknowledging you as emperors and sovereigns, praying that along with your royal power you may be endowed with sound judgment."[2] Respectfully pray for, yes, but worship, no. "I honor the emperor," declared Theophilus of Antioch (d. 185 AD), "not indeed worshipping him but praying for him…for he is not a god but a man appointed by God, not to be worshipped but to judge justly."[3] By the third century, however, Christians were beginning to argue that that fact of persecution by the state meant that the state was unworthy of the obedience due to a just sovereign. So asserted Hippolytus of Rome (d. 235) and Origen (d. 254).[4] As Origen explained, St. Paul's command to be obedient to authority (Romans 13:2) "is not of those in authority who persecute the Faith; of these it is said: 'It is better to obey God than men' (Acts 5:29). But Paul is speaking here of just authority…."[5] As persecutions against Christians heated up in the late third century and the beginning of the fourth, Christians felt Caesar was due very little, if anything.

But then the miracle of Constantine's conversion occurred, and Christians were faced with an entirely new question: What if Caesar asks to be baptized? What should the church render unto Caesar once he has become a Christian too?

The "Constantinian Question" is a prickly one: Did Constantine save the church by converting the empire, or ruin the church by absorbing it into the empire? Many Christians have argued that the beginning of the end of real Christianity came when a Roman emperor adopted it as his religion. The complaint is that with Constantine's conversion the church lost its pristine purity and independence and became an entirely subordinate tool of imperial power. Or, even worse, the church itself—now elevated to a position of imperial favor—became politicized and began to use spiritual goods for worldly gains.

The facts of the matter under Constantine aren't as important as the complaints themselves. They highlight the Christian rejection of twin evils: (1) the subordination of the church to friendly political power, culminating in the worship of the state, and (2) the corruption of the church by worldliness. Both evils became possible only with the conversion of Constantine.

We will not attempt to sort out all the complexities surrounding Constantine's conversion, or to give a detailed account of his imperial policies thereafter.[6] Our main concern will be *to discover what it was about Christianity that disallowed the fusion of sacred and friendly political power*. That's what has kept Christians from worshipping the state, from rendering unto Caesar what is due only to God.

I can't overemphasize the importance of this point. We tend to think of the distinction between church and state as somehow vaguely standing for the distinction between the state and any religion. We view it as a kind of general philosophical principle, universal and self-evident to everyone in every time. But that is profoundly misleading. The distinction between church and state, religious and political power is peculiar to Christianity, and the church invented it.

As the familiar phrase itself testifies, the distinction between "church and state" arose only under very particular historical circumstances. After all, it isn't "religion and state," "temple and state," "synagogue and state," "mosque and state," or "shrine and state," but *church* and state. The phrase doesn't describe the relationship of the state to any and every kind of worship or fit any other religion. It quite definitely points to the Christian institution of the church.

This isn't a quibble. Historically, the distinction between church and state, between religious and political power, didn't arise among the pagan Greeks or Romans, in Judaism or Islam, in Hinduism or Buddhism, among pagan Norsemen, or in regard to Japanese Shintoism. Like so many other things—the invention of the university; the rise of science; the ultimate rejection of slavery; monogamous and exclusive heterosexual marriage; opposition to abortion, infanticide, and suicide—the distinction of church and state is Christian in origin. The fundamental principle of the separation of church and state that we rely on today (even if we misunderstand it), was invented by the church long before the modern world.

But why did the distinction between church and state arise in Christianity alone? And why was it such an essential principle of the Christian religion that it survived both the savage attacks of pagan emperors and, even more curiously, the conversion of Constantine and the Christianization of the empire? The roots of that distinction are present in the very earliest Christianity—in fact, even before, in Christianity's Jewish roots in the Old Testament.

There's a very good reason we need to understand why and how the church originally made itself distinct from state power. Only with that understanding will we grasp why and how liberalism had to set about destroying this achievement so that it could absorb the church and its functions, creating the unfortunate situation we're living in today. If you know how something was done, then you know how to undo it. If we understand not only why and how the modern state became a this-worldly kingdom of God (even a god itself) but also exactly what was the arrangement it replaced (that is, the original Christian relationship between church and state), then we may have some chance of reversing the operation and disestablishing liberalism as our state religion.

So we're going to take a bit of time in this part of the investigation. In this and the two closely related chapters that follow, we will attempt to establish *what it was about Christianity that disallowed the fusion of sacred and friendly political power.*

Here we'll deal with the Biblical origins of the distinction between church and state. In chapter four, which follows, we'll look at Constantine's conversion itself. And in chapter five we'll treat the development of the church-and-state relationship from the time period after the fall of Rome to the High Middle Ages. If you follow the story from the Bible to the medieval popes and emperors, I guarantee you'll see our contemporary situation much, much more clearly.

The Authority of the Bible

We cannot comprehend how the distinction between church and state ever arose until we grasp this fundamental fact: Christians believed that the Bible really was the revealed truth of God, and so they treated what it said as the authoritative guiding source for their approach to everything, including the relationship of the church to political power. The distinction between church and state arose within Christianity, and nowhere else, because of the accepted authority of the Bible.

(A quick historical note: It took some time for the church to define the official canon of the Bible. But even the earliest Christians regarded the Hebrew Scriptures as authoritative. And the books that we know as the New Testament, including Paul's letters and the four Gospels, were circulated widely and read religiously by the early Christians.)

If you understand why the Bible kept the church from becoming a department of the state, you'll understand why, from the very first, liberalism attacked the authority of the Bible with such vehemence. Only the rejection of Biblical authority allowed the liberal state to dismantle the church and absorb its form and functions into its political aims—to make of the state, once again, what the pagan Caesars intended it to be.

It was the Bible that originally broke apart the ancient pagan fusion of religion and political power. We can begin to see where the distinction between the church and state came from by looking at the story of Moses in the Old Testament.

The Lesson of Pharaoh and Moses: Political Leaders Are Not Gods

Every ancient political entity of any consequence attempted to make its founder a hero of gigantic proportions who was either a god or descended from the gods, or who had been divinized. That was just the kind of claim made by the pharaohs of Egypt, who fancied themselves the incarnation of the Egyptian god Horus.

Against the Egyptian notion of divinized kings, Moses, the leader of the Israelites, is presented in the Bible as a very human figure—a man who kills someone and runs away, who is called back by God, and who, even after he witnesses an astounding theophany, goes about God's business with the grumbling acceptance of a man being forced to do things against his will.

The story of the plagues in Exodus and the founding event of the Passover are presented as a great contest between Yahweh and Pharaoh, *not* between Moses and Pharaoh. In this battle, all of the miracles are clearly done by God, not Moses, and the plagues show very clearly that Pharaoh is only a political king, not a god.

This sets the pattern for the rest of Scripture. Here and elsewhere in the Pentateuch, the divine is clearly distinct from the human. In fact, one of the most astonishing things about the Old Testament—something that sets it apart from other religious literature—is that the patriarchs, Moses, and even the earliest kings of Israel are all presented as so very human. All possibility of apotheosis is thereby cut off, that is, any possibility that a great Jewish leader-hero will later be divinized as a human-god founder. The faults of the men and women in the Bible are too plain. Yahweh is the only God.

God's Law Judges All Kings and All Nations

In regard to the Law, Moses is not presented as some kind of divine or semi-divine founder-lawgiver, as was the case with other mythical ancient cultural founders such as Romulus, Theseus, or Aeneas. Nor does he exalt himself as a great divinely-ordained king, the magnificent source of the benevolent law, as did Hammurabi.[7] Moses, a mere mortal, receives the Law from God; he doesn't grandiosely give it, but only very humbly passes it on.

The first of the Ten Commandments says, "You shall have no other gods before me" (Exodus 20:3). No divine-human kings, and that means—advancing to the prohibition of graven images—no sacred images of divine kings, or of anything else, such as a golden calf. (The bull-calf deity Apis was the most important of the sacred animals of Egypt, associated directly with the deified pharaoh as representing the virility and strength defining kingship.)

These commandments and the rest of the Law form a bulwark against absolute political power by forbidding the idolatry that is so often pushed by kings wishing to appear divine.

Even more astounding, the moral-theological commands of the Law stand in judgment above any actual human political regime and the will of any king—of any regime or king including those of the Israelites themselves. The word of the pharaoh was law; the word of a Jewish king was judged by the Law.

As the rest of the Biblical story unfolds in Joshua, Judges, and Kings, it is clear that the history of Israel is largely a tale of disobedience and severe judgment under the Law. The king's word is *not* law unless it conforms to *the* Law. Absolute theological and moral commands relativize any and every human kingship, and any merely human law. The revolutionary effects of this fact cannot be overestimated: any act of the king that goes against God's laws invites immediate rebellion on the part of the king's subjects—particularly on the part of the prophets who speak for the Law.

True Prophets of God Condemn Kings, Nations, and Even Priests

And that brings us to the prophets, beginning with Samuel. Samuel was, like the leaders immediately following Moses, a judge—a kind of political-military-priestly leader. But Samuel is also considered the first prophet.

Samuel, gift-child to the previously barren Hannah, was dedicated to the service of Yahweh under the priest Eli. Eli's own sons grew up to be "worthless men," specifically, worthless priests who "Had no regard for Yahweh," greedily stuffed themselves with the choicest sacrificial meat, and enjoyed themselves "with the women who served at the entrance to the tent of meeting" (1 Samuel 2:12, 22).

Like Moses, Samuel received a special, personal call by God (1 Samuel 3). He thereby became Israel's prophet (1 Samuel 3:20), his first task being the unpleasant one of having to tell Eli that God was about to smite his house for his sons' iniquity. God's Law judged even the priests.

Samuel didn't make out much better in this regard. While Samuel himself was blameless, his sons, whom he made judges over Israel, "did not walk in his ways, but turned aside after gain; they took bribes and perverted justice" (1 Samuel 8:1–3). Like the sons of Eli, they used their spiritual office for material gain and gratification.

The Israelites see that Samuel's sons are worthless. They ask Samuel to "appoint for us a king to govern us like all the nations," which both Samuel and God take as a sign of rejection of God's rule. Accordingly, Samuel makes a dire prediction of the kind of oppression that almost invariably follows upon giving one man the powers of a king: he nabs everything for himself (1 Samuel 8). The concentration of political power, whether in a king or a national government, almost always leads to use of that power for personal gain.

But the Israelites press for a king anyway. And so Samuel, the prophet and priest, reluctantly anoints the tall and handsome Saul. By pouring oil on the head of a mere man, the priest-prophet-judge raises him up to the stature of king, Yahweh's anointed one. In this act, we might say, Samuel hands over the office of judge, that is, of political-military leader, to the king, and Samuel becomes solely a priest-prophet.

A fundamental division of labor has been introduced (which admittedly, later kings such as Solomon will fudge), and in this division we have the faint historical beginnings of the all-important distinction of function between sacred and political power. *A priest is not a king, and a king is not a priest.* Applied to the context of Rome, this Biblical principle will one day mean that Caesar cannot also be *Pontifex Maximus*, the chief priest; and the chief priest cannot be a Caesar.

Moreover, the two functions are not equal. Implicit in this very act of anointing we can see that the prophet is really higher than the king. Saul receives his royal stature from a prophet, a man of God, and a priest. If there is any doubt in that regard, when King Saul takes it upon himself to offer a sacrifice as if he were a priest, Samuel accuses him of violating "the commandment of Yahweh your God," and so declares that the kingship is to be taken from him, and given to another (1 Samuel 13).

That other is David, whom God chooses and Samuel anoints: "and the Spirit of Yahweh came mightily upon David from that day forward" (1 Samuel 16). But that leads to another Biblical lesson.

Sin Spoils All the Kingdoms of This World, and Even the Greatest King Needs Salvation

David is *the* greatest of the Israelite kings, the one of whom God promises "I will establish the throne of his kingdom for ever" (2 Samuel 7:13). But even David does not stand above the Law. The priest-prophet stands ever ready to condemn the king on behalf of the Law. When David violates two commandments by first committing adultery with Bathsheba and then having her husband Uriah killed, he is reproved by the prophet Nathan. Nathan informs him of his punishment for violating the moral law that stands ever above him: the son born of the illicit union of David and Bathsheba will die, and God "will raise up evil against" David from his own house.

David's reply to Nathan's moral reproof is "I have sinned against Yahweh" (2 Samuel 12). The king acknowledges the supremacy of the moral commands from God, the commands that no one, not even a king, may violate. But in doing so, he also acknowledges the theological-moral authority of the prophet, the one who speaks on behalf of God to even the most powerful kings.

This mention of sin takes us all the way back to Genesis and the Fall. Sin affects everyone—every man and woman, every king, every kingdom, every nation. If David, the chosen king of the chosen people, was infected with sin, then there is no hope that politics will make things once and for all right and good here on earth. Sin spoils the whole world.

For the early Christians, as we'll see below from their use of Scripture, the political history of Israel became the template by which all human history was to be understood. They learned from the Bible what we must expect of every political entity, no matter how good—that "thorns and thistles it shall bring forth" (Genesis 3:18). This world is fallen. And that brings us to the New Testament, and the cure for the fallen world.

There Are Two Worlds, Two Kingdoms—and No Heaven on Earth

While this world and all its kingdoms are marred by sin, Christians are promised a new world and a kingdom not of this world, the Kingdom of God. In the Gospel of John (18:36) Jesus says to Pontius Pilate, "My kingdom is not of this world [*kosmos*]."[8] That was an astounding declaration, one that changed the entire course of history.

Whereas in Judaism there had been only one kingdom (the Messiah, David's son, would restore David's earthly kingdom), in Christianity there are two kingdoms. One is the temporal kingdom founded in and directed toward the things of this world. The other, the Kingdom of God, is not of this world, but rather is an eternal kingdom, of which Christ himself is king.

The ultimate allegiance of Christians—the allegiance that trumps all this-worldly loyalties—is to the Kingdom of Heaven. Because Christ had said that his kingdom was not of this world, there could be no heaven brought to earth, no political kingdom that could claim to be the Kingdom of God.

That great divide between the two kingdoms, founded in the great divide between two worlds, *is the very deepest source of the distinction between the church and state, and also of the church's independence from the state.* It is the great divide between the temporal and the eternal. But this source has its parallel in human nature itself, in the distinction between the mortal body and the immortal soul.

Body and Soul, Cross and Resurrection

Jesus makes it painfully clear that the cross defines one's ultimate allegiance. As he says in Mark 8:35–36, "If any man would come after me, let him deny himself and take up his cross and follow me. For whoever would save his life will lose it; and whoever loses his life for my sake and the gospel's will save it. For what does it profit a man, to gain the whole world and forfeit his soul."[9]

The distinction between the soul and body is a manifestation of the more comprehensive distinctions between the immortal and the mortal, the immaterial and the material, the eternal and the temporal. These distinctions are the source of the distinction between the church and the political power.

The church is mainly concerned about the ultimate fate of the immortal soul in the next world. Because the soul continues to live after bodily death, it is possible for Christians to lose their lives in this world and gain them in the world to come (paradoxically, gaining their proper bodily existence again, but in a transformed condition, as the soul is united to a resurrected body).

Note well: if there is no immortal soul, then physical death means complete extinction, and embracing the cross is foolishness—we'd all do better to throw our lot in with the kingdoms of this world.

But the church affirms the existence of the immortal soul. The eternal perspective taken by the church sets it apart from political power, which is of necessity focused on temporal things, the things of this world, largely defined by the needs of the body. Hoping for eternal life, Christians are able to submit themselves to the cross. They have the resurrection to look forward to, and eternal life in an everlasting Kingdom.

The Church in the World but Not of It, and in the Nations but Not of Them

That makes the position of the Christian in the world a startlingly new thing. The new Israel, the new chosen people, must regard the Kingdom of Heaven as the one and only promised land. The name of this community of believers who desire to be citizens of this Kingdom is the *ekklesia*, a Greek word which we translate "church."

Jesus himself declared that this community of believers is "not of the world, even as I am not of the world." Yet he also prayed to the Father that "I am not asking you to remove them from the world" (John 17:9–21). Like Jesus, who came into the world to save it, the community of believers, the *ekklesia*, is commanded to imitate Christ and go out into the world to try to save as many people as possible.

The *ekklesia* may not, then, simply withdraw from the world: "Go therefore and make disciples of all nations, baptizing them in the name of the Father, and of the Son and of the Holy Spirit, teaching them to observe all that I have commanded you" (Matthew 28:19–20). Christ's three-fold command forbids the church from turning all its attention to the next world.

To focus on the first command, to make disciples of all nations, the church did not—and still cannot—separate itself in the post-*Everson v. Board of Education* sense. The Christian *ekklesia* can't just "shut up and sing" hymns and retreat into private worship because it has been commanded to preach the Gospel to the whole world, to all nations. To cease preaching to the whole world, to all the nations, before the end of time would be to cease being the *ekklesia*.

But precisely because the church must witness to all the nations, the church is inherently *universal*, that is, *transnational*, and hence extends itself beyond any particular people, political regime, state, or nation, even while it strives to preach within every one of them.

Because of this universal mission, the church cannot be merely parochial, a political church of one political regime, an established state religion. The church must be *in* all the nations, but not *of* any one of them. Christians are, above all, citizens of the Kingdom of God.

Baptism, the Oath of Citizenship in the Kingdom of God

We cannot understand the later development of the distinction between church and Christian imperium without understanding baptism, the subject of the second command in Christ's great charge to the church. Whatever the disagreements today about the number and nature of the sacraments,[10] the early Christians understood baptism to be the rite that must be administered at the entrance to the church. It was through baptism that one became a member of the *ekklesia*. "For by one Spirit," St. Paul says, "we were all baptized into one body—Jews or Greeks, slaves or free—and all were made to drink of one Spirit" (1 Corinthians 12:12–13). Baptism was what made a Christian a member of the Body of Christ.

The command to preach to all nations was so successful that even kings became baptized members of the *ekklesia*. But being baptized meant submitting like everyone else to the doctrinal and moral standards of the church, as well as to discipline for transgressions. If even David, Israel's model of the messianic king, could sin and be called to account by a prophet, then so must a Christian king submit to the authority of the church.

Baptism had an essential initiatory function, and the question of who should administer it was a crucial one. As the church developed, it ended up following the same division of labor between priest and king that Christians found in the Old Testament. The division of labor was even clearer and more significant in the case of the Eucharist, in which the church took over and transformed the Old Testament Passover meal into its central communal act. Baptism made one a member of the Body of Christ. But the Communion meal was the sign and source of one's ongoing membership in that body, and the food that granted eternal life. "I am the living bread which came down from heaven," Jesus declared, "if any one eats of this bread, he will live for ever; and the bread which I shall give for the life of the world is my flesh.... Truly, truly, I say to you, unless you eat the flesh of the son of man and drink his blood, you have no life in you; he who eats my flesh and drinks my blood has eternal life, and I will raise him up at the last day. For my flesh is food indeed, and my blood is drink indeed" (John 6:51–55).

This startling claim was linked inextricably in Matthew, Mark, and Luke to Jesus's celebration of the Passover on the night before he was betrayed.

Hence the command, "Do this in remembrance of me" (Luke 22:19). The belief that ordinary bread and wine somehow became the body and blood of Christ demanded that not just anybody should officiate at this special communal meal. A priest must do it. Once again, a king was not a priest, and a priest was not a king.

Whether or not one accepts the sacramental nature of Communion, in the actual historical development of the distinction between the church and state the Eucharist reinforced the difference in function between what a priest could do and what a king could do, and hence the distinct powers and functions of the church as opposed to the state. Even more significantly it made possible excommunication, a powerful symbol of exclusion from the community for those who failed to live according to Christ's commands, even if they were kings.

Teaching Christ's Commands: the Extreme Holiness of the New Law

Finally, after the commands to make disciples and baptize them, comes Christ's command to "[teach] them to observe all that I have commanded you." Jesus's commands, the commands of the new law, are, to say the least, an intensification of the commands found in the Old Testament.

Jesus did not abolish the Law given to Moses; he made the commandments more severe. "Do not kill" became "Do not even be angry or insult anyone." "Do not commit adultery" became "Do not even lust," and divorce (allowed by the Mosaic law) was no longer permitted "except on the ground of unchastity." "Do not swear falsely" was now "Do not swear at all." "An eye for an eye" became "Turn the other cheek." And "Love your neighbor and hate your enemy" was changed into "Love your enemies and pray for those who persecute you." In short, being pretty good was no longer good enough. Believers were told, "You, therefore, must be perfect, as your heavenly father is perfect" (Matthew 5:17–48). When Jesus was approached by a rich young man who wanted to know what he had to do to possess eternal life—a young man who claimed to have kept all of the old commandments—he was told by Jesus, "If you wish to be perfect, go and sell what you own and give the money to the poor, and you will have treasure in heaven; then come, follow me" (Matthew 19:16–22). Christians were required to manifest a kind of otherworldly goodness, striving to be holy like God himself.

The old law was severe enough, and it stood in judgment above every king and every political regime. How much higher must the new law stand above the kings and kingdoms of this world.

And this new law could not be kept private. Jesus demanded that believers be "the light of the world": "Let your light so shine before men, that they may see your good works and give glory to your Father who is in heaven" (Matthew 5:14–16).

Obviously, a comfortable life in the present world is not the goal of the new law. This fact reinforces the essential distinction between the two kingdoms, temporal and eternal, and hence the difference between political power and the church. The new law commands not just goodness, but extreme holiness and this-worldly self-denial. Its commands are of such stringency and purity that they cannot be fully incorporated into this-worldly kingdoms, even while they are meant to influence them.

These commands therefore set the *ekklesia* at tension with all earthly kingdoms, all political regimes, until the end of time. The church continually offers an ideal of goodness beyond their reach. Since the church's demand for holiness exceeds what the temporal political power can demand of its citizens, the church has its own moral authority and domain above all political kingdoms, and this authority both influences and judges these mortal kingdoms.

But paradoxically the state is protected from the church as well—precisely for the reason that its demands for extreme holiness go beyond what is possible to incorporate in any temporal political regime. What the church demands of its members, the state cannot demand of its citizens;

that is to say, there can be no priestly theocracy, where the church tries to make the state a large monastery. The church cannot become the state; its kingdom cannot be made a kingdom of this world.

Perfection Is Impossible for Man—without Grace

There is a solution, the only solution, to the problems that plague the nations. As Jesus said to his downcast disciples when they heard him tell the rich young man that he must, to be perfect, give away his riches and follow Jesus, "What is impossible with men is possible with God" (Luke 18:27).

Sin makes earthly perfection, true goodness on the natural level, impossible; therefore, there can be no perfection through political action. But the commands of Jesus go beyond mere natural strength and call believers to extreme holiness, goodness raised so far beyond our temporal, natural capacities for good that all merely human effort is fruitless.

Hence the doctrine of grace, by which God makes possible what is impossible for men. But grace isn't something that the state can dispense. Grace is a gift from God, made known through his revealed Word as proclaimed by the church. The Gospel makes clear that, while grace and nature are related, the Kingdom of God made possible by grace must not be confused with any natural, political kingdom. Recalling what Jesus had said to Pilate, Christians knew that his kingdom is not of this world.

Modern political utopianism, as we shall see, is an attempt to discard the necessity of grace (and hence of the church), even while state power replaces grace as the instrument for perfecting man. Liberalism is more than the rejection of Christianity; it is the absorption and transformation of its doctrines. Before the Christian doctrine of grace, *no one would have dared think about perfecting the whole human race*—a few, select individuals, a small group or clan or class of society, yes, but not the whole human race. With Christianity, God's grace is indeed open to all, and so all may share in the perfection of holiness, but this offered grace takes full effect only in the Kingdom of God, that is, only in heaven. Liberalism takes the church's salvific mission and makes it a merely political goal, one to be achieved in this world by human power alone, a heaven brought down by force to earth, where we become the authors of our own salvation.

In the Bible, the author of salvation is Jesus Christ, who is, according to Christianity, the incarnation of God, the second person of the Holy Trinity made flesh. Many kings, from the pharaohs of Egypt to the emperors of Rome, had claimed to be the incarnation of a god. Christianity made the astonishing claim that there was, and could be, only *one* incarnation. No other man ever had been or ever would be God in the flesh. All deification was thereby denied forever to the political realm. All kings, all sovereigns, all people were mere human beings. There is only one God who is king, only one king who is God. That Biblical revelation would entirely change the course of political history.

Why Scripture Had to Be Discredited

It will no doubt come as a shock to those adamant secularists who demand, in the name of separation of church and state, that there should be no Bible reading in school, that Scripture itself is the most important historical cause explaining why the distinction between church and political power ever developed in the West. For understanding why that distinction arose only in Christendom, the study of its origins in the Bible is essential. Ironically, the current understanding of the First Amendment forbids studying such things in our public schools.

Modern secularism actually acknowledges this fact, in a twisted way. Secular revolutionaries realized that the authority of Scripture had to be knocked out before the secular state could control the church for its own purposes. The great architects of modern secularism spent much effort in carefully and relentlessly undermining the authority of Scripture, so that it couldn't function as a rival authority calling into question the aims of the modern secular state. The cultural demotion of the Bible from revealed truth to mere myth is the result of their labors.

What else would secular liberals need to do to have what the ancient Roman pagan state had, the full use of religious authority for their secular purposes? If we look back over this chapter, and see everything in Scripture that separated the church from the state, the necessary strategy is clear. Just undo the revolution that had been made by revelation. Eliminate the soul and the possibility of another world by implanting a purely materialistic view of the cosmos, eliminate the priest-king distinction by removing the priest or elevating the king to priesthood, relativize morality by making obedience to the civil law the highest and only moral code, make the state itself the "body" of a new, secular "Christ," eliminate sin, and finally grant to the state full redemptive powers.

That's just what liberalism did, as we'll see in later chapters. But first we need to trace the development of the distinction between religious and political power from its Biblical origins forward into the history of Christendom, so we'll understand what liberalism was originally rebelling against.

CHAPTER 4

FROM THE CONVERSION OF CONSTANTINE TO THE FALL OF ROME

T he distinction between the church and the state had its roots in the Bible, as we have seen. But how did the relevant Biblical principles actually play out in history? Interestingly, the distinction between church and state was established under the *least* likely conditions. It is no surprise that the church made itself distinct from the pagan Roman imperium that was out to destroy it. The real wonder is that the church made itself distinct from political power once that power was converted.

In this chapter we'll be looking at the pivotal period, the hinge century—as we might call the period of time beginning with Constantine's conversion in 312 and ending with Alaric's sack of Rome in 410—when the pagan empire tipped toward Christianity and away from paganism. This was the crucial point that later secularists such as Machiavelli and the historian Edmund Gibbon would rue, when glorious paganism gave way to the wretched church. To them, this was where history took a wrong turn— the turn that needed to be undone to wrest the world away from Christianity so it could return to the glories of paganism.

But the pagan world was already disintegrating on its own, even setting aside Christianity (though that hasn't stopped pagans, ancient and modern, from blaming Christianity for the empire's fall). Let's take a look at the condition of the Roman Empire at the time of Constantine's conversion from the Christians' point of view.

Caesar Renders His Soul unto Christ

We say that the pagan Roman emperor Constantine converted to Christianity in 312, but we have to qualify that because he wasn't actually baptized until just before he died in 337 at Nicomedia (located in modern-day Turkey). In calling Constantine the first Christian emperor we are actually reporting a kind of half-truth. For almost the entire duration of his reign, while he considered himself a Christian, he was not yet a member of the Body of Christ.

To become a member, he had to be baptized. And even after he became a Christian, a Christian emperor could not function as a Christian priest—in contrast to the situation in paganism, where the emperor had been a priest simply by virtue of his political office. (Still, the emperors would retain the empty title of *Pontifex Maximus* for some time.)[1]

Constantine couldn't circumvent the need for baptism because baptism made all the difference to his eternal fate. Eusebius of Caesarea, in his *Life of Constantine*, explains the difference that the dying Constantine believed baptism would make. "But when he became aware that his life was ending," Eusebius tells us, "he perceived that this was the time to purify himself from the offences which he had at any time committed, trusting that whatever sins it had been his lot as mortal to commit, he could wash them from his soul by the power of the mystical words and the saving bath."[2] When the emperor summoned the local bishops, he said to them,

> This is the moment I have long hoped for, as I thirsted and
> yearned to win salvation in God. It is our time too to enjoy the
> seal that brings immortality, time to enjoy the sealing that gives

salvation....So let there be no delay. If the Lord of life and death should wish us to live again here, even so it is once and for all decided that I am hereafter numbered among the people of God, and that I meet and join in the prayers with them all together. I shall now set for myself rules of life which befit God.[3]

Constantine laid aside the imperial purple once and for all when he took up the white robes of baptism. He died soon thereafter.

Such an act of humiliation and submission, laying aside earthly for heavenly glory, would have been unimaginable for a pagan Roman emperor. But as great as Constantine's powers were as the head of the state, he had come to believe that baptism—which was in the power of the church alone—was essential for inheriting eternal life in the Kingdom that would not pass away.

That brings us to an important point, one that we might expand into a kind of principle. As long as the emperor (or later, king, prince, duke, and so forth) *believed* that he had an immortal soul and *believed* that the church had power to grant eternal life in heaven, there would be a distinction between church and state.

Moreover—and this was what would so deeply goad modern liberals—as long as the church retained the power to determine believers' eternal destiny ("whatever you bind on earth will be bound in heaven," Matthew 18:18), then the church would ultimately be more important than the state because eternal bliss dwarfs temporal existence; or, to put it in the negative, eternal damnation outweighs any temporal success.

The Way, the Truth, and the Life: the Problem of Doctrine Becomes a Political Problem

Church-state relations under Constantine weren't perfectly aligned with Christian theology—far from it. It took some time for the full implications of Christian doctrines to transform the relationship between the church and the state. And Constantine, as we shall see, was not the ideal Christian emperor—even setting aside the fact that he waited to be baptized till the very end of his life, a not uncommon thing to do at the time.

But interestingly, even Constantine's greatest failures to respect a distinction between church and state illustrate the reality that church and state cannot be fused—especially that the church cannot be subordinated to the state. Consider Constantine's decidedly mixed record in the Arian controversy.

Christ had commanded his disciples to baptize all the nations in the name of the Father, Son, and Holy Spirit, and declared that he himself was "the way and the truth and the life" (John 14:6). But how was this great and mysterious truth to be understood?

As is well known, it was Constantine who called one of the most important church councils of all time, the Council of Nicaea (325), from which all Christians have received the Nicene Creed outlining the basics of the Christian faith.[4] At issue in this council was what came to be known as the heresy of Arianism—and, more generally, the question of how to sort out the nature of Jesus Christ, the Son, and his relationship to the Father. Was Jesus the Son truly divine, that is, begotten by the Father but co-eternal and one in being with him? (That was the orthodox position, defended most famously by Athanasius.) Or was the Son merely the first of all creatures, who did not exist before he was begotten? (That was the position of Arius, a presbyter from Alexandria, Egypt, for whom the heresy was named.)

Arianism had already spread rapidly, and orthodox bishops and Arian bishops were fighting over it. Scripture alone couldn't solve the issue. The New Testament canon had yet to be definitively established, and in any case the dispute arose from different interpretations of the same scriptural passages accepted as authoritative by all sides.

So Constantine, using his imperial authority, gathered bishops from all over the empire to clarify this essential point of doctrine. Had he wanted to follow in the footsteps of the pagan Roman emperors, he would simply have decreed which position the bishops should sanction. Instead, he deferred to the bishops, even while impressing upon them the importance of doctrinal unity for political unity.

The result of the council was that Arius was condemned and exiled. He ultimately fled to Nicomedia, putting himself under the protection of Constantia, the Emperor Constantine's sister, and the pro-Arian bishop Eusebius—the very bishop, ironically, who would later baptize the dying Constantine.[5]

But that is not the end of the story. Arianism continued to have many passionate supporters. Eventually Constantine, tired of controversy and wanting more than anything for doctrinal disagreements to quit disturbing the empire, attempted to mend fences and pushed Athanasius, the orthodox bishop of Alexandria, to readmit Arius into the church. Athanasius refused, and thence commenced a long, bitter struggle between Athanasius and Constantine, who exiled the orthodox bishop.

Arianism, as we have seen, had supporters in Constantine's own household. So it was that the Arian bishop Eusebius of Nicomedia baptized the dying emperor. That same Eusebius advised Constantine's son, Constantius II, emperor of the Eastern part of the empire, to use his imperial power after his father's death to reverse the decision of the Nicene council.

Constantius immediately began deposing orthodox bishops and installing Arian ones, and he spread his pro-Arian policies empire-wide when he became sole emperor in 355 AD. "The world groaned to find itself Arian," goes the famous quote from St. Jerome. It seemed that true Trinitarianism had been defeated by the imperium.

Political Unity versus Oneness in the Faith

Belief in a less-than-truly-divine Jesus opens the door a crack for re-divinizing the emperor. On top of that, Arianism meant a more compliant church. As historian Hugo Rahner rightly notes, "Arian Christianity was always more prone than the Catholic Church to submit to the state's authority because it lacked the counterweight of faith in Christ's divinity and thus a sense of transcendence, which could lead it to consider the state as only a thing of secondary importance compared with Christ's supreme power flowing from his participation in the divine nature."[6] No doubt the emperor understood the political advantages of Arianism. But Constantius wasn't some kind of a cackling megalomaniac like the divine Nero. He had—and we must understand the full force of such a criticism—good intentions. As historian Owen Chadwick notes,

> the consistent, overruling objective of Constantius' church policy was to find a formula on which the largest possible number could agree. Constantius was persuaded…that the right recipe for a united church throughout the empire was an imprecise and broad definition. The emperor was convinced by plentiful evidence [of conflicts between bishops] that the old Nicene formula of 325…was a cause of sharp disputes and not at all conducive to peace. It seemed sensible, therefore, to propose for everyone's assent a simpler creed…which was sufficiently wide to comprehend everybody but the intransigent extremists on either side.[7]

Politicians seek broad consensus with blurred edges (or no edges at all). Constantius was not seeking the truth about the nature of Jesus Christ, but rather a fuzzy creed with which anyone could agree, one so broad as to be acceptable to *both* those who asserted that Jesus Christ was eternal and fully divine *and* those who asserted that he was a mere creature.

But the church has to be concerned with truth, and Athanasius, the great champion of orthodoxy against political expediency, would not back down. It was, so it seemed, *Athanasius contra mundum*, Athanasius against the world.

Athanasius did not live to see the end of the battle, a battle in which there was all too much politicking on both sides in attempts to gain imperial support. Final victory for the orthodox came through another emperor,

Theodosius I (ruling from 379 to 395, the last three years as sole emperor). Theodosius accepted the anti-Arian Nicene Creed. He issued the so-called "Edict of Thessalonica" in early 380, which demanded that all subjects adhere to the faith as defined by the pro-Nicene bishops of Rome and Alexandria, and this creed (with additions) was officially reaffirmed in the Second Ecumenical Council of Constantinople (381).

The Christian empire was thereby brought back to orthodox Trinitarianism. (There were complications, though. The Arian Eusebius of Nicomedia had ordained a Gothic convert, Ulfilas, as bishop about forty years earlier, and he had set out as a missionary to his Germanic peoples, carrying Arianism with him. As a result, the Germanic Christians were Arians.)

While the story of Arianism is complex, the lessons learned, at least for our purposes, are not. While it may have been helpful for an emperor to force bishops to hash out and define orthodoxy, that same political power could just as easily confirm heresy as orthodoxy. Constantine called the Council of Nicaea, but Constantius called, and controlled, the Arian-affirming Councils of Arles (353) and Milan (355).

As the church found out, the truth of doctrine is something that must be defined and guarded by the church. If the state takes over the task, its concern for political unity will almost invariably drive it to water down the faith for the sake of political compromise. The source of unity of doctrine cannot be the emperor; oneness in the faith cannot be derived from the desire for political unity. Doctrinal unity must come from within the church *as distinct from* the imperium.

The Moral Transformation of the Roman Empire

Nevertheless, the distinction between the church and imperial power at the time of Constantine was not understood as a separation—certainly not in the modern, *Everson v. Board of Education*, sense. The church and political power were distinct in the Christian Roman Empire, but that didn't mean, either to churchmen or to Christian emperors, that the church should be walled off from a secular state. So even while we can rightly say the church invented the notion of the separation of church and state, we must be careful not to read modern secularist assumptions into ancient Christian thought.

A Christian emperor was Christian, and so Christian moral principles must inform his legislation. He himself would be judged according to how well those principles did inform his rule. As Christians, both priests and emperors naturally wanted the moral message of Christianity to be the basis of society and of law. They believed that it was their obligation to see that society was infused with Christian moral principles.

So, beginning with Constantine, we see a moral-political revolution taking definite shape in the Roman Empire, a revolution that will ultimately transform the moral-legal structure of the West. Both law and society, through the evangelizing efforts of the church, will move from smiling upon contraception, abortifacients, abortion, infanticide, prostitution, concubinage, divorce, pederasty, homosexuality, gladiatorial combat, and so forth, to rejecting all these things. Thus Christianity will bring about the single greatest transformation not only of conscience, but of public morality and law, in the world's history.

For example, brutality and military might were central to the maintenance of Rome's prestige, and gladiatorial combat was a traditionally sanctioned display of both power and courage. Against this long-standing tradition, in 325 Emperor Constantine wrote to one Maximus, a prefect, "Bloody spectacles displease us amid public peace and domestic tranquility. We therefore prohibit the existence of all gladiators."[8]

The pagan Roman right to commit infanticide was rejected; exposure of infants was now to be considered an act of homicide.[9] Penalties in the new moral-legal code were quite harsh. Constantine rejected both euthanasia and infanticide, counting both as equivalent in moral gravity to parricide, which had always carried an especially gruesome penalty. Thus,

> Whoever, secretly or openly, shall hasten the death of a parent,
> or son or other near relative, whose murder is accounted as

parricide, will suffer the penalty of parricide. He will not be punished by the sword, by fire or by some other ordinary form of execution, but he will be sewn up in a sack and, in this dismal prison, have serpents as his companions. Depending on the nature of the locality, he shall be thrown into the neighboring sea or into the river, so that even while living he may be deprived of the enjoyment of the elements, the air being denied him while living and interment in the earth when dead.[10]

But along with such severe punishments, Constantine also offered unprecedented positive charity to alleviate the situation. Recognizing that many parents were exposing their infants or selling their children into slavery because they were destitute, Constantine declared that officials of the empire would "bestow freely the necessary support on all persons whom they observe to be placed in dire need."[11]

Later Christian emperors were more explicit in uniting condemnation of the act of infanticide with pastoral care of exposed infants.[12] The concern for the abandoned infant marks an extraordinary difference between pagan Rome and Christianity. In pagan Rome, finders of such infants had usually sold them into slavery or prostitution. With the advent of Christianity, believers now had a moral obligation to baptize and care for such infants.[13]

Christianity brought with it other significant social-moral-legal changes. Because the church required monogamy (or celibacy), rather than giving sexuality license to express itself everywhere and anywhere, pornography and pornographic literature would soon all but disappear.[14] Men, and not just women, would be condemned for adultery. Women would gain property and contract rights, and divorce (which had been all too easy for men, at the expense of women) would be made much more difficult. Moreover, the law began to protect the weak from the strong, mainly by eliminating the judicial and administrative corruption that always favors the rich, and by allowing ecclesiastical courts to take on civil cases (the church being far more concerned than the state with the fate of the poor and oppressed).

The imperium itself, alongside the church, also began to take care of the destitute.[15]

We must add that the transformation was not just moral but theological, because the moral and theological, while distinct, could ultimately not be separated. Christian emperors considered questions of theological orthodoxy to be essentially related to the political order, as we've already seen with Constantine. This connection is especially clear by the time of the later Christian emperor Justinian (c. 482–565), whose famous *Code*, mentioned above, begins "In the name of our Lord Jesus Christ," and then proceeds to an imperial command for orthodoxy in regard to the Holy Trinity.[16]

The same close relationship between theology and civil law is found in Justinian's *Digest*, a Christian compilation and ordering of all the diverse enactments of Roman jurists.[17] The *Digest* would become the very core of all later European law, mediating the Christianized understanding of Roman law to the medieval and modern world. (As we'll see, it was precisely *because* Christianity had built its moral-legal structures on a foundation of Roman Law purified by Christian morality that modern liberals believed they had to find a completely different foundation, one that left no foothold for the church.)

By recognizing a moral code that stood above all merely human laws and judged them, the Christian Roman civil law instilled in the minds of the converted the profoundly revolutionary truth that the sovereign's will is only law insofar as it conforms to God's revealed moral law—and no farther. (Modern liberalism, as we shall see, begins with the assertion that the will of the king is law and ends with the assertion that the will of the people is law. Both alternatives represent a rejection of the Christian belief that the moral law is above and beyond *any* human will.)

The West Escapes Caesaropapism

The Christian distinction between the church and political power was fully realized only in the West. The reason for that, interestingly enough, is the fact that Constantine moved the imperial capital to the eastern part of the empire in 330 AD. Christian revelation, as we have seen, was the ultimate root cause of this distinction, but it took some time for Biblical and doctrinal principles to be put into actual effect in the circumstances that arose, providentially, in the history of the West.

The move of the imperial capital from Rome to Constantinople in the East allowed the Western church to come out from the shadow of the emperor and his imperial court. Thus the Christian and Biblical distinction between church and state could become established in the West where the church, absent the direct influence of a strong emperor, could develop free of excessive imperial control. By contrast, in the East the emperor did retain control over religious matters, and that control allowed him to subordinate the church to his rule. The situation that prevailed in the East, which approached a royal theocracy, is called Caesaropapism because it entails the effective rule of the emperor (Caesar) as a kind of pseudo-pope over the church.

Caesaropapism meant that the Eastern church would never gain the kind of independence that allowed it to be really, practically distinct from the state. (Hence the Eastern church would, many centuries later, come under the tutelage of Russian tsars and, in the twentieth century, remain an entirely ineffective force against the grim rule of the communists.)

But in the West, the Christian distinction between religious and government authority was able to prevail. The escape of the church in the West from imperial control was facilitated by two events. The first of these we have just mentioned: Constantine moving the imperial city to Constantinople. The second, to which we now turn, was the fall of the empire in the West.

The Fall of the Roman Imperium: St. Augustine Defends the Church and Defines the State

The sack of Rome by Alaric and the Goths in 410 was the beginning of the end of imperial rule in the West. The fall of Rome to barbarians made one point very clear: imperial Rome, even Christianized imperial Rome, was not eternal. The church remained while the city of Rome fell, proving that even the greatest political power was ultimately temporal and transitory—a point driven home and made a key part of the West's theological-political heritage by St. Augustine.

We must remember that at this time the pagan empire was not entirely Christianized. The sacking of Rome gave the still formidable pagans of the empire (especially those in the aristocracy) a powerful and apparently reasonable complaint against the Christians. Before Christianity came on the scene, Rome was great. Since Christianity's rise to power, Rome itself had been overrun by barbarians. Therefore the sack of Rome must be the result of the abandonment of the Roman gods, and of the malignant influence of Christianity undermining Rome's civic strength. Christians had destroyed the empire by weakening it, by attacking its gods as demons, and by shifting the ultimate loyalty of its citizens to a kingdom not of this world. Even worse, Alaric, the barbarian sacker of Rome, was a Christian (albeit an Arian). Didn't Christians have a greater bond with Alaric than with non-Christian Romans?

So claimed the pagans. The great African bishop St. Augustine rose to answer these pagan charges in his *City of God*, and, in doing so, this most influential of theologians greatly clarified and advanced the distinction between the church and political power. Importantly, Augustine's long defense is peppered with references to Scripture.

Augustine began by declaring that he was going "to defend the most glorious city of God against those who prefer their own gods to the founder of that city."[18] It was not Christianity that had brought about Rome's fall, argued Augustine. It was Rome's own pride, and "'God resists the proud, but gives grace to the humble' (Proverbs 3:34; James 4:6; I Peter 5:5)."[19] The entire history of Rome before Christianity had been filled with bloody internal conflict and turmoil that continued right up to the time of the Christian emperors. Even worse, Rome's imperial glory was based upon its having conquered and ruled through injustice, and "Without justice, what are kingdoms but great robber bands? What are robber bands but small kingdoms?"[20] It was not Christianity that had fatally weakened Rome. The empire had suffered a moral-political collapse long in the making.[21] "True justice," Augustine claimed, "does not exist except in that republic whose founder and ruler is Christ...in that city of which the Sacred Scripture says, 'Glorious things are said about you, O city of God' (Psalms 87:3)."[22]

And so, argued Augustine, pagan virtue was not the source of any greatness Rome could claim, and Christianity was not to blame for the fall of the empire. At its best, sinful Rome was an instrument of the "providence of the most high God," the God of the Christians, for "the wisdom of God says, 'Through me kings rule, and tyrants hold the earth through me' (Proverbs 8:15)."[23] And even though the empire was a tool of Providence, sin defined all Rome's efforts and aims, setting it against the city of God, which was the only truly just kingdom because it was ruled by the only true God. "The two cities [the pagan city of Rome and the heavenly city of God]," Augustine asserts, "were created by two loves: the earthly city by love of oneself" which is the root of sin, and "the heavenly city by the love of God.... The first glories in itself, the second in the Lord." Quoting St. Paul (Romans 1:21–25), Augustine asserts that the Romans' search for earthly glory led them into idolatry, so that they "'became fools, changing the glory of the incorruptible God into the images of corruptible man, birds, four-footed animals, and serpents'"—in other words, into pagan religion.[24]

Even aside from the effects of sin and idolatry on the earthly city, Augustine made clear that the aim of Rome could not compete with the aim of Christianity. While the Roman leaders ruled an earthly kingdom for earthly glory, the Christians' "city is everlasting," and there alone "exists true and complete felicity.... There the sun does not rise on the good and the evil (Matthew 5:45), but the Sun of Justice (Malachi 4:2) protects the good alone.... That city in which it has been promised to us to rule surpasses this one [that is, the earthly city of Rome] as far as heaven is distant from the earth, eternal life from temporal joy, solid glory from empty praise, the company of angels from the company of mortals, the glory of [him] who made the sun and moon from the light of the sun and the moon."[25] As Augustine makes clear elsewhere, in his *Confessions*, our longing for true and complete happiness is built into us by God, so that "our hearts are restless until they rest" in him.[26] We will always long for more than any earthly city can provide.

The church, defined by and aiming at the city of God, promises what no earthly city, no temporal kingdom, can ever provide. In this life, every Christian must live in an earthly city, but he will always possess a dual citizenship, and there is no doubt where his ultimate allegiance lies—to the city above and beyond this world.

The church is also supra-political in another sense, exactly the sense contained in the pagan charge that Christians had more in common with the invading barbarian Christians than they did with their fellow Romans who remained pagans. In aiming to convert all nations, Christians disregard political boundaries, uniting more intimately with non-citizens in the universal Body of Christ than with fellow citizens in any particular body politic. From the point of view of the earthly city, this is treason. From Augustine's viewpoint, however, this-worldly political orders are all merely transitory.

Here we must steer clear of a common confusion. The "Augustinian view" of the political order, of the city of man, is all too often presented as only negative, as exclusively a condemnation—as if any and every political order, pagan or Christian, was reduced in Augustine's thought to a band of robbers ruled by lust and crime. Such a reading is understandable, given some of the purple passages in *The City of God* where Augustine most passionately pummels the state. But Augustine did see an important difference between pagan and Christian rule, as he reveals in his assessment of Christian emperors. "Can Christian rulers be considered worthy and happy?," asks Augustine. His answer:

> Yes, insofar as they rule according to their own ultimate allegiance to the City of God, that is, if they make their power the

servant of God's majesty by using it for the greatest possible extension of his worship; if they fear and love and worship God; if they love that kingdom in which they are not afraid to share power more than their earthly kingdom; if they are slow to punish and ready to pardon; if they apply that punishment as necessary to govern and defend the republic and not in order to indulge their own hatred; if they grant pardon, not so that crime should be unpunished, but in the hope of correction; if they compensate with the gentleness of mercy and the liberality of benevolence for whatever severe measure they may be compelled to decree; if their extravagance is as much restrained as it might have been unrestrained; if they prefer to rule evil desires rather than any people one might name; and if they do all these things from love of eternal happiness rather than ardor for empty glory, and if they do not fail to offer to the true God who is their God the sacrifices of humility, contrition, and prayer for their sins. Such Christian emperors, we claim, are happy in the present through hope, and are happy afterwards, in the future, in the enjoyment of happiness itself, when what we wait for will have come.[27]

Note that the Christian emperor restrains himself *because* he looks to another kingdom for his reward. The best emperor in this world, Augustine argues, is the one who has his eye on the next. His hope to enter the kingdom of God makes him the most mild, just, benevolent ruler. The otherworldly kingdom of God is the most effective curb on the passions, ambitions, cruelties, and crimes of those who have unlimited political power in this world. Augustine gives the example of the Christian emperor Theodosius (347–395) who had massacred rioting Thessalonians. The bishop Ambrose of Milan had compelled him to do public penance for his sin.[28]

So contrary to what is often reported, in demoting the earthly city St. Augustine did not flatten necessary distinctions between good and bad political regimes or good and bad rulers in this world. That's why, immediately following the above-quoted passage, Augustine praises Christian emperors,[29] just as he condemns the pagan emperors.

But Augustine also avoids the error of thinking that the heavenly city and the earthly city can be happily united in a Christian imperium. Political rule of the transitory earthly city is always distinct from the kingdom of God. While the temporal realm can be ruled *for the sake of* the eternal realm, the presence of sin means that all earthly kingdoms are to some degree tainted. Even if a particular ruler happens to be a good Christian emperor, there will always be sin among his political subordinates, among the people he rules, and among his successors, and his kingdom will always be merely temporal rather than eternal.

St. Augustine turned out to be the single most influential theologian in the West, and his deeply wrought understanding of the distinction between the temporal earthly city and the heavenly city of God, which was the ultimate source of the distinction between the state and the church, had enormous impact. But while Augustine set the issue in good theological order, the distinction only took on living flesh and bones in history during the period running from the fall of Rome to the High Middle Ages, to which we will turn in the next chapter.

The Implications of This History
Seen from the Pagan Point of View

We began this chapter by noting that the fourth century AD, running from the conversion of Constantine to the sack of Rome by the Goths, is historically pivotal, the great turning point in world history when paganism gave way to Christianity. But if we look at things from the pagan side, it was the time when history took a terribly wrong turn. That assessment would be embraced by modern liberals, who would try—are in fact still trying, with a large measure of success—to turn history back again onto what from the liberal point of view is the right track, back to a form of paganism. Let's take another look at the ground we've covered, but this time *from the pagan-liberal side*, from the point of view of those who, seeing what was done in the christening of pagan society in the fourth century AD, ask "How can this be undone?"

First, it's clear that the church, which professes to stand above the state and hence looks down on earthly life as comparatively second rate, cannot be allowed to be independent. Christians, who profess a kind of dual citizenship, have only limited allegiance to the state. (You can't really get much obedience out of people who would rather die than comply with the laws of the state when they conflict with the laws of their supposed heavenly city.)

Something must also be done about belief in the immortality of the soul. That doctrine is at the root of the church's independence and power. It's what gives the priest power over the king, the bishop over the emperor. We must abolish the belief in the soul *at least* for our political leaders, because if they, like Constantine or Theodosius, are worried about their eternal fate, they'll always be in the power of the church. If we must have a "next world"—most people are incurably superstitious, you know—then everyone must be made to believe that they can get there simply by being decent, law-abiding people, good citizens of the kingdoms of this world.

We must jettison both the belief that there is supernatural happiness beyond this world—happiness that is incomparably greater than anything that can ever be experienced here—and also the moral intensity that raises the moral bar for Christians to a kind of perfection that mere human beings cannot achieve alone. As long as the moral bar is set impossibly high, Christians will feel they need supernatural help to make up for their failings ("sins," as they call them) and look forward to a supernatural realm where moral perfection is possible.

Thus the desire for happiness must be reduced to the yen for bodily comfort in this world. And the moral intensity of Christianity must be toned down to a more easy-going moral code that nearly everyone can follow with very little effort. Naturally, the return to the pagan regime will take a large-scale transformation of Christianized culture, one that both erases the desire for a greater happiness and eliminates the notion of sin so deeply embedded in art, literature, music, and in Christian doctrine itself. Christian morality must no longer be allowed to define law and culture. De-Christianization means replacing all this with an easy-going hedonism satisfied with what the state can give, so easy-going that the notion of failure or "sin" vanishes. In short, no more restless hearts; let all hearts rest in this world!

Further, the church must not be allowed to define doctrine or to control its own bishops. Instead, the state must become the definer of doctrine, and bishops and priests must be turned into civil servants. Doctrine itself could be demonized as the cause of political strife, and political compromise could be heralded as the right way to approach doctrine—make all sides happy by making all doctrinal disagreements seem trivial. If Christianity must survive in any form, let its creed be reduced to cheerfully getting along with everyone no matter what he or she believes. That was the Roman pagan approach—just obey Caesar's laws, and you can believe whatever you want, as long as you don't bother anyone else.

Obviously, in this thought experiment in seeing things from the pagan point of view, we're getting ahead of ourselves in the argument—and in history—looking ahead to what we'll uncover in more detail in later chapters. But before we explore the actual resurgence of paganism, which didn't really take off until more than a thousand years after Constantine's conversion, we need to understand more clearly how the relationship between church and state developed after this pivotal Christianizing period, as the church further evangelized the crumbling Western part of the empire.

CHAPTER 5

THE MIDDLE AGES: DEFINING THE CHURCH-STATE DISTINCTION

I n the previous chapters we've explored the Christian framework for understanding the relationship of the church to the state, and established why the church, to fulfill its mission, had to be independent from the state, but also had to evangelize the state as it evangelized all of society.

The real trick after the conversion of Constantine was, on the one hand, to avoid having the church absorbed by the Christianized state, and on the other, to avoid having the church, in its position of power and prestige, absorb the state. The two had to be kept distinct, even while on friendly and cooperative terms.

That's exactly what the historical wrestling match of medieval church-state relations was about. The implications of Christian doctrine and Christian life for the relationship between political and religious authorities had to be hammered out in practice, as well as in theory. We'll look first at some of that theory, and then move on to examine in some detail the historical conflicts in which the Christian arrangement between church and state was achieved in practice.

Two There Are by Which the World is Ruled

One of the most famous and influential passages ever written about church and state—quoted again and again by later popes and churchmen—comes from a protest by Gelasius, pope from 492 to 496, against the Eastern Emperor Anastasius's attempt to push a watered-down creedal compromise known as the *Henoticon*.[1] In 494 Pope Gelasius wrote to the emperor what became one of the most influential letters in history. Note that a practical controversy—the attempt by the emperor to water down doctrine—yielded an important theoretical principle:

> Two there are, august emperor, by which this world is chiefly ruled, the sacred authority of the priesthood and the royal power. Of these the responsibility of the priests is more weighty in so far as they will answer for the kings of men themselves at the divine judgment. You know, most clement son, that, although you take precedence over all mankind in dignity, nevertheless you piously bow the neck to those who have charge of divine affairs and seek from them the means of your salvation, and hence you realize that, in the order of religion, in matters concerning the reception and right administration of the heavenly sacraments, you ought to submit yourself rather than rule, and that in these matters you should depend on their judgment rather than seek to bend them to your will.[2]

Just as we've seen with Constantine, the sacramental power of the priest is ultimately more important than the political power of any ruler because that ruler's eternal destiny is in the hands of the priest.

But that did not mean, for Pope Gelasius, that the priest takes the place of the king or that the pope supplants the emperor. There are *two* powers, and the two powers and their two respective domains remain truly distinct.

In a later treatise *On the Bond of Anathema* (496), Gelasius explained the distinction further, asserting that before Christ, priest and king were often united in one man, "and so the pagan emperors were called supreme pontiffs [*Pontifices Maximi*]." This union of priest and king in the pagan emperor was, however, the result of the devil trying to imitate Melchizedek, the priest-king who prefigured Christ in the Old Testament.[3] But after the coming of Christ, "who was true king and true priest, the [Christian] emperor no longer assumed the title of priest, nor did the priest claim the royal dignity...."[4] For Gelasius Biblical history, culminating in Christ, determined political history.

After the Incarnation, the political and religious powers were forever and entirely distinct, each with its own proper sphere and functions, which the other must respect and not transgress. Both the church and the state were limited. According to Gelasius,

> For Christ, mindful of human frailty, regulated with an excellent disposition what pertained to the salvation of his people. Thus he distinguished between the offices of both powers according to their own proper activities and separate dignities, wanting his people to be saved by healthful humility and not carried away again by human pride, so that Christian emperors would need priests for attaining eternal life and priests would avail themselves of imperial regulations in the conduct of temporal affairs. In this fashion spiritual activity would be set apart from worldly encroachments and the "soldier of God" (2 Timothy 2:4) would not be involved in secular affairs, while on the other hand he who was involved in secular affairs would not seem to

preside over divine matters. Thus the humility of each order
would be preserved, neither being exalted by the subservience
of the other, and each profession would be especially fitted for
its appropriate functions.[5]

It's needful to say—*very needful*—that the word translated as "secular" here
did not, in the fifth century, have the modern implications associated with
secularism. That is, it did not mean "entirely devoid of any connection to
religion" or "bent on the removal of religion," or "materialist" or "atheist."[6]

In the time of Gelasius (and into the Middle Ages), secular (from *saec-
ulum* in Latin) simply meant *pertaining to the affairs of this world, of this life*.
It originally referred to the duration of a person's life, or to a particular
generation (as we say, "the present generation" or "future generations"),
and by extension, to the age (as in, the "present age"). It came to mean
worldly as opposed to divine, because divine matters are focused on the age
to come, when all merely temporal ages will give way to the eternal.

Secular was not, therefore, the opposite of religious. The temporal and
eternal, secular things and religious things, were not in fundamental opposition precisely because it was essential Christian doctrine that how people
lived this life in this age would determine how they spent eternity, as Christ
had stated most emphatically in Matthew 25:31–46, where the eternal fate
of both "sheep" and "goats" is determined by their charity (or the lack of it)
in this world. The temporal should aim at the eternal, even while being
distinct from it.

So now we've come up against a great puzzle. We find a fifth-century
pope stating decisively the distinction between church and state, assigning
each institution very definite functions that the other must not transgress,
and arguing that the division between the two was constructed by Christ
himself to keep both from pride by making each necessary to the other. This
is clearly no wall of separation between church and state in the post-*Everson
v. Board of Education* sense, that is, in the sense demanded by our modern
militant secularists.

So historically, our modern notion of the distinction between church and state is ultimately traceable to a theological argument made by a pope, who in turn claimed it was traceable to Christ himself, and based this claim on Scripture. What sense does it make to believe that the separation of church and state requires for Christianity to be walled off from the state as an alien contagion?

Pope Gelasius certainly did not see it that way, but he did argue that church and state must be separate in the sense of truly distinct. For the moral good of each, the church and the political power must each respect the independence of the other. Church and state are complementary, each supplying what the other lacks, so that there is an essential harmony without confusion between them.

This understanding of church and state as complementary was given its definitive form by Bishop Humbert of Silva Candida in the mid-eleventh century and Hugh of Saint Victor in the first part of the twelfth century. Taking up where Pope Gelasius had left off, Humbert argued,

> Anyone...who wishes to compare the priestly and royal dignities in a useful and blameless fashion may say that, in the existing church, the priesthood is analogous to the soul and the kingship to the body, for they cleave to one another and need one another and each in turn demands services and renders them one to the other. It follows from this that, just as the soul excels the body and commands it, so too the priestly dignity excels the royal or, we may say, the heavenly dignity the earthly.[7]

And Hugh of St. Victor asserted,

> There are two lives, one earthly, the other heavenly, one corporeal, the other spiritual.... Therefore [two] powers were established.... The one power is... called secular, the other

spiritual.... The earthly power has as its head the king. The
spiritual power has the supreme pontiff. All things that are
earthly and made for the earthly life belong to the power of
the king. All things that are spiritual and attributed to the
spiritual life belong to the power of the supreme pontiff. The
spiritual power excels the earthly or secular power in honor
and dignity in proportion as the spiritual life is more worthy
than the earthly, and the spirit than the body.[8]

The superiority of the priesthood to kingship was, for Hugh, rooted in the
Old Testament, wherein "the priesthood was first instituted by God and
then the royal power was established through the priesthood at God's command."[9]

By this point in the High Middle Ages, the entire intellectual structure
of the Christian distinction between church and state was in place. The
necessary separation of religious from political power was understood to
be firmly rooted both in Scripture and in the real metaphysical distinction
between the immortal soul and the mortal body. The church is defined by
the eternal good of the soul, and its activities are directed toward the city
of God, toward heaven. The state is defined by the temporal goods of the
body, and its responsibility is for the cares of earthly life.

But again church and state, even while truly distinct, are not separate
in the modern sense—for two reasons. The analogy to the relationship
between the soul and the body is illuminating here. First, while the soul and
body are distinct, they are still essentially united in the present life. Complete separation of the soul from the body—in the modern sense of absolute
separation of church and state—only occurs at death (just as the state will
pass away with the passing away of the world).

Second, precisely because a human being is an essential unity of soul
and body, the church must be concerned about the temporal, bodily welfare
of its members as well as their spiritual welfare. In fact the church is commanded by Christ to show real, very bodily charity to all, feeding the hungry,

clothing the naked, aiding the politically oppressed, serving the poor. In addition, given this essential unity of body and soul, the state must care for the good of the soul; that is, it must inculcate virtue and punish vice in its citizens because virtue leads to good political order and vice destroys it.

We've now got a general sense of the theoretical underpinnings of the distinction between church and state as it developed from the time of Pope Gelasius in the fifth century up until Hugh of St. Victor in the twelfth century. Now let's look at the gritty details of the historical context in which that understanding was actually hammered out during this same time period. We'll begin with the complexities of Pope Gelasius's time, the so-called Dark Ages after the fall of Rome.

Wrestling for the Truth in the Dark Ages

These times are known as "dark" because, as we've already noted, the political structure of imperial Rome in the West had collapsed under its own corruption and through external attack. Internal moral-political decay set the empire up to give way under successive waves of so-called barbarian invasions of Visigoths, Ostrogoths, Vandals, and Huns from the 300s to the 700s. Charlemagne—crowned by the pope at Christ's Mass (that is December 25) in the year 800—seemed a promising antidote to the political chaos, but after his death, his sons and lesser lords fought among themselves. Waves of attacks from without resumed, ensuring more complete political disorder. The attempt to create a unified Christian empire in the West dissolved.[10]

There were two important results of the dissolution of the empire: (1) bishops often became the default source of legal-political order wherever the imperial order had been destroyed,[11] and (2) with the imperial order gone, political order where it did exist was local—amounting to the rule by a duke or king of his personal *estate*, on which he often endowed a church or monastery.[12]

Both developments tended first toward confusing, but ultimately toward clarifying, the distinction between church and state. As we look at this historical process, we'll have a much better understanding of what went on if we substitute "estate" for "state," because after the collapse of imperial rule the political regimes in the West are defined by the rule of a person over his personal lands, that is, his *estates*. (Even when their reigns were dressed in imperial language, Frankish or Germanic "emperors" really amounted to Frankish or Germanic kings ruling over their own territorial estates.)

When Bishops Became Kings

In regard to the first development, bishops assuming political duties amidst a political vacuum, obviously Gelasius's distinction between the priestly and royal power was muddled when bishops were forced to function as kings, temporarily overseeing both ecclesial and temporal affairs.[13]

Things went beyond muddled to a state of corruption when bishops—or worse, popes—later became temporal rulers of their own lands, that is, their own estates. This happened not just because of a power vacuum that bishops stepped in to fill, but because temporal rulers often gave estates to the church as a form of genuine charity. The most famous of these donations of land was to the bishop of Rome—not the faked Donation of Constantine, but the actual well-intentioned and pious gift of Italian lands to the papacy in the mid-eighth century by the Frankish king Pepin, the father of Charlemagne. But despite good intentions, the result of these gifts was all too often bad. When the church assumed the domain and hence the powers of the estate, then church and estate, spiritual and temporal, were fused into one, and the church itself became worldly.

Hence the worst corruption in the church occurred during the time when the pope was not only the ruler of the church universal but also *at the same time* the political ruler of Italy, or more precisely, of the papal estates or states. The pope's loyalties became divided between conflicting aims as he tried to maintain a universal church *and* a very particular political kingdom at the same time. The sad result was that all too often he used the power of universal church to maintain his particular royal estate. And all over Europe, much the same thing happened with a great number of lesser bishops and their estates.

But that wasn't the worst of it. With the full force of the universal church's spiritual power backing a particular political regime, small wonder that the papacy came to be considered a great *political* prize. It was therefore sought after by ambitious Italian nobles who were eager to use the church for economic and political gains. Thus the scandal of the papacy in the fifteenth century—think of the Borgia popes—which was a repeat of the scandals in the ninth and beginning of the tenth centuries when the papacy fell under the control of "the gangster Roman nobility," to use historian Norman Cantor's apt words.[14]

We might say then, looking ahead, that the Reformation, as a reaction to the worldly papacy, was actually a reaction against a violation of the temporal realm by the spiritual, that is, a distortion of the proper relationship of church and political power as defined by previous popes themselves.

When Kings Established Estate Churches

When imperial order collapsed in the West and dukes and kings rose amidst the chaos as local guarantors of social order, they often did a very pious thing, something entirely admirable that contributed significantly to the further spreading of Christianity in the West. They built churches and endowed monasteries on their estates. But even with the best of intentions the local ruler all too often treated the church or monastery on his estate as *his own*—*his* church on *his* estate, and hence, his *estate church*, with a bishop or priest of his own choosing who was ultimately answerable to him.

In this situation, the church was subordinate to the ruler and his estate, and the allegiance of the priest or bishop was to the estate owner in a kind of vassal-to-master feudal relationship. Perhaps he was a pious duke or king, as was often the case. But even in that best-case scenario, the church's independence was severely compromised.

Much worse abuses occurred when a less than pious king or duke viewed the church on his estate as a handy means of revenue. Perhaps he might have recently acquired the estate, whether by fair means or foul, and might consider the local monastery as simply part of the booty. He might rake off tithe money for himself. Or he might use his power to fill clerical positions as a means for advancing his kin—appointing indolent or ambitious sons to bishoprics, churches, or monasteries. These sons might very well have no interest in holiness and see their positions in the church only as providing a very this-worldly opportunity to live it up.

The utter corruption of the church by worldly laymen was the result. "Lay investiture," as it was called when temporal rulers could appoint clergy, naturally led to "simony," the sale of clerical offices, and also to "concubinage," that is, clergy living in quasi-marital relationships with women, and fathering children whose temporal careers they would naturally want to assist by using the church's resources. As historian Brian Tierney notes, "Few of the men who acquired ecclesiastical positions in this way cared anything for the spiritual duties of the offices."[15] Since their concerns were only temporal, they acted like feudal rulers rather than priests. So, for example, we have the complaint of one Berengar, viscount of Narbonne, against Wifred, archbishop of Narbonne. Berengar's family had sold the bishopric to Wifred's father, so that the son could be installed. (Wifred was ten at the time of the sale, and the price was a hundred thousand gold *solidi*.) Of course, Berengar had hoped that Bishop Wifred would remain a loyal friend. "But then, arrogant as a devil, he unexpectedly provoked me to anger and harassed me," complained Berengar to a church council in 1056, "and built castles against me and made cruel war on me with a vast army, so that on account of him almost a thousand men were slaughtered on both sides."[16] The bishop was acting like a duke, and a treacherous one at that. In the Middle Ages, it became patently obvious that if the church was to avoid being corrupted by the state, the two needed to be kept separate.

The Great Church Reform

The understanding of the right relationship between spiritual and temporal power as sketched by Christian thinkers from Pope Gelasius to Hugh of St. Victor actually emerged from the historical events of this period. Those theological principles were solidified in the process of trying to set things right, to separate the church from the estates, and the estates from the church, and keep them distinct. The right theory came largely from the church trying to reestablish the right practice, making spiritual and temporal rule distinct but complementary, the church and state each minding its own business, and each depending on the other without usurping the function of the other. Darkness, we might say, led to light, corruption to clarification, perversion to proper principles.

The evident corruption in the medieval church was answered by a great surge of enthusiasm for reform among the clergy, zealously supported by the laity. Monastic reform, the first phase of the renewal, began in the early 900s with the foundation of a new abbey at Cluny for monks who were truly committed to poverty, chastity, obedience, and enthusiastic about following St. Benedict's Rule—at a time when wealthy monks had earned a bad reputation for living luxurious worldly lives. They were reacting to the worldliness by turning away from the world. What helped make Cluny different from other monasteries, and proof against the rampant corruption of the church in its age, was that William of Aquitaine, the temporal ruler who donated the land to the monks in 910, ensured that their abbot would be elected by the monks themselves, so that no lay leader might somehow gain control of the abbey. "And, through God and all his saints, and by the awful day of judgment, I warn and objure," thundered William, "that no one of the secular princes, no count, no bishop whatever, not the pontiff of the aforesaid Roman see, shall invade the property of these servants of God, or alienate it, or diminish it, or exchange it, or give it as a benefice to anyone, or constitute any prelate over them against their will."[17] As we shall see, the Cluniac monastic reform, which soon spread across Europe, would be integral to saving and deepening the distinction between church and state. The turn to radical Christian holiness would slowly bring about the restoration of the proper, distinct domains of the church and temporal political power.

Why? The Cluniac reform produced a line of reform-minded bishops, the most important of whom were two popes, Leo IX (pope 1049–1054) and Gregory VII (1073–1085). Because of their position within the church, and their status in Christianized society, they could push through reform of the church from the top down.[18]

The papacy itself had fallen into the worst corruption as an embattled prize for Italian nobles. But ironically the religious reform that had begun in Cluny was made effective in Rome because the German king, Henry III—called Henry the Pious and soon to become Holy Roman Emperor— had installed a pope of his own choosing after booting out three rival claimants to the papacy because he was so disgusted with the condition of the church in Rome.

Henry believed he was fully within his rights in choosing the pope because Rome was part of *his* domain, *his* political estate, and therefore he had the right to appoint its bishop. Since he was in fact quite pious, he appointed a reform-minded pope (who soon died), and then another (ditto). Many people at the time suspected that the first two popes Henry had chosen were poisoned by nobles resisting both reform and the intrusion of a German king in the affairs of Rome. But the third time proved to be the charm. Henry appointed a third pope, Leo IX, who immediately set in motion a great reform that was carried forward by Pope Gregory VII.

The reform had two key aspects, both of which helped to separate the confusion of church and estates, and cement their proper division.

First—again ironically, given how Leo IX got his job—the reformers wanted to put an end to lay investiture, that is, to lay rulers choosing and installing bishops. That, it was hoped, would put an end to kings and dukes choosing their wanton or greedy sons to be their "bishops" so they could milk a living from the church, and an end to treating churches and monasteries as political prizes or trading chips (they were, as we've seen, quite literally bought and sold). The church must choose its own clergy, the reforming party demanded, and that must begin with the church at Rome. No more emperors or nobles choosing popes. The College of Cardinals was created with precisely this end in view, to take the election of popes out of the hands of ambitious and scheming Italian noble families or even well-intentioned emperors, and put it into the hands of reform-minded bishops.

Since less-than-holy bishops and abbots had concubines or were even married, and doled out churches or monasteries to their equally unworthy sons, the reforming popes demanded strict clerical celibacy. That would keep churches from being considered part of temporal estates to be passed on to sons as family legacies.

And neither Pope Leo nor Pope Gregory was content with merely issuing decrees from Rome. The goal was to actually eject unworthy bishops, priests, and abbots and to clean up dioceses and monasteries—so that a holier-minded church, having shed its worldliness, could once again care for the souls that it was charged with guiding into the next life. The whole church needed a cleaning.

The attempt at reforming the church from within meant standing firm against further intrusions by political rulers, the chief of whom were the German Holy Roman Emperors.

The Emperor Claims Rome as His Estate

If you look at a map of Europe you'll see more clearly the geographical reason for the continual political conflicts between church and estate that followed. While the Roman Empire in the West had actually died with the fall of Rome in the fifth century, continual attempts to revive a political imperium marked the centuries after Charlemagne. By the time of Pope Gregory VII, the center of such attempts had shifted from France to Germany, with German kings continually laying claim to be Holy Roman Emperors—that is, the successors to Charlemagne and the Roman emperors of ancient times. But the estate of a Holy *Roman* Emperor would necessarily stretch down from Germany itself to cover Italy. And so we have the interesting powder-keg result, the cause of so much unhappy conflict to come, that the Germanic Holy Roman Emperors considered Italy to be part of their estate, and the church at Rome to be *their* estate church.

That is why Henry III believed he was fully within his rights to boot out bad papal claimants and put in his own man. Happily for history his man, Leo IX, was a zealous and holy reformer, and his reforming zeal was taken up with even more passion by Pope Gregory VII. But Henry's son,

Henry IV, was not known as Henry the Pious Jr. Henry IV wasn't interested in the reform of the church; he wanted control of Italy and especially of the spiritual and material treasures of the church.

The Epic Clash between Pope and Emperor: Church and State in the Balance

Henry IV and Pope Gregory VII got into one of history's most famous clashes—all over who should have the right to appoint a bishop (in this case, the bishop of Milan in Italy). But there was much more at stake: Who would control the church? The whole distinction between church and state that we now accept as a given was balanced on the outcome.

If Henry IV's candidate for bishop of Milan was successfully appointed, it would prove that the Germanic king, the state, was in control of the church. Bishops would be reduced to mere political appointees with the requisite political loyalty to the emperor and his designs. Henry clearly believed that political unity and strength depended on subordinating the church to his political ambitions. As historian Brian Tierney rightly notes, "Henry could not give up the right of appointing bishops without abandoning all hope of welding Germany into a united monarchy."[19] His great political plans depended on a loyal church under his royal control. It would greatly strengthen Henry's political hand if Henry's bishops in Germany were loyal appointees, and that meant that they could not be chosen by, and answerable to, an Italian pope.

Moreover, to completely obviate any possibility of conflict with the papacy, Henry realized that he needed to control it. For his political strength as a German king, with alleged estate rights as the Holy Roman Emperor, Henry needed not just to have his own loyal bishops in Germany, but to own the papacy itself.

If Henry got his way, then Europe would take the path to Caesaropapism, and the consequent history of the West would follow the path the East had taken, into royal theocracy, with the church serving the sovereigns' political ambitions. Church and state would have been fused into a state church—there is no church "and" state in such an establishment.

If, on the other hand, Pope Gregory won out in the conflict and his candidate became Bishop of Milan, the church would retain its independence, and it could proceed with much-needed reform from worldliness to holiness. Tierney makes clear what was at stake: "Gregory could not acquiesce in the imperial claims, which included a claim to appoint the popes themselves, without jeopardizing the continuance of the entire reform movement, for Henry showed none of his father's spontaneous zeal for the task of revivifying the church."[20]

In this contest Pope Gregory had a trump card—excommunication. Because even a king must realize that his eternal destiny overshadows any potential political gains in this world, the church has ultimate spiritual authority over him. In a letter written in December 1075, Gregory reminded Henry of Christ's own words to St. Peter in the Gospel of Matthew: "I will give you the keys of the kingdom of heaven, and whatever you bind on earth shall be bound in heaven, and whatever you loose on earth shall be loosed in heaven" (Matthew 16:19).[21]

Henry's reply the following year began with the prickly salutation, "Henry, King not by usurpation, but by the pious ordination of God, to Hildebrand, now not Pope, but false monk." (Gregory's name, prior to ascending to the papal chair, was Hildebrand.) Rather than backing down, Henry made a counter-claim, one of the utmost importance for understanding later developments in the early modern world, when kings would claim to rule by divine right. "The Lord, Jesus Christ, has called us [here Henry was using the royal "we"] to kingship, but has not called you to the priesthood." Henry claimed that he was king by God's call alone, and answerable to God alone. He, too, could quote Scripture: "The true pope Saint Peter…exclaims 'Fear God, honor the king' [I Pt 2:17]."[22]

The second part of Henry's counterattack was the charge that Gregory was a false monk, rather than a true pope. In a stirring finale, Henry thundered, "I, Henry, King by the grace of God, together with all our bishops, say to you: Descend! Descend!"[23] "Our bishops," of course meant "*my* bishops in *my* Germany, *my* estate." Gregory was no pope, asserted Henry—the implication being that the King would very soon be appointing a proper pope of his own choosing.

But Pope Gregory played his trump card, informing Henry that he was excommunicated: "I deprive King Henry...who has rebelled against thy [God's] Church with unheard-of-audacity, of the government over the whole kingdom of Germany and Italy, and I release all Christian men from the allegiance which they have sworn or may swear to him, and I forbid anyone to serve him as king."[24] A king who attacked the church put himself outside the church, and therefore, as an enemy of God, was no longer a king. As Gregory would later declare, kings are members of the church and must accept its discipline. "Or are they not of the sheep which the Son of God committed to St. Peter?" asked the pope rhetorically, referring to the passage from the Gospel of John in which Christ tells Peter, "Feed my sheep" (John 21:17).[25]

This was not a mere display of the pope's own arbitrary will in a battle of wills, but was based upon the understanding that an unjust ruler was no ruler at all—the very same principle that we would use to bring a morally wayward president to his knees by the power of impeachment. Our notion that no man is above the law is, in fact, indebted historically to this display of power by a pope over a king, or at least to the principle he was invoking. And this Christian principle was, as we've seen, rooted in the Biblical understanding that no king—not even David himself—was above the moral law of God.

Henry cracked because he was afraid of rebellion (rather than of hell, or so it seemed). The German bishops were loyal men of their king, but they trembled at the theological implications of excommunication and went over to Gregory's side. If that weren't enough, the various princes in Germany, always waiting for a chance to weaken the already tenuous hold of their overlord, were only too happy to hear that any oaths of allegiance had just been canceled by Rome.

And so, Henry did an unspeakably strange thing, something possible only in the historical context of a Christian society. In January of 1077 he betook himself to Canossa in northern Italy, where Pope Gregory happened to be staying, shed his royal garb outside the fortress, and humbly donned the rags of a penitent. Standing outside in the snow, barefooted and bare-headed, Henry wailed and pleaded three days for Gregory to absolve him of his sins.

Gregory's trump card had worked. But now Henry was, ironically, playing his own. Gregory had grave doubts about Henry's sincerity, with good reason, as we'll see. But Gregory, too, was bound by the laws of the church, by the mercy of Christ himself. A priest cannot deny a penitent absolution. As Gregory later reported to the German princes, who were less than enthused at the pope's clemency, "we released him from the bonds of anathema and received him into the grace of Holy Mother Church."[26]

Henry took an oath that he would henceforth behave—and broke it soon enough. In 1080 Henry would march on Rome, and install his own pope (or anti-pope, as he is called), Clement III, an imperial-party bishop who had always opposed Gregory's reforms. Pope Gregory fled Rome and died in exile. Before his death, he issued a kind of defense of his policy toward the emperor, which was filled with multiple "convincing proofs…to be found in Holy Scripture," He cited Matthew 4:9, 11:29, 16:18–19; Mark 10:44; John 8:50, I Corinthians 6:3, among others, and leaned especially on the story of the prophet Samuel anointing Saul in I Kings 15:17.[27]

In all this historical mess, confusion, and apparent defeat, a great principle was firmly established—the church and state must be kept distinct.

The Light Dims Again

We don't need to go into detailed accounts of the succeeding battles between popes and would-be Germanic emperors, except to note that

the more heated the battles got, the more stridently the popes claimed to
have authority over kings and emperors. Such heat did not produce light.
Innocent III (pope 1198–1216) is usually regarded as the pope who went
too far in his claims, thereby usurping political power. Historically, this
is not quite accurate, or at least, it's not that simple. In several instances,
Innocent made it clear that he did not wish to usurp the rightful power
of the political ruler.[28] At the same time, Innocent did assert that both
ecclesiastical and political authority rested in him, and that he conferred
political authority on the king. Just as in Christ, in whom priest and king
were united, so also in the pope: "Jesus Christ…has so established the
priesthood and kingship in the church that the kingship is priestly and
the priesthood is royal," and so "he has set over all one whom he appointed
to be his vicar on earth so that, just as every knee on earth and in heaven
and even under the earth is bowed to him, so all should obey his vicar
and strive that there be one fold and one shepherd…so that kingship and
priesthood, like body and soul, should be united in the one person of the
vicar of Christ.…"[29]

This certainly appeared to be a declaration of papal theocracy (the
complete subordination of the state to the church) even if it was made in
an attempt to fend off royal theocracy (complete subordination of the
church to the state). Such claims seemed to upset the framework hammered
out during the time from Pope Gelasius to Hugh of St. Victor, the understanding that there were two, distinct powers, ecclesiastical and political,
each with its own proper realm, and each respecting the other's authority
by not trespassing on it. (Pope Boniface XVIII's famous papal bull, *Unam
Sanctam*, issued in 1302, made the subordination of state to the church
even more emphatic. Yet even here there were political complexities and
theological nuances, given that one of Boniface's main concerns in calling
for the unity of the church was to counteract the tendency of temporal
rulers to create what amounted to politically subordinate national
churches.)

But we should mention that while Innocent III may seem to have gone
too far, upsetting the delicate balance of church and political power, he was

still one of the great reforming popes. It was, after all, Pope Innocent who received a bedraggled Giovanni Francesco di Bernardone, pleading for recognition of his poverty-loving religious order. Innocent truly believed Giovanni to be the man God had sent to save the church from crumbling, and so he gave his papal blessing and permission to the man who would become St. Francis of Assisi.

Later popes, however, used the alleged papal powers over kings to rule in splendor as kings of their own estates, thereby fulfilling Pope Gelasius's prophecy that bishops who usurped the powers of kings would be swollen with pride and corrupt their office.

Leading Up to the Reformation

By the 1400s, the century before the Reformation, the papacy had once again become a political prize, the possession of Italian noble families such as the infamous Borgia and Medici. The Christian distinction between church and state had been obscured again, with the same disastrous results. Innocent III had crossed the dividing line between church and political power with good intentions, but the unintended consequence was, ironically, political power regaining complete control of the church and even more completely corrupting it.

What was the solution to this mess? Three distinct answers to the problem can be traced in the history of the West.

The first was another attempt at reform from within the church, as under previous reforming popes such as Gregory. Holy-minded bishops, priests, and monks worked for reform from below, trying to push up a holy, reforming pope to take the place of the worldly Renaissance popes.

The second was an attempt at reform through a revolution in the church; that was the Protestant Reformation.

The third kind of reform was the most radical. But it has had the most staying power. Its triumph has resulted in the now familiar secularizing separation of church and state, whereby the church is ousted from any public role and reduced to impotent silence, and the state absorbs the church's functions, structure, and even doctrinal authority, redirecting all those things to its entirely this-worldly goals. That is the reform that has been effected by modern secular liberalism.

Our concern in this book is with the last "reform," and so we'll begin the next chapter with Machiavelli and the invention of the modern secular state. But first some concluding reflections about the distinction between church and state.

Liberals Take Credit for the Church-State Distinction—and Set Out to Undermine It

Let's focus on an important historical irony, one that I hope occurred to you while you've been reading this chapter. Modern liberalism poses as the inventor of the distinction between church and state, as if liberals had been solely responsible for prying the church away from state power and erecting a wall of separation to keep the church from assuming dictatorial political rule. Or, looking to the Reformation and its fallout, they claim that liberalism had to wall Christianity off from the public square because otherwise the various Christian sects would still be using state power today as a weapon in their theological disputes. So liberals claim credit for creating the distinction between church and state, and for the exclusion of the church from political power.

But as we've just seen, that distinction was already well-established in the Christian Middle Ages. Catholic theologians, not secularizing liberals, were the first to argue that the church should not wield political power. The distinction between church and state was invented long before the arrival of liberalism. It was set forth by the church itself—to keep both the church *and* the state from corruption. The Establishment Clause of the First Amendment in our Bill of Rights (in its proper interpretation, at least) is historically indebted to theological developments in the Middle Ages, to the efforts of reform-minded popes, and to the holy monks of Cluny.

Ironic, isn't it, that the contemporary secular liberal understanding of church-state separation should be used as an instrument to drive Christianity, which is the ultimate historical source of the church-state distinction, into extinction?

If it wasn't clear enough from the events of Constantine's reign, one final point, well worth pondering, should surely be obvious from the history of church-state relations in the Middle Ages. If the secular power wishes to throw off all the church's influence—to remove any obstacle that Christianity might offer to the state's sole domination, unconstrained by any principle—then it must remove all the sources of the church's independent power. Henry IV felt the sting of excommunication and was forced to humiliate himself to regain control of his political realm. If the state were to become the only power, somehow the sting of possible exclusion—from the sacraments, the church, and the hope of heaven, from the respect and loyalty of Christian citizens—must be removed.

Some obvious ways this might be accomplished may have already presented themselves to the reader's mind. The political sovereign could gain control of the church, so that its hierarchy was entirely beholden to him, thereby creating an established state church. He could declare that he himself was a priest, uniting priestly and kingly power in his own person, so that he was answerable to God alone. Or he could deny the reality of the power of excommunication as wielded by bishops; that is, he could simply deny that there *are* any sacraments. He could engage in a smear campaign against the church, so as to entirely undermine the church's moral and spiritual authority. Or, since the Bible was the authoritative foundation of the church's independence and authority, he could engage in a smear campaign against the Bible, or declare that the state was the only legitimate interpreter of Scripture. Or, most radical of all, he could deny that there is any such thing as a soul, or any such otherworldly realm as hell, and even that there is a God—so that there is only material reality, only this world, and our salvation lies within the power of the state alone. Each of these options, as we shall see, will be tried from the 1500s on, with the most radical of them being attempted at the dawn of the sixteenth century. To that origin of modern liberalism we now turn.

PART III

THE RISE OF LIBERALISM AND THE RE-PAGANIZATION OF THE STATE

CHAPTER 6

MACHIAVELLI INVENTS THE SECULAR STATE (AND ITS CHURCH)

I have a confession to make. I was lying to you all along when I told you that the church invented the distinction between the church and state.

Well, I wasn't really lying, but I wasn't being completely accurate either. But it wasn't really my fault. The problem is the word "state." I had to use it, because it's the word we use today to refer to any political entity. But, in truth, it can't really be applied before the time period we're now discussing in this chapter. The term "state" didn't exist before the 1500s—at least in the sense in which we understand it today. As political historian Quentin Skinner rightly notes, "no political writer before the middle of the sixteenth century used the world 'State' in anything closely resembling our modern sense."[1]

What is that modern sense? We think of the "state" today as a kind of abstract, impersonal entity that exists independently of whatever concrete human beings happen to live in it—a neutral system of laws and offices, a set of structures that affects the individuals flowing under or through it, but which itself remains supremely unaffected.

This abstract modern conception of the state is, however, something that developed only *after* the actual invention of the state. We need to go back to Niccolò Machiavelli (1469–1527) to understand why it's misleading to say that the church invented the distinction between the church and state in the Middle Ages. It is entirely accurate to say that the church invented the distinction between the church and political power, and gave us, as a heritage, the understanding that each must have its own distinct functions and realm of authority. But the "state"—that's the invention of Machiavelli.

And Machiavelli also invented the absolute separation of church and state that is the hallmark of liberalism. The church distinguished religious and political power, but Machiavelli built the first wall between the church and the *state*. In fact, his very purpose in inventing the state was to exclude the church from any cultural, moral, or political power or influence—to render it an entirely harmless subordinate instrument of the political sovereign. Moreover, the sovereign's aims, in Machiavelli's view, were to be entirely secular, entirely bent upon this world, with no concessions to the next. Our contemporary notion of excluding Christianity from any public influence by separating it from the entirely secular state, even while the secular state co-opts the domain and functions of the church—that's Machiavelli's creation, the modern secular liberal state.

So let's go back to Machiavelli and see exactly what he had in mind in inventing the "state," a term we're so used to using, that it may be shocking to witness its original construction. In fact, let's go a little further back, before Machiavelli, so we can understand the notions that Machiavelli received from the past, and built on—or tore down.

The "State" and Church before Machiavelli

The original usage of the word for "state" as it was developing in the Middle Ages—that is, as the word was actually used during the period covered in the previous chapter—is best understood if we take into account its etymological connections to the words *status* and *estates*. Someone's status is very personal, reflecting who he is and what he has made of himself, what power, wealth, influence, and land he has. (Land ownership was an especially important aspect of status in the Middle Ages.) A medieval king or duke's estate was a manifestation of who he was. It represented his power and prestige, his accomplishments, his personality and his abilities as a ruler.[2] All of this was not impersonal and abstract, but very personal and concrete.

That's why it was misleading (my apologies, again) to use our modern abstract and impersonal word "state" to describe the estates of kings and other rulers of the Dark and Middle Ages. During this period, if we want to be accurate, we cannot yet talk of "church and state" but, as I often did in the last chapter, of the church and the various rulers' *estates*.

The singular "church" is important as well. In the West there was, up until the sixteenth century, only one church, even while there were many estates. The universal rule of the Roman Empire was gone for good with the collapse of Rome. So there were many kings and princes throughout Europe who paid little or no attention to the Frankish and German attempts to reestablish a universal imperium, or Holy Roman Empire, as it came to be called. To them, the Holy Roman Emperor was just another king trying to muscle in on their territory. Thus during this period we have one church but multiple estates in Germany, France, and England—estates that would soon be growing into distinct nations.

Two developments in the 1500s transformed this situation. First, with the Reformation in the sixteenth century we have the rise of multiple doctrinally distinct forms of Christianity. Thus, the West moved from church and estates to church*es* and estates. Second, as just noted, we have the rise of nation-states out of the various competing personal estates of local rulers. It is in the 1500s that we enter the era we are now in, the modern era of churches and nation-states. We must now speak in the plural, and as we'll soon see, plurality compounds the whole problem of "church and state."

Machiavelli's "Stato"

To understand what Machiavelli was up to, we must put ourselves in the position of the humiliated Henry IV standing outside in the snow at Canossa, begging Pope Gregory to absolve him from his sins so he could regain his crown and his control over the rebellious German nobles.

That is the exact situation that Machiavelli set out to cure with the invention of the secular state. For his purposes, the church had to be stripped of its power to control a ruler. The ruler must be freed from such invisible shackles once and for all, so that he could be the real and effective master of his own estate without interference from the church.

The church's notion of dual harmonious powers—priestly and kingly rule, the church and political realm understood as soul and body, the city of God and the city of man—all that had to be undercut, Machiavelli thought, because the duality really meant that the church ruled the king's, prince's, or duke's estate by an invisible spiritual hand. The estate, Machiavelli believed, must be reinvented so that it could be entirely independent of the church. That reinvention is the modern secular state. Machiavelli introduced the liberal notion of the separation of the church from the state in order to leave a purely secular state by subtraction of the church.

Or, to put it another way, Machiavelli took over the medieval notion of "state" as *status*, as estate, as representing the effective personal ruling power of princes, kings, dukes, or even the oligarchs[3]—and made an all-important addition. Now the state must *not* be linked to the church as body to soul. The state, the political body of which the ruler is the head, must be the projection of his this-worldly power alone.

Why? The world was full of mess and misery, Machiavelli argued, precisely *because* temporal rulers were Christians, because they believed they had immortal souls and an eternal destiny in heaven or hell. This belief constrained their actions, forcing them to subordinate their estates to the church and its interests. And the church wielded this power over rulers only because it was the gatekeeper of morality, holding the keys to heaven.

In order to regain his independence—an independence enjoyed by pagan, pre-Christian kings and emperors—a ruler, Machiavelli believed, must be a secular in our modern sense. He must free his estate, his state (*stato* in Machiavelli's native Italian), his personal rule, from the church and its morality. He must create a secular *stato* by creating an entirely secular ruler, hence Machiavelli's well-earned reputation as a shocking teacher of atheism and immorality, indeed, a "teacher of evil."[4]

This sense of a secular state is captured very exactly in a famous passage from *The Prince*, Machiavelli's book of clever and wicked counsel to rulers: "A prince, and especially a new prince, cannot observe all those things for which men are held good, since he is often under a necessity, *to maintain his state*, of acting against faith, against charity, against humanity, against religion" [emphasis added].[5]

That is Machiavelli's revolutionary teaching—to make good *in this world*, a prince sometimes has to do evil things, even unthinkable things. He can't be bound by the invisible chains of a morality linked to some supernatural destiny. When he has to choose between the maintenance of his kingdom in this world and those things that the church holds to be necessary for entering unto the kingdom of the next world—faith, charity, humanity, and religion—Machiavelli advises the prince to choose to maintain and enhance his state, his status, his estate *in the here and now*.

Lesson number one from Machiavelli: this world is the *only* world. A prince must prefer what is in front of his own eyes to some imaginary kingdom known only by faith. What we see with our own eyes is that well-calculated brutality and actions that most people consider evil are often the best, most effective means for achieving one's political goals in *this* world. In Machiavelli's even more famous words,

> many have imagined republics and principalities that have never been seen or known to exist in truth; for it is so far from how one lives to how one should live that he who lets go of what is done for what should be done learns his ruin rather than his preservation. For a man who wants to make a profession of good in all regards must come to ruin among so many who are not good. Hence it is necessary to a prince, if he wants to *maintain himself* [that is, his state], to learn to be able *not to be good*, and to use this and not use it according to necessity.[6] [emphases added]

Gone is the Christian principle that one must never use evil means, even to achieve a good end. Machiavelli's teaching is that the prince must use *whatever* means work—good or evil, fair or foul. *Whatever.*

Machiavelli and Materialism

The implications of this teaching are revolutionary. In order to free the prince, the temporal ruler, to do the things that really need to be done for the glory of his own earthly estate, Machiavelli has to convince him to shed the belief that he has a soul. That will free him from the hold Christianity and morality have on his actions. But this means, of course, that the prince ceases to be concerned about heaven and hell. He is thereby *liberated* from the next world. (Here we get a hint of the real foundation of modern *liberalism*'s essential connection to modern secularism.) For Machiavelli's prince, there is no longer any tension between his temporal, earthly kingdom and the kingdom of God, because there is no kingdom of God.

Machiavelli thereby initiated both a revolution in politics and a revolution in cosmology, that is, in the ruler's view of the whole of reality. For Machiavelli's kind of politics to succeed, the prince or king had to be convinced that *material, bodily reality is all there is*, and rule accordingly. Machiavellianism as a political revolution and materialism as a cosmological revolution—these two modern revolutions go hand in hand, with the political revolution leading the cosmological one.

In Machiavelli's view, accepting a purely material view of the world would make the prince a much more effective ruler in this world. Since he has no soul to worry about, he has no fear that his temporal actions will affect his eternal destiny. His more effective power in this world will be manifested in his greater *status*, his earthly glory, his estate, his state. And that state will be an entirely secular, soulless one, a state ordered to his personal this-worldly prosperity, glory, and power, rather than one that is hampered and hamstrung by belief in the soul's ultimate destiny in some imaginary world to come.

Machiavelli, centuries before Justice Black wrote the opinion in *Everson v. Board of Education*, advocated the strict separation of church and state that is at the heart of our contemporary constitutional jurisprudence. But the wall of separation that Machiavelli erected between them was a psychological one. It is the prince's complete skepticism about the spiritual realm that walled the church off from his state. The Machiavellian prince understands that the things the church speaks of incessantly, the very things that it claims give it authority—the existence of the soul, the truths of Christianity, the reality of a judging God, eternal bliss and eternal damnation, the absolute necessity of acting with faith, charity, humanity, and religion—all these things are simply not real because the only reality is material, bodily reality. There is only this life; when the body dies, that is the end. And a prince must rule and order his estate in the here and now accordingly.

The Church as a Tool of the Prince's State

So Machiavelli is the first proponent of a secular state. Thus it makes sense to inquire: Did Machiavelli favor an aggressively atheist state along the lines of what Lenin and Stalin achieved in the Soviet Union? Or would he have favored the gentler secular state such as what we find in European liberal democracies today?

Neither, although both the harder and the softer version are later developments from Machiavelli's foundation, as are other forms of the modern liberal state. But for Machiavelli, secularism is only for the prince, not for the people. Machiavelli makes religion a tool of the prince's state, a tool that helps him to rule the masses who still believe in God. That is the first historical step toward liberalism creating an established state church.

As the title of his infamous work suggests, Machiavelli's *Prince* was not intended to be a popular book addressed to the masses but a book addressed to princes, the rulers of the masses (and even speaking to princes, he is careful how he speaks, since outright atheism at this time would bring severe punishment). The prince *himself* must have an entirely secular outlook. He must ultimately order all his policies from this secular outlook. But in order to be effective, the new secular prince must *appear* to be religious and moral. Machiavelli was a teacher of duplicity as well as atheism and immorality. Nowhere is this clearer than in his counsels about how a prince must use religion to his earthly advantage.

As Machiavelli advises, a prince "should *appear* all mercy, all faith, all honesty, all humanity, all religion." He adds that "nothing is more necessary to *appear* to have than this last quality" [emphasis added]. Why? As we noted before, a ruler "cannot observe all those things for which men are held good, since he is often under a necessity, to maintain his state, of acting against faith, against charity, against humanity, against religion."[7] But he will be most effective in his ruthlessness if he *appears* to be innocent and pious. Outward piety must mask inward amoral, irreligious Machiavellianism.

So with Machiavelli the wall of separation between church and state is entirely interior and invisible. It's a wall inside the prince's mind, separating what the prince actually believes from what he wants to appear to his subjects to believe. He alone is liberated from belief in the next world, and he uses his subjects' belief to control them.

There are three reasons Machiavelli erected this wall of duplicity dividing the private atheism of the prince from his public piety. Most obviously Christianity was still publicly powerful at the beginning of the sixteenth century, so that to argue directly and publicly against Christianity was to risk not just political but quite literal suicide—since you could be sent to the gallows as an atheist. It was safer to pretend to believe in God. (Machiavelli himself, understanding this danger very clearly, wrote with calculated duplicity in this regard.)[8]

Second, precisely because Christianity was still culturally powerful at the time, Machiavelli understood that it could be a powerful *tool* for the really clever atheist who had perfected the art of duplicitously using public piety for his own purposes.

The third reason, closely related to the second, is that Machiavelli agreed with certain of the ancient Greek and Roman pagan philosophers and historians (such as Polybius, Livy, and Plutarch) who believed that, while popular religions are not true, they are useful for controlling the masses because the masses are generally stupid, and hence incapable of true Enlightenment.[9] (And to release those who *aren't* stupid from the bonds of Christian morality would only be to create equally ruthless political opponents for yourself.)

Christianity from the (New) Pagan Point of View

We're all aware that there was a resurgence of interest in the Greek and Roman pagan world in the Renaissance, an attempt to reconsider and appreciate pagan thought and culture on its own terms. For many Christians, such as Erasmus, this just meant a deeper appreciation of pre-Christian thought within the context of an all-encompassing Christian worldview.

But for others in the Renaissance—Machiavelli chief among them—reading the ancient pagans brought them to think like pagans again. They adopted the pagan view of the world, and hence saw Christianity *from the outside*, in the same way as the Roman pagans had viewed it.

For these new pagans, the Christian view of history was upside down. Christianity wasn't the truth that had saved the world, salvaging a few valuable scraps of pagan culture along the way. It was a foolish superstition that had destroyed the glory of Greece and Rome. Christianity was a great interruption, an historical detour that had sent human history off course into the Dark Ages of murmuring irrational monks. From the pagan view of things, Christianity was a mistake.

Intellectual pagans in the ancient world had believed that all religion was based on ignorant superstition, but it was useful superstition. And Christianity was just one more religion (if a peculiarly intractable one). Thus, in the new pagan outlook, which was most decidedly Machiavelli's outlook, Christianity was just one more silly superstition, but one which must somehow be made useful.

The re-paganization of the Western mind was the origin of liberalism's demotion of Christianity to one more superstition, one that could be transformed into a useful tool for its this-worldly aims. (Note that it is also the ultimate cause of theology departments and Biblical studies departments in universities being transformed into religious studies departments. "Theology" and "Biblical studies" treat Christianity as true. "Religious studies" treats Christianity as one more religion, a species of the genus, no better or worse than any other superstition or folk belief. As a matter of fact, the term "religion" in the modern sense was invented as part of the campaign to demote Christianity—a "genus" name deliberately created so that Christianity would be just one more "species" of religion.[10])

Reasons of State

With Machiavelli, then, we have a revival of the pagan notion that Christianity is just another religion. The concern is not its truth, but how to make it useful to the state, just as Roman paganism was useful to the Roman Republic, and emperor worship was useful to the Roman Empire. Secular rulers' actions may have a veneer of Christianity, they may use words or phrases familiar to Christians, but they are actually animated by a hidden disdain for Christianity.

But Machiavelli knew that Christianity wasn't really just one more religion. The Christian religion was especially impossible to reconcile with an entirely this-worldly approach to political life, given its overriding emphasis on the world to come. The intensified demands for holiness were also an obstacle. Machiavelli was counseling the use of evil means to achieve desired political ends, and thus he thought Christian morality directly interfered with the ruler's political effectiveness. Christianity refused to exempt the ruler from the commands of Christ.

In freeing the ruler from these commands (by freeing him from worry about his fate in the next world), Machiavelli allowed him to do, as we say today, "whatever it takes" or what later, though not all that much later, came to be called "reasons of state,"[11] and even later than that, *realpolitik*. *Realpolitik* is Machiavelli-style politics not bound to Christianity or its morality—but still using it for public relations.

The church as a tool of secular policies is, we might say, Machiavelli's established secular church, the state liberated from the church but using the church for its own purposes. Liberation from Christianity and liberalism are essentially connected. As early as Machiavelli we can see the notion that the church should be used as a tool or instrument of liberalism, and so rightly speak of an established liberal church of the state—at least in principle, if not yet in practice.

Soulless Politics and the Original Blueprint for the Established Secular Church

The modern secular state was not at first an impersonal state. It began with the ruler's very personal acceptance of the secular worldview—the belief that material reality is the only reality, that there is only the body and no soul, and hence that the prince has no heaven to hope for or hell to fear. As we have seen, the ruler's abandonment of faith undermined the original distinction between the church and the political power.

Remember, the original division between church and political power as it developed in the Dark and Middle Ages had been rooted in the distinction between soul and body. The reality of the soul had given the church its power, and hence its authority over any Christian king.

So all that was needed to destroy the authority of the church over Christian kings was for the king to shed his Christianity and his belief in the existence of the soul. With the soul gone, only the body was left, and hence, only the temporal realm, only political power, remained. Politics became everything for the Machiavellian ruler.

And the new, all-encompassing politics was literally soulless, in a sense quite alien even to pagan philosophers such as Aristotle and Plato. The old paganism had heartily affirmed the body, but many ancient pagans had also praised the goods of the soul. (Think of Plato, Aristotle, and Cicero.) Christianity affirmed the essential goodness of creation even while rejecting hedonism, but it took the pagan acclaim of the soul and its virtues up into its own supernatural framework. For this very reason, modern liberalism had to destroy or reject even the pagan thought that had proven compatible with Christianity. Modern liberalism affirms the old pagan this-worldliness, the embrace of the body, but it rejects the existence of the soul as something that might continue to lead people right back to Christianity. As a result, the new paganism is entirely materialistic, and that materialism is meant to destroy any foothold for the church in the world. Insofar as we've accepted materialism, it has done just that.

So the new paganism introduced into the politics of the West by Machiavelli is quite different from the old. Liberalism's return to paganism could not be an innocent return. The reversion to paganism amidst a completely Christianized culture was an explicit rebellion against Christianity.[12]

Christianity was no longer formative for the Machiavellian prince himself, and his rule ultimately (if secretly) aimed entirely at the ruler's earthly glory, attending only to the needs and desires of his body (not his eternal destiny), to the health of the body politic (not the salvation of his soul), and to the rewards of temporal life (not eternity in heaven).

But as we have seen, religion was not done away with. Machiavelli's secular prince ruled entirely for the preservation of the body politic *as a body*, as his very earthly, very personal realm, even while he *used* religion as a necessary support to that rule. Religion therefore became an instrument of the ruler's secular state.

Thus religion took a new form under the manipulations of Machiavellian princes. Since Machiavelli was advising princes in Christian lands, his advice was concerned with *establishing a secular church*, one that had the outward appearance of Christianity even while it was actually defined from within by secularism. In giving us the blueprint, Machiavelli represents the first phase of the establishment of the secular church, the church as the tool of an ultimately secular state.

This secular church was liberal in the sense we've seen above—it was an agent of liberation from the next world, the intense moral strictures of Christianity, the demands of doctrine, and worry about the fate of one's soul, and thus liberation to enjoy whatever pleasures the world has to give. But at first the secular church was an agent of liberation for the prince only, not the people. The liberation of the people (liberalism for the people) lay in the future, but a future essentially connected to Machiavelli's revolution.

Machiavelli, the Reformation, and the Wars of Religion

Machiavelli was writing his *Prince* in the context of pre-Reformation Catholic Italy. But it should be clear that it doesn't actually matter *what* religion the secular-minded prince has at hand, as long as it is ultimately defined and controlled by him—as long as the ruler determines the religion of his state.

That fact brings to mind a phrase that arose just a few decades after Machiavelli's death when conflict was tearing apart Europe: *cuius regio, eius religio* ("whose realm, his religion"). This famous Latin phrase describes the compromise of the Peace of Augsburg (1555), the agreement of war-weary Europeans that ruling princes would thenceforth determine whether their particular domain would be Catholic or Lutheran. (With the Peace of Westphalia in 1648, the same principle was extended to include Calvinism.) This compromise represents a great victory of the state over the church because the established church of each state is defined by the ruler of that realm.

Cuius regio, eius religio was originally a war-weary compromise, not a Machiavellian ruse. Yet it played into the hands of Machiavellian rulers and hence helped lead to the development of the secular state. A ruler could now choose whichever kind of Christianity proved most useful for him.

But note that Machiavelli pre-dated the Reformation. He wrote *The Prince* about five years before Martin Luther posted his *Ninety-Five Theses* on the door of the castle church in Wittenberg, Germany, on October 31, 1517. Thus Machiavelli invented the modern secular state *before* the outbreak of the Reformation and the ravaging of Europe by the religious wars that followed in its wake.

That's an immensely important point. Contrary to the Enlightenment assumption shared by Thomas Jefferson, contrary to Justice Black's reasoning in *Everson*, contrary to the assumptions of radical secularists today, the secular state is not something that was proposed in response to religious conflicts and wars. The entire intellectual framework of the secular state was set out by Machiavelli before the religious wars of that post-Reformation era; it was not created as the solution to those conflicts. Machiavelli separated the church from the secular state for a very different reason. He wanted a return to pagan Rome. We've touched on this point, but it is so important and so often overlooked that we need to reinforce it.

The Superiority of Pagan Religion to Christianity

Machiavelli's complaint against Christianity was not that it led to wars, but that it led men away from them. Christianity made men effeminate cheek-turners, monks pining for a heavenly city rather than bold warrior kings, princes, and citizens willing to fight for their earthly city. As Machiavelli explains in another work, Christianity,

> having shown the truth and the true way, makes us esteem less the honor of the world, whereas the Gentiles, esteeming it very much and having placed the highest good in it, were more ferocious in their actions.... Our religion has glorified humble and contemplative men more than active men. It has then placed the highest good in humility, abjectness, and contempt of things human; the other [the religion of the pagans, or Gentiles] placed it in greatness of spirit, strength of body, and all other things capable of making men very strong.[13]

Pagan kings and heroes were therefore superior to Christian saints and martyrs. In short, the glories of paganism were emasculated by Christianity. Proud pagans would fight for glory and political freedom. Meek Christians refused to fight because they feared losing eternal life and thereby undermined the glory of the state and its security against ruthless enemies only too willing to run roughshod over pious dupes. As Machiavelli argued, Christianity

> asks that you have strength in yourself, it wishes you to be capable more of suffering than of doing something strong. This mode of life thus seems to have rendered the world weak and given it in prey to criminal men, who can manage it securely, seeing that the collectivity of men, so as to go to paradise, think more of enduring beatings than of avenging them.[14]

Who is really to blame for making Christianity "effeminate," for making Christian men into defenseless sissies? This state of affairs "arises without doubt more from the cowardice of the men who have interpreted our religion according to idleness and not according to virtue."[15]

Christianity *not* built on virtue? But hasn't Machiavelli complained that Christian rulers are hobbled by virtue? Well, from Machiavelli's pagan perspective, Christianity is built upon a wrong understanding of virtue. What is the right one? Machiavelli certainly doesn't mean virtue in the sense of goodness, as we think of it. How could he, given his advice to the prince about the necessity of doing evil? Virtue for Machiavelli means the manliness of the spirited warrior (the *vir* in "virtue" means "man" in Latin), the virtue that manifests itself in the fight for earthly glory and honor, the kind of virtue found among the great Roman heroes. These pagan heroes must replace the meek, other-worldly Christian saints as the men we esteem.[16]

Machiavelli was making the exact same complaint about Christianity as the ancient pagans did: Christianity is bad because it undermines the glory of the state. Machiavelli asks nothing less than for the West to make a return to pagan Rome, where religion was entirely subordinate to the earthly state.

Pagan Religion, Pagan Education

That brings us to a deeper level of Machiavelli's revolution. All of these criticisms just quoted from Machiavelli were made in the context of his

comparison of ancient pagan (or "Gentile") religion to Christianity. What
"makes men less strong now," as opposed to the time of the glories of pre-
Christian Rome, Machiavelli argues, can be traced to "the difference between
our education and the ancient," which is "founded on the difference between
our religion and the ancient."[17]

The implications are as startling as they are illuminating to our situation
today: Machiavelli was suggesting that to reverse the ill effects of Christianity, religion must be re-paganized and the control of education must be
wrested from the hands of the church and put into the hands of the state.
The state will reeducate the people in a re-paganized view of religion.

This has a direct effect on the church. The established secular church
must appear to be Christian, but in reality it must be rebuilt on the pagan
model of religion that was so marvelously effective in ancient Rome, when
religion directly and completely supported the state's earthly security and
glory. The state must educate and form its citizens to esteem and hence
desire this-worldly glory and the good of the state as the supreme good.

But since the Christian church is so powerful, the return to pagan religion cannot be direct and immediate. It must be accomplished by an entire
reconstruction of Christianity from within, by removing or transforming
precisely those elements of the church that set it at odds with the kingdoms
of this world, so that it can serve the state as ancient Roman religion had.

The strange beast that was created by Machiavelli's alchemy is the established secular church, in all its different forms. Some of the secular churches
that followed upon Machiavelli's revolution don't look very liberal at all;
some look startlingly like the most liberal churches of today; and there are
some in between. We'll be looking at several different examples in the next
few chapters. But first, some concluding reflections on Machiavelli.

Some Historical Repercussions
of the Machiavellian Revolution

We've uncovered a new understanding of the "state"—not a neutral
political structure, but a political body devoted to the exclusively secular

goals of its rulers. And we've encountered a new understanding of the "separation" between it and the church, as well. The current belief that the church must be separated from the state and walled off in private impotence—leaving, by its subtraction from the public square, the liberal secular state—all that is Machiavelli's invention. The playing out of this principle in our courts today is in keeping with his goal of creating a state liberated from the Christian worldview.

We must emphasize that the oft-repeated claim that the secular state was made necessary by religious conflicts among Christians is simply false history. Machiavelli conceived the secular state before Luther had ever nailed up his *Ninety-Five Theses*, and long before the division of Christianity resulted in religious wars.

Given these facts, perhaps we should see the infamous religious wars that occurred after Machiavelli in another light. We may well wonder whether the bloodiness of these later religious wars, such as the infamous Thirty Years War (1618–1648), was caused by princes and kings *using* religious differences, *using* the multitude of churches created by the Reformation, as political tools to advance their own ambitions as builders of nation-states. The national churches established under *cuius regio, eius religio* were of the precise sort Machiavelli had envisioned, entirely subordinate to their respective states.

Certainly Christians cannot absolve themselves of the blame they must shoulder for the atrocities of the so-called "Wars of Religion" of the sixteenth and seventeenth centuries. But because Machiavelli's thought spread so rapidly around Europe, and was so influential among both rulers and modern philosophers, we should recognize the secular causes of these wars as well—rather than, as we now do, seeing these wars as the cause of secularism itself.

We've also uncovered at least a part of the explanation for the strange fact that the current situation of Christians so closely resembles that of the first Christians in the pagan Roman Empire. Machiavelli set in motion a strategy for re-paganizing the West. Secularization is re-paganization. It puts the church (at least the churches that refuse to be liberalized) right back in the same situation of antagonism to the state.

We should now recognize why modern liberal secularism advances and the church retreats wherever ideological materialism gains acceptance. As the notion that we have no soul is accepted, the power and influence of the church decrease. With this decrease comes the eclipse of Christian morality as well. Morality is re-defined in this-worldly terms, either by bodily pleasure and comfort, or, on a more elevated level, by this-worldly political glory that can require rigorous sacrifices and sufferings for the success of the state. Thus Machiavelli's secularism will eventually bring us two kinds of states liberated from Christianity—the modern soft liberalism that we're intimately familiar with, aimed at bodily comfort; and the hard liberalism of, for example, Fascism, which obviously has far more affinity with Machiavelli's praise of the virtues of the Roman pagans.[18] While both share a common root in Machiavelli, they are, as it were, different shoots. In this book, our concern is more with the former than the latter. Fascism has been thoroughly discredited, but soft liberalism is still in the ascendant.

As modern people, we tend to look back on the liberalization of Christianity as a rationalization of religion, a shedding of ancient superstitions. But understanding Machiavelli means recognizing that what was really happening was instead a secularization intended to reshape Christianity so that it would serve the secular project rather than hinder it, affirm the secular state from below rather than judge it from above. Liberal Christianity is the form that the established religion of the state takes—perhaps not its final form, but its most visible, obvious form.

FROM HENRY VIII TO THOMAS HOBBES: THE STATE CHURCH, LEVIATHAN, AND THE SOVEREIGN INDIVIDUAL

Machiavelli was by no means singly responsible for re-paganizing Western culture. The Renaissance in general, as is well known, was marked by a return to pagan literature and to the glory of pagan Greece and Rome, and by a recovery of the wisdom, the art, the entire outlook of the ancient pagan world. Some Renaissance Christians, such as Erasmus and Thomas More, tempered their appreciation of paganism, ultimately subordinating the good to be gathered from the ancient world to the truth of Christianity. Others, such as Machiavelli, shed their Christianity and embraced paganism whole-heartedly, deciding that Christianity had to be re-formed, forced back into its ancient pagan position of subordination to this-worldly political power and glory.

To adherents of the neo-pagan view, the very things that made Christianity distinct from pagan religion were obstacles that had to be eliminated in order to make Christianity the tame religion of the new secular state. Machiavelli started a revolution, but much more work had to be done to finish it, both on the theoretical and on the practical level.

In this chapter we will examine Henry VIII's church as the first practical step toward the established secular church in the West, a step taken under the influence of Machiavelli. And then we'll look at the great theoretical leap that this practical step made possible. A century after Henry VIII, England gave the world the immensely influential political philosopher Thomas Hobbes, author of the *Leviathan*, who constructed an entirely secular foundation for Henry's church, and therefore gave us the first truly secular established church in a major modern state—more exactly, an absolutist, autocratic version

Since Hobbes's theoretical model was based in significant part upon the very practical achievements that preceded him, we need to explore the actions of the infamous Henry VIII and his daughter Queen Elizabeth I in some detail in order to understand the political and ecclesiastical context of Hobbes's state church.

Henry VIII and His Church

There is no reason to rehearse the famous cruelties of Henry VIII in regard to his six wives, or the brutality of his reign, or the evident glee with which he snatched up church and monastery property to fund his own extravagant reign and buy off a new set of nobles. These are all well enough known to make him a good candidate for being considered the consummate Machiavellian king.

I am not using the adjective "Machiavellian" loosely. In fact, there are very good reasons to believe that Henry VIII's policies were actually influenced by the counsels of Machiavelli.

Machiavelli's *Prince* was written in 1513, about four years after Henry VIII became king of England. But Henry enjoyed a long reign, dying in 1547. Machiavellianism is known to have become a factor in advice given to the king after the fall of Cardinal Thomas Wolsey in 1529. Waiting in the wings to step in after the Catholic cardinal's fall were a group of young scholars who had been studying at the University of Padua in northeastern Italy, where they had absorbed Machiavelli's teachings, which were circulating in clandestine manuscripts at the time. Richard Morison and Thomas Starkey were probably the most important in this group that returned to England after the fall of Wolsey to aid Thomas Cromwell in defining Henry VIII's policies. Reginald Pole, who had also attended the University of Padua but was a stout critic of Henry's policies, accused Cromwell himself of using Machiavelli's *Prince* as the prototype for Henry's rule.[1]

In 1527 Henry had begun seeking ways to annul his marriage to Catherine of Aragon so that he would be free to marry his mistress Anne Boleyn. Cardinal Wolsey proved unable to secure the annulment from Rome, and his downfall ensued soon thereafter.

Thomas Cromwell took Wolsey's place as the chief architect of Henry's policies, including this very interesting solution to the marriage problem: make Henry *himself* the head of the church in England. In 1534, a compliant Parliament did just that in the Act of Supremacy, declaring the king to be "the only Supreme Head on earth of the Church of England, called *Anglicana Ecclesia*."[2]

Behold the established state church, with the king as its head. In one fairly swift move, Henry was able to set up his monarchy in the West along the same lines as the Eastern Byzantine monarchs. He had made himself a Caesaropapist by ridding himself of the actual papacy. In so doing, Henry ensured that the church's invention of the real distinction between the church and the political power was undone, at least in England. Political and religious power were once again fused, with the political power in control.

We Americans need to remember this moment. This fusion of church and state under control of the English nation-state was rejected 250 years after Henry by the American colonists, as the First Amendment attests. We must understand, very clearly, what we rejected.

The first question we might ask is, was this a *secular* development on Henry's part? We may doubt whether Machiavelli's counsels were the entire cause of Henry's establishing his own church. But we should not doubt that Machiavelli's approach to politics, and to the ruler's use of religion, provided justification and guidance among his advisors after the fact. Thus it is entirely plausible that Machiavellianism was integral to the complete subordination of the church to the policies of the English king (or, later on, queen).

We cannot doubt that Henry meant to assume the full powers and functions of the church. Henry put himself directly below (but not far below) God, with everyone else beneath him—churchmen and civil servants alike, all in absolute, unquestioned obedience to their king as head of both church and state.

This included complete control over Scripture and its interpretation, as was made visually clear in the frontispiece picture for the 1539 Great Bible, the official English Bible translation of the realm. The engraving featured King Henry on his throne, handing *down* a copy of the Bible to both the archbishop of Canterbury, Thomas Cranmer, and Henry's chief minister, Thomas Cromwell, the two quite subordinate and loyal appointees guiding the English church and state, respectively—both under Henry's watchful eye.[3]

With the king just below God, and the church firmly beneath the king, a kind of partial divinization of the monarch crept into English culture. To cite one vivid example from just a bit later on, Queen Elizabeth I ordered the Anglican priest presiding over her coronation mass in 1559 not to elevate the host, so as not to allow any competition with *her* elevation to the throne. And during her reign, as William Cavanaugh notes, Elizabeth suppressed Corpus Christi feast celebrations where the consecrated Eucharist was carried in an elaborate public procession under an ornate canopy, even as "she was appropriating significant symbolic aspects of the feast with herself substituted for the host. Elizabeth made a frequent practice of being processed around under a canopy modeled after those used for Corpus Christi feasts. A royal cult complete with shrines and pilgrimages grew up around the person of Elizabeth."[4]

Elizabeth is rightly famous for shaping the Church of England according to political expediency. It was a church with a mixture of Catholic and

Protestant elements so as to keep political discontent to a minimum, a church always aimed entirely at supporting the state, a church whose doctrine was not defined by truth but by political compromise, a church whose clergy were, in effect, civil servants of the royal sovereign.

Divine Right Kingship in Europe

We do not want to be unfair and single out the Church of England. Elizabeth wasn't the only monarch engaged in political exercises of self-divinization. This kind of thing had already occurred in Catholic France in the previous century and would soon occur in Germany and the rest of the continent as well, marking what historians John Bossy and William Cavanaugh call a "migration of the holy" during this period, a shifting of religious symbols and titles from the church to the state.[5]

This migration of holy symbols and authority occurred during the time that modern nation-states were emerging, with monarchs who wanted the church of *their* state to be *their* established church, to be (as under Henry VIII) a pliant instrument for the building of their particular political aspirations.

The interesting result of putting the church under the state, wherever this occurred, was that sacred authority was thereby absorbed by the king. Thus during this period we have the emergence of what came to be called the Divine Right theory of kingship, a reassertion by Western monarchs of the kind of royal theocracy that had prevailed in the pagan Roman Empire and dominated the East since Constantine had moved the capital of the Christian Empire to Constantinople—complete royal supremacy over the church, the state, the aristocracy, and the people, with the monarch's word as law. The quasi-divinization of the king was an integral part of his claim to absolute supremacy in his realm.

Historians usually associate the beginning of the modern claim that the king rules above all as a matter of divine right with the French monarchy. Jean Bodin (1530–1596), who had provided the original Divine Right-style justification for the French crown, is generally considered the first apologist for the modern theory of Divine Right kingship. Interestingly, while Bodin began by denouncing Machiavelli (such denunciations had, even by then, become a standard pose), in fact "Machiavelli's influence on Bodin is omnipresent."[6] It is fair to say that Bodin's theory is not fully Machiavellian, and so not really secular in a precise sense, but his account certainly was influential among other monarchs, including English monarchs, whose aims were secular.

The Divine Right theory of kingship doesn't by itself get us to an established secular church. Divine Right monarchy often took the form of a kind of return to Constantinian rule, the rule of a Christian king over his realm.

The full *secular* theoretical justification for the creation of an autocratic established state church would come from the pen of the Englishman Thomas Hobbes, one of the most influential modern political philosophers. Hobbes would give the secular sovereign everything he needed to be the complete master of the church.

The Church of Hobbes:
Established, Autocratic, Secular

Hobbes was almost certainly an atheist. There is no doubt that he was a materialist, and he rightly understood that full-bore materialism was essential to cutting the church off from all power and bringing about the real secular revolution that was necessary to undermine the "seditious" influence of religion—that is, to finally root out any strength that the church might still have to resist the absolute power of the king. Loyalty to the pope or to the Bible above the civil sovereign meant that citizens were divided in their loyalties, with the king coming in second. The kingdom of God trumped the political king. That is the situation that Hobbes sought to cure.

It is not surprising that Hobbes's greatest and most influential work, the *Leviathan* (1651), was written during the English civil wars of the mid-seventeenth century. These civil wars were in no small part religious wars: the Puritan faction, ultimately led by Oliver Cromwell, beheaded an Anglican king, and during the mayhem of civil war even more radical religious factions (such as the Diggers and the Ranters) pushed for a public voice and political power, many basing their rebellion on the Bible.[7] All were in some way calling upon God to justify rebellion against the king.

In assessing this situation, Hobbes concluded that *the* political problem was the existence of any notion of religion *independent* of the political power. Religion that was not subordinate to the state could serve as a base for a challenge to the sovereignty of the king, thus being a cause of rebellion and civil war. Note that the problem, in Hobbes's view, wasn't Christians fighting each other but Christians challenging the state. Christianity itself had to be re-formed in a Machiavellian way so that it would support the state rather than continually challenging it.

Hobbes was calling for a radical, secularizing re-formation of the church. Anything that could possibly disturb the king's political power or support any notion of the church's independence had to be ruthlessly and systematically eliminated. Everything that had allowed the Christian church to claim a distinct existence and function must be eradicated.

In with Materialism, Out with the Soul

First, Hobbes eliminated the soul, and every other possible immaterial entity. "The World, (I mean not the Earth only…but the *Universe*, that is, the whole mass of all things that are) is Corporeal, that is to say, Body…." he claimed, "and consequently every part of the Universe is Body; and that which is not Body, is no part of the Universe: And because the Universe is All, that which is no part of it, is *Nothing*; and consequently *no where*."[8]

All is matter and nothing but matter. Thus there simply is no spiritual realm for the church to exercise power over. Everything that exists is physical. The old medieval system of dual authorities—the church looking after the people's souls while the ruler took care of their physical well-being—is thus collapsed, with all of the power being awarded to the ruler.

As the absolutism of Hobbes makes clear, materialism implies totalitarianism (since there is nothing above or beyond the state). And so materialism is the ultimate source of the later totalitarian regimes that demand full obedience and minute control over every aspect of everyone's lives. But as we'll see in his unfolding argument, Hobbes turns out to be, oddly enough, more liberal in his absolutism than later totalitarian states. To understand this, we need to turn to his account of morality, the second aspect of his secular revolution.

Complete Moral Relativism

Hobbes eliminated good and evil, that is, any moral standard derived either from God or nature that could stand above and hence against the civil sovereign. Hobbes's moral relativism followed upon his materialism. Matter isn't good or evil—it just is. Since human beings are bodies made up of much smaller invisible atomic bodies, our actions, thoughts, and desires are all reducible to the mechanical actions and reactions of our constituent atoms.

What we call good and evil are, then, merely our subjective physical responses to outside stimuli. If it feels good, we call it good. If it feels bad or painful we call it evil. In Hobbes's startling words,

> whatsoever is the object of any man's Appetite or Desire; that is it, which he for his part calls *Good*: And the object of his Hate, and Aversions, *Evil*; And of his Contempt, *Vile* and *Inconsiderable*. For these words of Good, Evil, and Contemptible, are ever used with relation to the person that uses them: There being nothing simply and absolutely so; nor any common Rule of Good and Evil, to be taken from the nature of the objects themselves....[9]

Sin No More

Third, Hobbes eliminated the Christian doctrine of sin, and any notion of natural justice or injustice. This point pretty obviously follows upon his elimination of good and evil, but a fuller explanation of it involves a slight detour into Hobbes's invention of modern natural rights theory.

To begin with, Hobbes declared that the "Desires, and other Passions of man, are in themselves no Sin. No more are the Actions, that proceed from those Passions, till they know a [civil] Law that forbids them...."[10]

In other words, there is no original sin. There is no sin of any kind at all in our original natural state, in what Hobbes famously called the "state of nature"—not until government comes along and creates wrongdoing by passing the first laws. "Right and wrong" are, then, purely artificial, mere human creations of the sovereign of the state. To understand this, we need to look at Hobbes's account of "rights."

The Infamous "State of Nature" and the Right to Anything and Everything

In the natural, pre-civil, pre-social condition of the human race, Hobbes asserted, each individual had a *right* to anything and everything he desired. He could do anything he wanted to get whatever he wanted. Hobbes based this claim on the notion that we have a "natural right" to preserve ourselves: "THE RIGHT OF NATURE...is the Liberty each man has, to use his own power, as he will himself, for the preservation of his own Nature: that is to say, of his own Life; and consequently, of doing anything, which in his own Judgment, and Reason, he shall conceive to be the aptest means thereunto."[11] The notion that human beings in some primal state had a *right* to whatever they happened to want, a *right* to do anything at all to get it, and a *right* to do absolutely anything to preserve their own lives—all of this depends upon the assumption that there is no sin and no objective right and wrong. And that's why today we heirs of Hobbes emphasize our "rights" in our civil discourse, rather than talking about right and wrong.

Hobbes also introduced another, related aspect of modern liberalism: the "Liberty each man has" to decide for himself what he shall seek as desirable, and hence call good. This purported "liberty" to define good and evil for oneself is directly related to the liberation that was already central to liberalism going back to Machiavelli: liberals can claim this liberty to decide for themselves what good means only if the church's understanding that God has already determined good and evil has been eliminated.

Hobbes's "state of nature," which takes the place of the Genesis account of our original condition, accomplishes exactly that. Since there is no sin and no good and evil in the "state of nature," "notions of Right and Wrong, Justice and Injustice have…no place. Where there is no common Power, there is no [civil] Law: where no Law, no Injustice."[12] This is a claim made against the power of the church. Hobbes was saying that there is no justice built into creation, and hence no claims of natural or divine justice can be made against the individual in the state of nature (or against the civil sovereign, as we'll soon see). On Hobbes's premises, all of the prophets of the Old Testament were really rebels whose claims to be speaking on behalf of God's justice against the injustice of Israelite kings were entirely groundless.

With no notion of sin, no natural good or evil, and no justice or injustice, our original natural condition was simply frantic individuals feverishly trying to get whatever they wanted by any means possible, with no civil power to keep them in check. As a result this natural state was chaotic, to quote Hobbes's famous words, "a war as is of every man against every man.…And the life of man, solitary, poor, nasty, brutish, and short."[13]

The Sovereign Saves the Day

Enter the sovereign. Government was invented to put an end to this miserable state of nature. To avoid violent death, according to Hobbes's account, each person must give up his absolute right to define good and evil to a king, who then arbitrarily determines the rules that everyone else (except for himself) has to live by in his state.

But importantly, as noted above, there was *no sin and no right and wrong* until the sovereign declared them to be so, that is, until the king declared something to be illegal. If it's against the will of the king and his law, then it's a sin. But if the law doesn't forbid something, then it's not a sin. And no one—certainly not the church—can declare something to be a sin that the king allows.

One might well ask why anyone would want to put himself under a sovereign with such absolute arbitrary power. Hobbes's answer is ingenious, and it sheds light on the confusions of our own times. The belief that we each have a natural right to whatever we want paradoxically bolsters the power of the absolute sovereign, because we need the sovereign to protect us from everyone else—from all others who so passionately believe that they have this same right to do anything *they* want. The notion that there is no right or wrong, but only "rights" that the state must protect gives the state complete power over all the individuals claiming rights. Individuals are powerless to express their "rights" without the state's protection.

As a matter of strategy, a secular state does all that it can to convince its citizens that they have these "natural rights," because the more they claim them, the more they need the secular state's arbitrary power to settle their interminable conflicts and keep peace. Each individual claims the fundamental but arbitrary right to determine what is right or wrong for him or her, but since all claim that right, then someone has to set boundaries, or there will be, once again, the chaos of the state of nature. That someone is the sovereign. And the will of the sovereign, the king, is just as arbitrary as anyone else's—the only difference being that *his* will happens to be law. That is, it is enforced by his state. (Recall how personal the "state" was for the Machiavellian prince.)

The King Makes His Own (Secular) Church

It's not difficult to see why Hobbes wanted to undermine the church's power to declare something a sin. If the spiritual power (the "*Ghostly* Power," as Hobbes calls it) can claim "the Right to declare what is Sin" then the church can "challenge by consequence [the civil sovereign's authority] to declare what is Law." Think of our own situation today, with Christians saying that murder is a sin, abortion is murder, and therefore laws that allow abortion are unjust and must be overturned.

The "Right to declare what is Sin" had therefore to be taken from the church, and given to the political sovereign. To eliminate any challenge from the church, "Sin" had to be reduced to "nothing but the transgression of the Law." If the sovereign says it's a sin, it's a sin; if not, then it's not. Otherwise, there would be "two Masters," the church and the state. When they disagree about what is a sin, subjects can't obey both—that's "impossible."[14] A house divided cannot stand. Therefore, divine law could not be allowed to exist as distinct from and potentially antagonistic to the civil laws, and citizens had to be brought to tolerate whatever anyone does, as long as the law allows it. Thus in our post-Hobbesian world, each of us has the right to do whatever we want, as long as it doesn't violate the law, and as long as we don't bother anyone else.

This account of our "rights" may sound comfortably familiar, but Hobbes's new secular formula is absolute political power built upon complete moral relativism. That means there's no appeal to any moral standard against the king because Hobbes has eliminated any moral standard, period. In a clear echo of Machiavelli, the king's might quite literally *makes* right.[15]

Hobbes therefore gives the West absolute Divine Right monarchy, but without the "God" part—a purely secular-based absolute monarchy, not given by God but built from an entirely materialist, amoral, relativist foundation.

That does not mean, however, that religion has no place in Hobbes's scheme. Like the Machiavellian prince, the Hobbesian sovereign must *use* religion as an instrument of state. Religion cannot be dispensed with because there is a "natural Seed" of religion in human beings, insofar as their ignorance of natural material causes leads them to suppose that there are immaterial or spiritual causes at work.[16] If the king doesn't learn to use this "seed" of religion to his advantage, then it will be used against him. The sovereign cannot allow a rival spiritual kingdom to arise amidst and against his earthly kingdom, so he cannot allow any distinction between church and state, spiritual and temporal power, to be asserted.

The sovereign must therefore have the power to define everything about the state's established religion, or the church won't truly be under the state's control, and it will exist as a potential rival power. Thus there must be only "one Worship," and this "Public Worship" must be "*Uniform*," and under complete control of the sovereign, to the extent that only those "Attributes [of God] which the Sovereign ordains" are to be allowed.[17]

Moreover, the king must decide which books of the Bible will be allowed in the official state version. Since "Sovereigns in their own Dominions are the sole Legislators," then "those Books only are Canonical...which are established for such by the Sovereign Authority."[18] (Hobbes practiced what he preached, boldly declaring "I can acknowledge no other Books of the Old Testament, to be Holy Scripture, but those which have been commanded to be acknowledged for such, by the Authority of the Church of *England*."[19])

The king, the civil sovereign, also determines the official interpretation of the Bible, judges any and all alleged prophets, and decides whether there will or will not be any sacraments. The single mark of a true prophet, declared Hobbes, is simply that he not teach "any other Religion than that which is already established."[20]

Hobbes was a materialist who did not believe that miracles were actually possible. But since so many people in his day still believed in miracles, and since they occur throughout the Bible, Hobbes had to deal with them. He therefore put his own decidedly political spin on miracles. By a rather roundabout and dubious exegesis of the Bible, Hobbes proved that the only reason miracles occurred in Scripture was to render "men...the better inclined to obey" their political leaders.[21] Miracles, he argued, may not ever be a cause of political revolt.[22]

But anyway, said Hobbes, miracles "now cease"—that is, they simply don't happen any more.[23] And just in case that weren't enough guard against the miraculous intruding into the political realm, Hobbes declared that the civil sovereign is the judge of the legitimacy of any alleged miracle—including the alleged miracle of the Eucharist.[24] As judge of all doctrine and sole arbiter of the legitimacy of the sacraments, the sovereign can't possibly be excommunicated.

Hobbes's church is entirely a state church, completely under the king's power: "I define a CHURCH to be, *A company of men professing Christian Religion, united in the person of one Sovereign; at whose command they ought to assemble, and without whose authority they ought not to assemble.*"[25] United not in Christ—according to St. Paul's definition of the church as "the Body of Christ"—but in the political sovereign. Obviously, for Hobbes, there is no "universal Church" beyond each nation's state church. There are *only* established state churches.

With no independent spiritual power, necessarily there is "no other Government in this life, neither of State, nor Religion, but Temporal." Hobbes reasoned that if we allow any real, independent spiritual power, then "there must needs follow Faction, and Civil war in the Commonwealth, between the *Church* and *State....*" The church must be entirely subsumed under the state so that the "one chief Pastor is...the Civil Sovereign," that is, the king.[26] The king is now the supreme pontiff—just as in pagan ancient Rome. All lesser pastors are the servants of the king, and may only teach and preach what the "chief Pastor" allows.[27]

In short—since we are talking about England here—the Church of England is the church *of England*, that is, a wholly owned and operated subsidiary of the nation state, aimed entirely at supporting the government of England as identified with the person of the king. England is his estate, and the church is his estate church, entirely beholden to him.

But what about heaven and hell? Don't they continue to present a real challenge to the supremacy of the king and his political regime? Won't eternity trump this world in the end? Hobbes realizes that the question of the afterlife is a most serious problem for his secular project.[28]

His solution was to try to persuade the king's subjects (again, through a clever manipulation of Scripture) that the road to heaven is through obedience to the king, and that ultimately the kingdom of heaven was really only a kind of metaphor anyway—the "Kingdom...of God" is really "a Kingdom upon Earth," a "Civil Kingdom."[29] Since it won't be significantly different from or better than what we've got in this life, it shouldn't inspire us to disobey the king.

Just as heaven isn't all that good, hell isn't all that bad either. Since we don't have souls, we won't exist to be tormented eternally. After we die, we cease to exist, asserted Hobbes. Then at judgment day, God will magically recreate us, putting those who were obedient to their civil sovereign into some kind of jolly old eternal England, and immediately snuffing out the damned completely (a doctrine called annihilationism). Not much to fear there.[30]

So Hobbes gives us a refined version of Machiavelli's established secular church, based in part on what Henry VIII, Elizabeth I, and other English monarchs had already achieved. As with Machiavelli, the secular political power is in complete control of the church and forms the church accordingly, as a secular institution under the thumb of the king. But Hobbes takes a step in the secularizing direction beyond the Machiavellian. Hobbes's re-formation of the church—covering worship, the attributes of God, what books will be allowed in the Bible and how they will be interpreted, and what is a sin and what isn't—is exceedingly thorough. But what's truly revolutionary is Hobbes's materialist premises. Unlike, say, Constantine's church or the sixteenth-century French church, Hobbes's church is even more radical than royal theocracy or Divine Right monarchy, where the king imagines that God has placed him on the throne. Hobbes was very careful to build his new secular political order not from God down to the king, but upwards from a mechanistic, materialist substrate. In Hobbes's *Leviathan*, the king's ultimate power comes from the alleged materialist facts that there are no souls, there is no good or evil, no justice or injustice—just physical bodies in perpetual motion and arbitrary wills seeking to enjoy the pleasures of bodily life and avoid its pains (especially the pain of a violent death, the very kind the early Christian martyrs willingly endured).

Hobbes's Established Church Is Secular, but Is It Liberal?

The established church as Hobbes conceived it was clearly a secular church. Henry VIII had already made the church in England entirely subordinate to the state, and Hobbes saw the purpose of that church as the support of the sovereign. But was it a *liberal* church?

I think we can cut through a lot of tedious debate by noting that modern liberalism simply transfers to the individual the kind of absolute autocratic power Hobbes ascribed to the king. Thus liberalism today awards the individual the power to decide how to live free of the interference of the church or Christian morality (the very power Hobbes gave the sovereign). Hobbes had the state ruling with an autocratic hand from above. The modern liberal state tends to treat all individuals as if they were Hobbesian sovereigns and protects their "right" to decide good and evil for themselves, as long as they aren't hurting anyone else. A difference, yes, but a slight one. Modern liberalism's dispute with Hobbes is like a disagreement between a son and a father—it's still the same family. Liberalism today shares the same secular, materialistic aims, the same emphasis on rights, the same assertions of moral autonomy so carefully laid out in Hobbes's secular political philosophy.

Moreover, contrary to their own self-image, contemporary liberals are not quite as democratic as they think they are. They show a marked tendency to use state power to effect political and cultural change from the top down, especially through the courts. If they can't get their proposals through the duly elected legislature, they resort to executive order or regulation by unelected bureaucrats. They also have a tendency to try to rule society through "experts" who deny the legitimacy of common opinion, especially religiously informed opinion, and substitute "scientific" knowledge, which somehow always seems to end up being secular and secularizing. Finally, very much in tune with Machiavelli, liberals tend to want to remold society by co-opting public education, another mode of top-down imposition of the secular worldview, forming individuals in accordance with state-sponsored secular goals.

This kind of autocracy is not all that far removed from Hobbes's. There is good reason to consider Hobbes the founder of modern liberalism and his established secular church to be the first model of the established secular church of liberalism.

From Leviathan to the Sovereign Individual

There are other obvious parallels between Hobbes's sovereign and the liberal sovereign individual. Modern liberals agree with Hobbes that miracles can't happen. They claim that there really is no heaven, but if there is to be heaven and a kingdom of God, it must be on earth, in the here and now. They also assert there is no sin. They claim that each individual has the right to determine the attributes of God, and that each individual has a right to define doctrine for him or herself. And the litany of self-proclaimed Hobbesian "rights" in regard to religious belief goes on: each individual now has the right to decide if there will be, or will not be, any sacraments for him or herself; a right to interpret the Bible for him or herself; the right to define his or her own relationship to God, or not-God; the right to declare and live by his or her own views of morality.

These propositions were all first put forth by Hobbes—but he applied them only to the sovereign. The only difference is that in modern liberalism they apply to each sovereign individual. Whatever squabbles there are between the father and his sons, the family resemblance between Hobbes and modern liberalism is so strong that paternity is undeniable. Hobbes's autocratic secular church is the source of later liberalism's secularized liberal church. And insofar as the liberal state and the liberal church seem today to share the very same goals—so that liberal Christianity supports a state-imposed liberal agenda—there is every reason to suspect that the liberal Christian churches have become the established churches of the secular liberal state.

Despite his autocratic absolutism, Hobbes is clearly responsible for modern secular liberalism—and for the liberal church. The obvious objection to calling Hobbes a liberal is not so obvious anymore. Not only is he the founder of the liberal notion of "rights," of moral relativism, and of an entirely secular-materialist foundation for politics, he also spells out all of the basic assumptions of liberal Christians, and, we should add, of those who have left even secular liberal Christianity behind to become their own gods.

But Leviathan Wins—and Builds Liberalism's Wall of Separation

We conclude this chapter by making some connections from Hobbes to our own present-day situation. The key to recognizing Hobbes's essential role in the development of liberalism is seeing that later liberalism simply transferred all the powers and privileges Hobbes claimed for the sovereign king to the sovereign individual. The goal of the liberal state thereby becomes, in an interesting twist, the protection of the individual's claimed right to define his own religion. It is for this reason, so we are told, that there must be a "separation of church and state"—so that each individual's right to define God for himself may be protected. So today the Leviathan state protects all the little, individual Hobbesian sovereign individuals.

But Leviathan actually comes out on top. Why? The practical result of individual sovereignty in religious belief is to foster a kind of doctrinal chaos, a religious state of nature where each individual claims the absolute right to define God—the effect being a kind of doctrinal war of all against all, so that the state must step in and bring order by excluding them all, and pushing religious belief entirely into the private sphere. The exclusion of religious belief from the public square with the erection of a wall of separation between church and state thereby creates a fully secular state, a state that, in equally excluding all beliefs, orders the public realm according to *un*belief.

Notice that the claimed *right*—or, as we might say today, the *liberty*—to define one's own religious beliefs actually brings about the result that all religious beliefs are privatized and rendered powerless. Thus the claimed right or liberty ends up feeding the power of the secular state, in fact creating the secular state by the subtraction or absolute "separation" of religion. The ingenious effect is that religious individuals, feeling threatened by the secular state, claim more fervently the *right* or *liberty* to define their own religious beliefs. But that claim only confirms and deepens all religious differences, resulting in an increase in the secular state's power to remove any vestige of religion from public life, so that no one's personal religion can impose on anyone else's. Religion understood in this way actually becomes the engine of secularization. I don't think Hobbes quite saw this ingenious possibility, but I'm fairly sure that other, later liberals did, including Benedict Spinoza, the generally acknowledged founder of modern liberalism, to whom we will turn in the next chapter.

But first, a few more parting thoughts about Hobbes. We have discussed his complete moral relativism and his assertion that we have a primitive natural right to do anything we want. These two positions together completely undermine the church's status as keeper of Christ's moral commands—commands that are above every state and every individual, and that define good and evil. After Hobbes, the right of the political sovereign (and later, of the sovereign individual) to define morality trumps the church's moral authority. The predictable result of the acceptance of Hobbes's assumptions was the eclipse of Christian morality as the defining morality of the West. This helps explain why Christians find themselves, quite startlingly, facing today what appears to be the same pagan moral situation faced by the early Christians. Hobbes's invention of natural "rights" (in opposition to Christian morality) has, more than almost anything else, returned us to pagan Rome, and even taken us beyond it to a new, more radical paganism.

In case anyone doubts Hobbes's role in creating our current situation, take a close look at just one issue, abortion. Abortion, as we have already seen, wasn't even a moral question among the ancient pagan Romans. It was so acceptable as to be a non-issue for them. Only Christianity made abortion a moral issue, both then and now. To see the connection between society's return to affirming abortion and Hobbes's assertion that we each have the "right" to define our own personal moral reality, our own subjective view of good and evil, witness the following statement from our own Supreme Court in *Planned Parenthood v. Casey*, a case focused on abortion "rights": "At the heart of liberty is the right to define one's own concept of existence, of meaning, of the universe, and of the mystery of human life. Beliefs about these matters could not define the attributes of personhood were they formed under compulsion of the State."[31]

The problem with the flourish at the end of this extraordinary statement is that the state *has* taken upon itself the power to impose on us the belief, through the power of the Courts, that we each have the right to define our own concept of existence, of meaning, of the universe, and of the mystery of life. The state is not neutral. It imposes Hobbes's entirely relativist view upon us. And Hobbes's view acts as an acid dissolving the central Christian doctrines—that our existence is defined by God, that meaning is defined by reality and not by our subjective inclinations, that the universe was created by God, and that the mystery of life has already been determined by the author of life.

Let's look at one final point—the relationship of Hobbes's thought to pagan thought. Hobbes reaffirms pagan thought explicitly *against* Christianity. Christians, we recall, had sifted through pagan philosophy, taking the good and throwing away whatever was incompatible with Christianity. So they accepted much of Plato, Aristotle, Cicero, and the Stoics, who focused on virtue and the immortal soul's destiny, but they cast aside the materialists such as Democritus, Epicurus, and Lucretius, who denied the soul and affirmed a kind of materialistic hedonism and moral relativism. Like Machiavelli, Hobbes accepted the pagan notion that religion was destructive but useful nonsense. But he was much more explicit than Machiavelli in rejecting the pagans that Christians had found compatible. Hobbes didn't want any aspect of the reappropriation of pagan thought to inadvertently lead back to a reaffirmation of Christianity. So he favored the very pagans that Christians had jettisoned—principally the materialists and the hedonists.[32] That goes a long way to explaining why modern liberalism is so thoroughly defined by both materialism and hedonism, and why it preaches both in its church.

CHAPTER 8

SPINOZA:
THE LIBERAL ELITE
AND THE ESTABLISHED
SECULAR CHURCH

H obbes gave the West the autocratic established secular church,
which I've argued can also rightly be called liberal because it is
grounded in the desire to liberate the state from the church, this
world from the next, and morality from the intensified demand for holiness
commanded by Christ. In Hobbes's *Leviathan*, the sovereign has complete
control of every aspect of his church, from the number of books in the
Bible and their official interpretation, to the number of sacraments (if any)
that are allowed, to the number of miracles (if any) that can be believed,
and even to the very attributes of God. *What* was believed didn't matter to
Hobbes, as long as it served the king and the king's state. Needless to say,
bishops, priests, pastors—or whatever the sovereign decided to call those
under him in Hobbes's established church—would be very loyal political
appointees.

Hobbes theorized on the basis of an English church that in practice,
under Henry VIII and Elizabeth I, had already opted for doctrinal compromise governed entirely by political expediency at the expense of truth, and

even of consistency. Machiavelli's influence had played a role, as had the perennial tendency of political sovereigns to use whatever is at their disposal for the sake of their political goals.

But Hobbes offered the established church in England the intellectual framework for a truly and thoroughly secular foundation, thereby eliminating any possible conflict between the state and its church. All power was in the king, the king defined his religion, and his religion was the religion of the realm.

While Hobbes's established secular church was entirely autocratic, Benedict Spinoza (1632–1677) moved the established secular church toward something resembling the modern liberal or mainline church we're familiar with, the one that seems entirely at home in the world, holds ever fewer doctrines (and those, very lightly), and focuses on "social justice," that is, the advance of radical causes and the welfare state.

Not coincidentally, Spinoza is often called the father of modern liberal democracy. He has also been called the father of modern Scripture scholarship—as has Hobbes, interestingly enough. Spinoza is the father of the radical (versus the moderate) Enlightenment. How all this patrimony fits together will be the focus of this chapter; all of it will help us to understand the church Spinoza founded.

Spinoza's Radical Life and Philosophy

Spinoza was a descendant of the Marranos, Jews from Spain and Portugal who had been forced to convert to Christianity but secretly practiced Judaism. His family had emigrated from Portugal to the Netherlands, the most liberal state of the time, in hopes of living openly and without persecution as practicing Jews. Spinoza was born in Amsterdam where he was able to study the Torah in peace.[1]

It would be all too easy to blame Spinoza's radical views on the anti-Semitism that he and his family experienced, but his radicalism, which surfaced very early, was opposed first of all to his own Judaism. At a mere twenty-four years old, he was excommunicated by his fellow Jews.[2] His radicalism had been rubbing them the wrong way for some time.

Spinoza's rebellion against Judaism had surfaced in his teens. The French philosopher René Descartes was an important influence. Descartes had proposed a kind of dualist philosophy, putting forth a completely materialist physics that explained everything (including how bodies move), but also asserting that there were purely spiritual aspects of reality as well.

Descartes saw a human being as a mechanical body yoked to an immaterial soul—the so called "ghost in the machine." But Cartesian dualism created a dilemma: if the human body moves itself by entirely mechanical means, what does the ghost, the soul, add?

Descartes affirmed, though not without considerable ambiguity, the existence of God as an immaterial spirit. But here again, Descartes' dualism posed a dilemma. What do we need God for if the world can be entirely explained as a self-contained, self-running mechanism?

Descartes' dualism suffered from a set of inner contradictions. The spiritual realm seemed to be added on as an afterthought. (Or perhaps he had retained it disingenuously, only to avoid persecution by religious authorities, who would rightly suspect materialism as tending to atheism.)

Spinoza's answer: cut the dualism in half, ditch any notion of immaterial realities, and embrace complete materialist monism. Spinoza became an even more radical materialist than either Machiavelli or Hobbes. As we'll discuss in more detail below, he identified God and matter, the creator and creation.

Descartes' wasn't the only influence on Spinoza. Machiavelli also deeply informed Spinoza's radical philosophy, especially his approach to the state's use of religion.[3] Spinoza scholar Edwin Curley calls Spinoza "arguably the most Machiavellian of the great modern political philosophers."[4] And Spinoza himself praised Machiavelli as "that most farseeing man."[5]

Anyone reading Spinoza's most famous work, the *Tractatus theologico-politicus* (the *Theologico-Political Treatise*), will also see Hobbes's footprints all over it. Hobbes's *Leviathan* was immensely influential among the radical circle in Amsterdam of which Spinoza soon became the center.[6] Let's begin our exploration of Spinoza's thought with his most radical idea.

God Is Everything: the Deification of the World and the State

Spinoza identified God with nature, thereby deifying nature and naturalizing God, a philosophical position often called materialist monism (because it cuts out any dualism of matter and spirit) or more accurately, pantheism (because God is all things). "There can be, or be conceived, no other substance but God," declared Spinoza in his *Ethics*.[7] Thus for Spinoza, everything in nature, everything in the world, the entire unfolding of human history, the political state itself, and every individual human being— all of these things were and are manifestations of God.[8] God isn't above creation or above history; he *is* creation, he *is* history. In direct contrast to Christianity, an immaterial God never became flesh. For Spinoza, all flesh (that is, all matter) always was and is God.

The implications of Spinoza's pantheism are far-reaching. First of all, Spinoza collapsed creator and creature, destroying the essential distinction introduced at the very beginning of the Bible. Pantheism makes a god of this world and thus completely undermines the entire Judeo-Christian understanding of reality that flows from the creator-creature distinction in Genesis. Removing that creator-creature distinction allows for a reintroduction of pagan animism and idolatry, the worship of the divine in creatures. Spinoza's "monism" was a radical rejection of the First Commandment.

Spinoza's rejection of "Thou shalt have no other gods before me" paved the way for the Romantic idolatry of nature. The Romanticism of the late eighteenth and nineteenth centuries was not only a reaction against the mechanistic Enlightenment view of nature—the conception of nature as a clock and God as the distant clockmaker. Romanticism was also a full embrace of Spinoza's pantheism, a pulling of God into nature.

Pulling God into nature meant pulling God into history. Under the influence of Spinoza, history, especially human history, would itself come to be considered the "manifestation" of God. For Spinoza, God is revealed *in* nature, *as* nature. This has the effect of the divinizing of human history since human nature and human activities are thereby manifestations of God. So as a result of Spinoza's pantheism, history becomes God, and human beings worship their own actions and efforts as divine. And since the political state is the most powerful expression of collective human action, the state itself becomes the greatest manifestation of the divine.

An obvious result of pantheism's deification of the state is that nothing stands outside the state, or outside human history, to criticize or correct it. Moreover, if God *is* the world, obviously there cannot be any heavenly kingdom in another world. Spinoza cut off that possibility and ensured that the devotion previously paid to a spiritual God would be lavished on the material kingdoms of this world. Even though Spinoza himself directed his devotion to nature, the historical result of his pantheism was uncritical religious devotion to the state. The secular state was thereby sacralized, made divine itself; it became, in the minds of its devotees, a real manifestation of the divine in and through history. The pantheistic state that had its seed in Spinoza would come to full flower in the ruminations of Georg Wilhelm Friedrich Hegel (1770–1831), who declared that the Prussian state was the fullest manifestation of the immanentized "spirit" of God.

Obviously, the sacralized state has no need of the church, except perhaps as a department of the state. When the creator is collapsed into the creature, the church is collapsed into the state. The distinction between church and state is entirely lost, and the state absorbs the form and all the functions of the church. With Spinoza we have, then, the origin of the most radical form of the established secular church—the state *as* church, devoted to the worship of itself. Spinoza's is a *liberal* established state church because it is defined precisely by liberation of this world from the next, liberation of the state from a critical church standing outside and above it, liberation of individuals from the demands of a morality defined by God.

Spinoza's pantheism is at the bottom of all his arguments, and it was immensely influential in history. We must keep it in mind as we sort through the rest of his philosophy, beginning with Spinoza's actually very undemocratic foundation for liberal democracy, which is the kind of state he envisions as appropriate to his grand vision.

Spinoza's Human Pyramid

You can't understand Spinoza's role in the foundation of modern secular liberal democracy until you grasp his very undemocratic starting point, which we might call Spinoza's pyramid. Spinoza believed that the population always has been and always will be made up of three different classes of people: (1) a very small number of rational people with real intellectual vision, the philosophic elite; (2) a middle-sized group, larger than the philosophic elite (but much smaller than the vulgar, below), who might best be called scientists, experts, or intellectuals rather than philosophers and who, while they reason like the elite, aren't of the same great intellectual caliber and vision; and finally, (3) a very great number of stupid or vulgar people, incapable of reasoning, who are led by their imaginations, passions, and superstitions.[9]

Imagine the whole population as a pyramid, with the three classes stacked up in order of size. The philosophic elite are at the pointy top, with the more numerous scientific followers of the elite in the middle, and finally at the bottom are the most numerous of all, the vulgar, unscientific masses, making up the much broader base of the pyramid.

If things ran the way that they should in Spinoza's thinking, the philosophic elite at the top would govern everyone below them on the pyramid—especially the vulgar masses. Only the reasonable would rule.

And what does Spinoza mean by reasonable? For Spinoza, Spinozan mechanistic-materialist pantheism defines what it means to be philosophic and truly rational. To be rational *is* to deny immaterial reality. Only Spinozan monists are rational, so only they have the right to rule.

The scientists, the class in the middle of Spinoza's pyramid, dutifully follow the lead of his philosophic elite. To be rational means to be a materialist, so to be a rational scientist (is there any other kind?) means to be a scientific materialist who firmly believes that only matter is real, and that any notions of spiritual or immaterial realities are foolish, the kind of thing only the vulgar masses believe.

So the vulgar masses at the bottom of the pyramid are supposed to bow to the edicts of the scientific elite, or as we now call them, the scientific "experts." These experts define reality for the masses. They make sure that the vulgar masses believe that "science" proves that reality is entirely mate-rial, and that any notion of immaterial reality is so idiotic as not to be worthy of consideration by intelligent people. The Christian distinctions between immaterial and material reality, soul and body, next world and this world, city of God and city of man, and church and state are all ridiculed out of existence.

The Church Gets in the Way of Spinoza's Pyramid-Building

That's how Spinoza wanted the pyramid to work, and we might even imagine Spinoza as a kind of early modern Pharaoh in charge of its con-struction. But the problem is—or so Spinoza argued—that what we actually find throughout human history is that the pyramid is upside down, and the stupid, irrational, superstitious, vulgar masses are ruling everyone else, including the philosophers like Spinoza.

How did this happen? How did the ignorant masses get the upper hand?

Spinoza has a clear answer: in the West it happened through Christian-ity, through the Bible, through the fear of hell and hope for heaven, through the belief in the existence of the soul, through the church's control over the state. The church stands squarely in the way of Pharaoh Spinoza's pyramid-building project.

That is *the* theological-political problem, according to Spinoza. The goal of his *Theologico-Political Treatise* is to set the pyramid up the right way, so the Spinozan philosophic elite can rule. The church that stands over and against the state, teaching all the wrong things, must be firmly subordinated to the state—and hence to the rule of the philosophic elite. Secular liberal democracy and the established secular liberal church are the historical results of Spinoza's very successful pyramid-building project.

Why the State Needs Its Own Church and Its Own Bible

Spinoza's project involved not the rejection of the Christian church, but its complete re-formation, not the rejection of the Bible, but its complete reconstruction. In the words of Spinoza scholar Yirmiyahu Yovel, the "overall aim" of Spinoza's *Theologico-Political Treatise* "is to establish mental and institutional mechanisms" that will channel and transform the irrationalities of the vulgar masses to accord with the rationality of the philosophic elite, "using state power and a purified popular religion as vehicles of a semirational civilizing process."[10] The philosophic elite must regain control of the state and put the church completely at its service; the church itself must be transformed so that it becomes an instrument of the secularizing liberal state.

"Mental and institutional mechanisms." "State power." "Purified popular religion." These are the tools that will enable the followers of Spinoza to put the pyramid right side up again, with the ineradicably stupid masses at the bottom where they belong. They stay there obediently because of the influence of the church that has been "purified" by secular liberalism.

This all may seem fantastic to us today. We, who are now surrounded by rather bolder atheists, assume that secularism and outright atheism go hand in hand. How could the denial of the reality of the next world *not* mean atheism? And so we think that secularists pushed for the complete elimination of the church and Christianity from the very beginning.

But Spinoza wanted to construct an established secular church (rather than abolishing religion altogether) precisely because he believed that universal enlightenment was impossible. The mass of mankind would always be led by ignorance, fear, passion, imagination, and superstition: "I have recognized that it is equally impossible to take away superstition from the vulgar as to take away dread," dread or fear of the unknown being the very thing which feeds superstition.[11] We all can't be philosophers like Spinoza. The philosophic elite form a very small cadre, and always will. Alas, ignorance, fear, passion, wild imagination, and superstition (like the poor) will be with us always, Spinoza lamented. So we will always need a church to govern the foolish, irrational masses.

The same is true for the Bible. Spinoza thought the Bible was a book written *by* the vulgar *for* the vulgar and aimed only at whipping up "devotion in the psyches of the vulgar,"[12] that is, in the minds of the great mass of men who are moved by their passions rather than by reason. It therefore "only narrates matters in the order and phrases by which it can move human beings—and mainly the plebs—to devotion in the greatest degree...." Since the Bible isn't philosophic, "it speaks of God and of matters quite improperly, no doubt since it is not eager to convince reason, but to affect and occupy human beings' fancy and imagination."[13] At best, it's a kind of rousing fairy tale.

But that's all that the "plebs"—the common people—are capable of understanding. And thus the Bible is a necessary instrument for controlling them. As Spinoza, drawing a lesson from ancient pagans, notes in the very beginning of his *Tractatus theologico-politicus*, "Nothing regulates a multitude more effectively than superstition."[14]

Don't wipe out superstition; *use* it to rule the incurably superstitious masses. Don't abolish the church; *use* it. Don't completely discredit the Bible; *use* it. Secularize every religious institution so that it will be a pliant tool of the secular philosophic elite. A look at what Spinoza intended in regard to the Bible will help to illustrate how it all works.

Reconstructing the Bible by Rejecting Miracles

Spinoza, as was mentioned above, is known as the father of modern scriptural scholarship. In Steven Smith's words, Spinoza's *Tractatus* "stands at the beginning of what would later become known as the 'higher criticism' of the Bible. This higher criticism aims at nothing less than the historical understanding and reconstruction of the Bible. Spinoza's biblical criticism is, then, historical criticism; its goal is the historicization or secularization of the biblical text."[15]

To put it another way, the "scientific" study of scripture—what modern Biblical criticism claims to provide—ends up being "scientific" precisely in the special Spinozan sense: the vulgar class's access to the Bible is mediated by "scientific scholars" from the middle part of Spinoza's pyramid, all in service of the aims of the philosophic few at the pyramid's pointy top. Historical-critical Bible scholars are, as it were, the intellectual civil servants employed in Spinoza's project, the "experts" to whom the common people must defer in any attempt to read and interpret the Bible. These experts provide a wedge between the Bible and the reader and, even more importantly, between the reader and the orthodox Christian church.

Spinozan Biblical criticism therefore produces a secularized Bible, which serves as the founding text of the established secular liberal church. Spinoza's strategy for effecting the secularization of Scripture arose out of his pantheism. With God collapsed into nature, and nature into God, the Bible could be de-supernaturalized. That is, all the miracles could be removed from the Biblical text—or at least discredited, so that liberal Christians believe a sort of watered-down version of the Gospel. "Scientific" scriptural scholarship begins with the assumption that miracles are impossible, that nothing supernatural can occur.

Why? This is Spinoza's argument: If God is nature, and nature is God, then the laws of nature are not something created by God, but rather expressions of his very essence. Therefore it is impossible that God could ever act *against* or *outside* the laws of nature. God *is* nature, and God can't act against or contrary to himself. And so there can't be any miracles:

> If something were to come about in nature which did not follow on the basis of its law....it would necessarily conflict with the order that God has set in nature for eternity through the universal laws of nature; and so it would be contrary to nature and

its laws; and, consequently, faith in it would make us doubt everything and lead us to Atheism....a miracle, whether contrary to nature or above nature, is a mere absurdity.[16]

Belief in miracles leads to atheism—because it makes us doubt the laws of nature! Spinoza's rhetorical excesses to the side, the bottom line is that miracles are impossible. Therefore, the apparent miracles in the Bible must have some other explanation besides God's supernatural intervention in the world.

The most common source of the miracle accounts in the Bible, in Spinoza's opinion, is ignorance. An alleged miracle is "nothing else but a work whose natural cause we cannot explain on the mode of some other, usual thing; *or, at least, that the one who writes or narrates the miracle cannot so explain*" [emphasis added].[17]

What else can one expect from a book written by the vulgar and unscientific? Thus the "scientific" Biblical exegete spends his time removing miracles from the Biblical text, or at least explaining them away as the result of the ignorance of the apostles and evangelists.

The Fruit of Spinoza's Plan: the Mainline Churches

But how does this wholesale rejection of miracles fit in with Spinoza's political plans? We recall that belief in the supernatural, in the miraculous, in God's being other than and above nature, was essential to the authority of the church, and even to its existence as distinct from the state. The church has its source in a supernatural being and supernatural revelation, and it is aimed at a supernatural goal—the kingdom of God. All that is needed to undermine the church's authority is to persuade people that it is impossible for anything supernatural to erupt into the world and disturb the secular order. Once the church's authority is undermined, the church can be completely subordinated to the secular aims of the state.

But Spinoza didn't just declare that miracles were impossible and expect everyone to agree immediately. His campaign against the miraculous was a carefully crafted plan depending on instituting "mental and institutional mechanisms," as Yovel calls them, to control the vulgar masses by transforming how they think and how they act.

The first mental mechanism that Spinoza's project depends on is the habit of thinking of everything according to the materialist view of the world, a set of mechanistic assumptions that makes miracles impossible, or more accurately, unthinkable. Materialist-minded scientists and materialist-minded Biblical scholars continually reinforce materialist assumptions in the populace, until this-worldly materialism becomes an ingrained habit. These "experts" stay busy telling the populace what they can think—about the world, and also about the Bible.

The authority of these experts is bolstered (and thus the secularizing revolution is pushed forward) by a host of institutions: scientific societies, scientific training, scientific methods of scriptural scholarship, university curricula. All of these, especially the last, which directly affects the largest number of people, act as *institutional* mechanisms that continually reinforce the *mental* mechanisms of the materialist worldview. And the trickle-down effect from all of these institutions forms the entire approach of public education, the main institution for mental-mechanism-formation that shapes the minds of the masses from their very earliest years, especially where state-guided education is mandatory.

We can see the implications of Spinoza's radical revolution. As the minds of the populace become increasingly secularized—increasingly formed by the view that all is matter, that this world is all there is, and that no irruptions of the supernatural can possibly occur—the church will lose more and more of its authority and, thus weakened, will much more easily be made into a useful tool of the secular state.

That is exactly what has happened historically since Spinoza. Spinoza's plan to weaken the church by undermining faith in the supernatural has been hugely successful.

The materialistic mindset has increasingly taken hold, and the church has become correspondingly anemic. The church weakened by unbelief in the supernatural is what we call the mainline or liberal Christian church. That church has total faith in materialist science, fully embraces the "scientific" study of Scripture fathered by Spinoza, and professes a completely de-supernaturalized form of Christianity that is entirely at home in this world and only vaguely and non-threateningly associated with the next.

This is a church that poses no challenge whatsoever to the secular state. In fact, it serves the cause of secularization at every turn. It's a church with the bodily form of Christianity but devoid of the soul. In modern times, this secular church has been accurately described in H. Richard Niebuhr's biting summary of its theology: "A God without wrath brought men without sin into a kingdom without judgment through the ministrations of a Christ without a cross."[18]

There are more radical forms of Spinoza's church, in which the connection to Christianity is entirely abandoned. These Spinozan churches often appear under the name "Unitarian," but they sometimes take even more radical forms in which the object of worship is no longer God at all—but rather nature, or the deified human race.

But our main concern here is with the liberal or mainstream church, which may be soulless and anemic, but which is still recognizably Christian. If that's all that's left of the church once Spinoza is done with it, what exactly is its purpose? Why keep it around? Or the Bible, for that matter? What—what of any use, at least—is left of the Bible after the "scientific" Spinozan Scripture scholars have completed their work of Biblical reconstruction? If you think so little of the Bible, we might ask Spinoza, why not just toss it out?

Making Stupid People
Good Citizens of the Secular State

The short answer is that a de-supernaturalized and weakened church, stripped of any dogmatic claims based upon the miraculous, makes an excellent moral prop for the secular state. Thus the Bible is reduced to a bunch of old stories from which we may, very carefully, extract moral lessons, or to be more accurate, build up an entire secularized version of morality.

Making the Bible into a morality tale—that's Spinoza's revolutionary goal. It's hard for us to consider this goal revolutionary now. We're so used to the notion that religion isn't about the nature of reality, that religion has no connection to science, and consequently that religion is *only* about morality, that we don't recognize how revolutionary Spinoza's reduction of religion to morality originally was.

The Bible, Spinoza argued, was written by and for the ignorant, the vulgar, and the superstitious. "Scripture does not contain grand theories or philosophical matters, but only very simple matters, which can be perceived even by the slowest."[19] In other words, the Bible is for dummies.

Needless to say, these dimwits aren't philosophers or scientists. But they can at least appreciate a good, stirring moral tale. And that's helpful. The simple-minded need to be taught how to behave. But they need to be taught in a way that suits their less-than-sharp intellectual abilities. The Bible can be a useful tool for that purpose, as long as it doesn't give the vulgar plebs any pretensions to knowledge of truths above reason.

That's the kind of thing that makes the plebs uppity. If they think they possess supernaturally revealed doctrinal or moral truths that stand above and judge the state, they're actually dangerous. That's why the Bible has to be reduced to the role of moral cheerleader.

All You Need Is Love

Vulgar people must be taught by the Bible, but in a way that makes them more, not less, obedient to the state. For Spinoza, that means reducing the entire message of the Bible to one simple platitude: "obedience toward God consists only in love of neighbor...."[20]

Declaring that Christianity is *entirely* defined by love of neighbor allows Spinoza to wipe out all sources of doctrinal conflict. Everything else is entirely inconsequential, including all the intricate doctrinal differences that Christians over the centuries have thought were so momentous because the salvation of souls might depend on them. All that counts is being good. Or more accurately, as we'll soon see, being nice.

Spinoza gives us a new, virtually dogma-free church, a universal form of Christianity based on the single command to love one's neighbor: "this very commandment is the sole norm of the whole catholic faith; and all the dogmas of the faith...are to be determined through it alone."[21] On the basis of his argument that "the whole law consists in this alone: in love towards one's neighbor,"[22] Spinoza insists that "*we are bound to believe nothing else* on the basis of the bidding of Scripture but what is absolutely necessary for executing this commandment" [emphasis added].[23]

To sum up Spinoza's kind of Christianity: *You don't need the Nicene Creed if you're nice*. People who fight over inconsequential dogmas are not nice. They're *intolerant*.

And the Greatest of These Is Tolerance

St. Paul's words about the theological virtues of faith, hope, and love (or charity) are well known: "but the greatest of these is charity"(I Corinthians 13:13). In elevating the love of one's neighbor to the greatest and only needful doctrine of Christianity, Spinoza would seem to be in essential agreement.

But Spinoza's kind of love is a noticeably tamer virtue than St. Paul's. Spinoza's love is not the kind of self-sacrificing charity that drove the saints and martyrs such as Paul to lose everything, even to suffer death, in order to bring the truth about salvation to their fellow man. Quite the contrary. By love, Spinoza meant minding one's own business, not bothering others but just getting along—in a word, tolerance. Faith is, therefore, recast by Spinoza as granting "to each the highest freedom of philosophizing," that is, as an affirmation of complete freedom of thought, rather than of specific theological truths. The reason, given by Spinoza quite frankly, is that faith is fundamentally irrational, concerned only with "nothing but obedience and piety."[24] Be good and let others think as they please. Spinoza enshrines doctrinal tolerance as the supreme virtue in the established secular liberal church. The complete insignificance of belief in Spinoza's version of Christianity is highlighted by the fact that Spinoza sets his view out as a complete antithesis of Luther's view that we are saved by faith alone, not by works. For Spinoza, precisely the opposite is true: "We can judge no one to be faithful or faithless except on the basis of works. Namely, if the works are good, however he may dissent in his dogmas from the other faithful, he is still faithful. And on the contrary, if the works are evil, however he may agree in words, he is still faithless."[25]

For Spinoza, differences in theology are utterly inconsequential. All that matters is that you are externally moral and hence law-abiding. And even atheists can be law-abiding citizens. Later, Spinoza's disciples would point out that Spinoza himself was both perfectly law-abiding and at the same time an atheist (on the theory that his pantheism amounted to a disingenuous way of saying that nature is everything and there is no God). Therefore, as his philosophy spread out and became influential in the eighteenth century, Spinoza's followers argued that atheists should be tolerated rather than persecuted.

The Secular State Enforces
the Liberal Dogma of Tolerance

But if someone's faith is to be judged only on external works, *on law-abidingness*, then the civil sovereign becomes the judge of Christian morality. In other words, the morality of the church will be determined by the secular state, which governs the external actions of the citizens.

In Spinoza's scheme, the state is also the enforcer of the notion that anyone can believe anything he wants, as long as he is law-abiding. Faith is essentially irrational, and can never be expunged from the vulgar multitude. When the adherents of the various beliefs try to gain political control, civil wars follow. "For avoiding these evils," Spinoza asserts, "nothing safer can be devised for a Republic than to place piety and Religious worship solely in works, that is, solely in the cultivation of charity and justice, and to leave each a free judgment concerning other things."[26] The government inculcates into its citizens the belief that the chief of all the virtues is tolerance—the affirmation of everyone's right to believe anything he wants as long as he behaves himself in public. To put the principle in a form that's familiar to us, dogma is subjective. What people believe is entirely a personal matter. What matters is whether they disturb the peace or physically hurt someone else.

The result is that, ultimately, the political sovereign (or imperium, as Spinoza calls it) determines what "religion" can mean. In Spinoza's words, "Religion receives the force of right solely from the decree of those who have the right to command." Spinoza backs up this assertion with an argument that should sound familiar from Hobbes: "God does not have any special kingdom over human beings except through those who hold the imperium." Civil power defines the church. "Religious worship and the exercise of piety has to be accommodated to the peace of utility of the Republic and, consequently, be determined solely by the highest powers— who thus have to be its interpreters as well."[27] The highest powers, again, are those of the imperium, the state. And what is most useful to the state is religious tolerance.

Spinoza's re-shaping of Christianity has an immense and obvious effect on the relationship of the church to the state. If doctrine doesn't matter, then the church doesn't matter. If the secular state defines belief as entirely relative and inconsequential, then ultimately the church is only a private club for the like-minded, whose shared beliefs are entirely subjective. By pushing the notion that doctrine doesn't matter, and that anyone should be able to believe anything as long as he obeys the civil laws, the state ultimately undermines the church as an authoritative body and puts the authority to define doctrine entirely into the hands of individuals. Instead of a duality between church and state, we now have only a duality between the individual and the state. The church as an effective intermediate institution is neutralized. *Now the individual must face the state alone.*

Note Spinoza's cleverness. In his scheme, the state doesn't actually define doctrine. But it does continually undermine the church's authority to define doctrine by inculcating in its citizens the view that each individual has *a right to believe anything he wants*—and by claiming to protect that right.

How the Right to Believe Anything Pushes the Church Out

What I'm going to say here may sound so strange—it's so completely counter to what we've all been told—that I'm afraid you may have trouble believing it, let alone digesting its full import.

Here goes. It is by asserting the "right" of each person to believe in God in the way he or she sees fit that Spinoza, the founder of modern liberalism, was able to achieve the complete exclusion of the church from the public square.

Even more disturbing, the belief in this individual right actually *creates the need* for the secular state. The more that right is believed and acted upon, the more we need the secular state to protect our right to believe what we want, against other people's conflicting religious beliefs. So maximizing the diversity of beliefs, based upon this right, maximizes the power of the secular state. Or, to put it another way, continually undermining the unity of Christianity destroys the ability of the church to stand against the state, to judge the state, to speak for God's commands against the machinations of the state.

This can all be validated in our own experience. We are more Spinozan than we think.

Today we passionately hold to the principle that we have a *right* to believe, to worship, as we each see fit—each of us individually. But that means that everyone else has the same right, too. Therefore, in order to protect our own rights from the threat of some other believer using government power to dictate beliefs to us, we cannot allow anyone's faith to define or even inform the state. In short, the multiplicity of competing and contradictory beliefs leads us to embrace a secular state—a state defined by no one's belief, that is to say, a state defined by *unbelief*.

The same dynamic brings about the entire privatization of belief. Since belief is entirely relative to individuals—what else *could* it mean to claim that each of us has a right to determine what we believe?[28]—belief is entirely privatized. Christian faith, instead of being unified and universal, is atomized, relativized, and privatized.

To put it another way, the more churches there are, the stronger the secular state becomes. This is an excellent strategy for secularizing society. Fomenting divisions among Christians and promoting religious diversity beyond Christianity serves to advance secularism by maximizing religious disunity.

In a Spinozan society (such as our own), the only church that retains any hold on public power is the secularized liberal church—the church that rejects miracles and the supernatural, preaches love (but only of the watered down tolerant sort), treats doctrine as inconsequential and subjective, promotes diversity of belief, and exalts tolerance as the chief virtue. In short, the only church with power is the church Spinoza created, the church defined by the goals of the secular state, the church that ensures that the church is powerless, and that the powerless church serves the state.

If that doesn't astound you, then perhaps taking a closer look at how Spinoza establishes this right of the individual to believe anything will shake you up.

The Creation of the Right to Believe Anything about God

Ask yourself this: where in the Bible, where in the history of Israel so completely defined by the Law, where in God's continual anger at Israel for mixing themselves up in the alien religion of the Canaanites, where in the words of Christ who claimed that he was the Way, the Truth, and the Life, where in the words of St. Paul who railed against tampering with the doctrines about Christ, where in the first seven centuries of the church carefully and painfully hammering out the details of the doctrines about Jesus and the Holy Trinity, where among Christians who believed that Scripture is God's Holy Revealed Word—where in all this would you possibly derive the notion that somehow the goal of Christianity was to inculcate the principle that each person has a right to believe anything he wants?

If we are honest, we have to admit that if anything defines the history of the Judeo-Christian tradition, and hence the church, it is the obsession with *believing the right thing*, with having and protecting the truth—not the idea that each individual has a right to believe anything he wants.

If such a right had been accepted among the Jews of the Old Testament, there would have been no Jews, and no Hebrew Bible. If that right had been assumed among the Christians of the early church, there would have been no distinction between orthodox and heretical, no councils, no creeds, and indeed, no Bible—since the biblical canon was put together in response to heretics (like Marcion, and the Gnostics) asserting alternative versions of Christianity. There would certainly have been no church—a definite, distinct Body of Christ with a definite set of beliefs, as distinct from the state, and in fact, challenging the pagan empire at its heart.

As we've seen in some detail, the original, historic liberty claimed by the church was actually the freedom from interference and control by political power, the freedom to define doctrine, the freedom to choose its own priests and bishops, the freedom to administer its own internal affairs. It was a liberty rooted in the distinct functions that the church and political power each had, and so it also protected the political realm from being taken over by the church. The understanding of liberty that protected the church from the state in Christendom was grounded in an understanding of faith fundamentally at odds with Spinoza's notion that faith is essentially irrational, and so there is no right or wrong in regard to what one believes. The liberty of the church was a liberty rooted in the recognition of the deepest human desire for seeking the highest truths. That is a much different foundation than Spinoza's complete theological subjective relativism. To explain the contrast in a slightly different way, the right to seek the truth is not the same as the right to define the truth in whatever way one happens to fancy or desire. There's a world of difference between respecting religious liberty because you believe that human beings have a fundamental need to be persuaded by truth, and hence to freely and sincerely assent to it, on the one hand, and, on the other, thinking with Spinoza that, since religion is irrational and based merely on one's subjective feelings and desires, it should be confined to the realm of taste, "to each his own."

If we're honest, we have to admit the notion that we all have the right to define our own religious beliefs whatever way we please—a principle that so many of us modern Christians accept as an integral part of our Christianity—must actually come from somewhere else, rather than from Christianity. And wherever it may originally have arisen, we certainly find it in Spinoza.

Where did Spinoza's relativist version of religious liberty come from? More or less straight from Hobbes,[29] but buttressed by Spinoza's pantheism.

Spinoza, like Hobbes, denied the reality of objective good and evil. But Spinoza based his argument against moral absolutes upon the notion that God is everything—and therefore everything and everyone is God. Since God has "the highest right to everything," and everyone is a manifestation of God, then "each individual has the highest right to everything it can do." Since God is above the law, then each of us (in our natural, pre-civil state—another idea Spinoza took from Hobbes) is a law unto himself, with a right to do anything he likes.[30] Just as God cannot sin, so individuals, in the "state of nature" cannot sin. The "natural state is…without religion and law, and consequently without sin and wrong," a truth that Spinoza tells the reader is "confirmed by the authority of Paul."[31]

Just as each person has a right to *do* anything, he has a right to *believe* anything, for in this "natural" condition there is, Spinoza claimed, not yet any formal religion. Each believes as he sees fit. So many individuals, so many beliefs, so many gods.

This religious pluralism would seem at first to contradict both Spinoza's pantheism and his pyramid. Surely the correct belief about God, from Spinoza's pantheist point of view, is that God is nature and nature is God.

That's what the elite philosophers know by reason, whereas the religious beliefs of most people, the vulgar people, are based on ignorance, superstition, and fear. Why should the vulgar have a *right* to believe what is clearly, for Spinoza anyway, erroneous and irrational?

He confers that right on them *as a matter of strategy*. From Spinoza's perspective, as we've noted, the vulgar mass of men will always be with us. They will never embrace the rational, materialist pantheism of the philosophic elite. They are incapable of understanding it. In fact, they will always view their betters' rational belief with the greatest suspicion. But if they cannot be overcome by reason, they can be vanquished by flattery. The flattered multitude will, ironically, protect the philosophers from persecution. Here we should note that in Spinoza's own day, freethinkers were in actual physical danger from both governments and mobs (so we rightly have some sympathy with Spinoza here, even while rejecting his solution to the problem). Spinoza himself carefully concealed his radical opinions, allowing them to be published only after his death.

So that's Spinoza's plan. Flatter the vulgar. Tell them they *have a right*, just as much as anyone else, to believe whatever they wish about God. If everyone believes he has that right equally with everyone else, then everyone's right to believe whatever he wants will be equally protected. Including Spinoza's. The atheist or freethinker is protected by this right above all (assuming, as noted above, that he is law-abiding).

Spinoza's right to believe whatever one wants has the same effect as Hobbes's natural rights. These rights maximize the number of competing claims, thereby creating a kind of "state of nature" or "state of war" where each individual needs the secular state—the Leviathan—to protect him or her from the possibility of being politically controlled by someone else's beliefs. Let me repeat that the secular state is the state defined by no one's belief, that is to say by *unbelief*. The secular state thereby increases its power precisely by protecting each individual's right to believe anything, a right which has the effect of maximizing the diversity of competing beliefs and increasing the need for the secular state. Unbelief thereby becomes the default view, enforced by the political power. Secularism becomes the state religion, the state belief system, the state worldview.

Thus the church is disabled as an authority distinct from the state. Encouraging the passionate belief in the right to believe whatever one wants has the effect of atomizing the church, splintering its one distinct body into countless competing churches—none of which can stand against the state, and each of which needs the secular state to protect it from any other church's belief gaining political control. The more churches there are, the more powerful and more secular the state becomes.

The Liberal Church and the Secular State: a Perfect Fit

But doesn't this pluralism of many churches contradict the notion that liberalism has established one secular church? Isn't the liberal church just one more competing church among the ever-increasing multitude?

No, it's not. Liberal or mainstream Christianity is a special form of Christianity that perfectly coincides with the liberal state's secularizing aims. The liberal church is de-supernaturalized, it takes the Bible as (at best) a morality tale, it looks to satisfaction in this world and not the next, it regards belief itself as something that is defined subjectively and therefore rejects the notion of authoritatively defined doctrine, it looks to the state as the organ of this-worldly charity and progress, it holds all the same basic moral positions as secular liberalism, it looks for salvation in and through history, and it views materialist science as providing the definitive view of the world. In short, liberal Christianity makes no difference; its views are indistinct from purely secular liberalism.

Since the beliefs of liberal Christianity are indistinct from those of secular liberalism, the secular liberal state ends up, *de facto*, supporting liberal Christianity with the powers of the state. How could it be otherwise? The liberalized church and liberal state share the same assumptions and aims.

While liberal churches themselves do not use their own authority to impose their beliefs by force, the state does impose secular liberalism.

Liberals have tended to impose a top-down revolution, using especially the courts and the universities as organs of change. That is, of course, in keeping with Spinoza's plan—the top of his pyramid must impose its views on the bottom of the pyramid using any of a number of mediating middle-men and middlewomen: the cultural intellectual elite, the various "scientific" experts in biblical studies, sociology, psychology, and so forth, buttressed by scientific materialists in the hard sciences. The revolution is carried on by the liberal elite, the two top parts of Spinoza's pyramid, and thus we may rightly call the church that follows this lead the Liberal Elite Established Secular Church.

CHAPTER 9

ROUSSEAU'S RADICAL LIBERALISM: ESTABLISHING CIVIL RELIGION

I
n the past few chapters we have covered revolutionary thinkers whose aim was to turn Christianity into a religion that would be useful to the secular state. Their reconstructed versions of Christianity tended to break down the original Christian distinction between church and state that had been established in the Middle Ages. But in their schemes there was still a role for the Christian church, and even a kind of separation of church and state, insofar as Hobbes, Machiavelli, and Spinoza in their different ways encouraged secular rulers to erect a wall between their private secular aims and their public use of Christianity. Even in the liberal state religion constructed by Spinoza, the Bible is still considered to be a useful tool, as long as it is interpreted according to the scholarly, scientific "experts" of the new Biblical criticism.

But with Jean-Jacques Rousseau we turn an important corner. Rousseau is the first architect of the secular church to explicitly declare what before him had been only implicitly, secretly held—that Christianity is wholly incompatible with the new secular world order and that it cannot be salvaged but must be superseded, replaced by an entirely new religion completely defined by the secular political project.

In short, what is needed is a *civil religion* with its own secular worldview unchallenged by any alien Christian otherworldliness, a religion with its own morality, its own dogmas, and its own creed.

Rousseau gave us the blueprint for that secular liberal civil religion. It was this blueprint that was used by the radicals of the French Revolution, and it has remained influential to our day. As will become apparent, we can identify several different incarnations of Rousseau's civil religion.

To understand Rousseau's civil religion, we must grasp how thorough his rejection of Christianity was. Like all deep-thinking radicals, Rousseau knew that he couldn't take any half-measures if he were to succeed. And he meant to entirely displace Christianity. So he had to go back to the beginning, and provide a counter-myth to the Biblical account in Genesis.

Rousseau's New Eden, New Adam, and New Eve

In *Discourse on the Origin and Foundations of Inequality* (more popularly called the *Second Discourse*), Rousseau offers his own version of Genesis.[1] In his telling of the tale, man is little more than an animal, "an animal less strong than some, less agile than others, but all things considered, the most advantageously organized of all." Rousseau envisions his version of Adam "satisfying his hunger under an oak, quenching his thirst at the first stream, finding his bed at the foot of the same tree that furnished his meal; and therewith his needs are satisfied."[2] This Adam is not created by God. God is conspicuously absent from Rousseau's account of the beginnings of the human race—in fact, a century before Darwin, Rousseau offered his own version of evolutionary theory to explain man's origin (albeit in an endnote).[3]

To create a kind of anti-Genesis, Rousseau erases or denies everything one finds in the Biblical account of human origins. Human beings are not made in the image of God; that is, they are not rational by nature. Indeed, "the state of reflection is a state contrary to nature and...the man who meditates is a depraved animal."[4] Man's natural, non-depraved condition is to savor "the sentiment" of his own "present existence without any idea of the future."[5] Man is naturally a feeling animal, not a rational animal, a being absorbed in the here and now, and hence oblivious to eternity. In Rousseau's account there is no primitive religion, no care or concern for— or even mention of—God. For Rousseau, belief in God is not natural, and religion is somehow part of the depravity that comes in later, with meditation.[6]

In this fictional Eden, for which Rousseau admits he has no evidence,[7] there is plenty of food, and since the desires of Rousseau's Adam are minimal, feeding himself requires almost no effort. He doesn't build shelters, and he wears no clothes. He needs nothing, so he owns nothing. Thus private property is shown to be unnatural. This Adam lives in idyllic idleness in a laborless paradise.[8]

> His desires do not exceed his physical needs, the only goods he knows in the universe are nourishment, a female, and repose; the only evils he fears are pain and hunger. I say pain and not death because an animal will never know what it is to die; and knowledge of death and its terrors is one of the first acquisitions that man has made in moving away from the animal condition.[9]

We shouldn't get the notion that this Adam needs an Eve to complete him, that marriage and the family are somehow natural. That would take us back to the original Genesis, and affirm Christianity's starting point. And Rousseau, especially here, is careful to provide an anti-Genesis. For Rousseau, in our original condition, "Males and females united fortuitously, depending on encounter, occasion, and desire…and they left each other with the same ease." There is no romance; just the fleeting satisfaction of brute sexual desire: "any woman is good for him." The mother leaves the child as soon as she can wean it, feeling no emotional attachment. Needless to say, the father, long gone, "does not recognize even his children."[10]

Since this is all natural, according to Rousseau, then quite obviously marriage and the family must be considered entirely artificial, as is the sexual morality that Judaism and Christianity affirm.[11] Given that the connections between male and female and parent and child are taken by Rousseau to be artificial, we are not surprised to find that he denies that human beings are social or political by nature.[12] By nature we are happily unconnected individuals with no obligations, moral or otherwise.

Morality itself is not just missing from Rousseau's account; it is explicitly denied. There are neither moral commandments nor a God who commands in Rousseau's Eden. Rousseau's Adam and Eve are neither moral nor immoral, but amoral: "men in that state, not having among themselves any kind of moral relationship or known duties, could be neither good nor evil, and had neither vices nor virtues...."[13] Yet, according to Rousseau, "man is naturally good."[14] Natural man, being amoral, is without sin. He does not fall by disobedience. On the contrary, his entry into civilization as it develops—as he loses his natural animal goodness and his enjoyment of spontaneous pleasure—is his fall. Morality that limits our enjoyment of sensual pleasure is artificial, hence morality is bad. Behold the origins of the modern sexual revolution, which tries to take us back to Rousseau's sexual Eden.

In Rousseau we also have the source of modern radical egalitarianism. Before the fall from Eden, Rousseau's Adams and Eves are also naturally equal, and for much the same reason that they are amoral. Just as natural man is so satisfied with his small animal pleasures that he is neither virtuous nor vicious, so also, in aiming to satisfy only the simplest pleasures, he is entirely undeveloped. In their original crude simplicity, all human beings were originally equal—including men and women. But since natural talents are unequal, when human beings introduced private property, notions of beauty, more expansive and complex pleasures, reading, writing, artisanship, art, and all that goes with human development beyond the primitive state, then inequality developed, both in what people could do and what they had.[15]

With this fall from equality arose the notion that one man should be linked with just one woman—a notion that came about, Rousseau imagines, because a man and woman happened to stay together long enough in a thrown-together shelter to understand that their sexuality was connected with the effect of producing a child. The man thus spent his time out hunting for food for all of them, taking on the role of provider, and the woman stayed in the hut taking on the role of wife, a role that made her softer than the man. Her physical degeneration brought dependence on his strength, and so the sexes became complementary, related to each other in a family where male and female have become physically and functionally distinct. Even worse, this all led to notions of mine and thine—not only to possessive (rather than free and spontaneous) sexuality, but also to private property born of the desire to care for *my* wife and *my* children. Family and property meant the loss of our original goodness, and even more, of our original spontaneous freedom to satisfy our desires with no obligations, no moral duties, and no labor. The inequality of the sexes, the family, the home, the man as provider, private property, the necessity of work—all these are signs of our loss of original goodness and equality.[16]

Anti-Genesis as Liberal (Political) Paradise

Rousseau's anti-Genesis myth is essential to understanding the direction in which radical liberalism takes politics. Human beings always order their lives according to what they deem to be the *good*, what *should* be.

In the Judeo-Christian tradition, Genesis provides a template that defines the proper ordering of moral, social, and political affairs. To take a quick and obvious example, the ideas that men and women are made for each other and that sexuality is meant for an exclusive union created by a covenant inform the Judeo-Christian understanding of sexuality. Natural sex differences and heterosexual marriage define how we act morally and also how our laws treat marriage—or how they did. Heterosexual marriage is *good*. Violations of or deviations from it are *bad*.

But in just the same way, Rousseau's anti-Genesis account is definitive for liberalism. Rousseau defines what liberals consider to be *good*. Radical political liberalism will therefore aim to re-create through technical and political power, insofar as it can, the original "good," the "natural" condition of man and woman as outlined by Rousseau. Rousseau's anti-Genesis thus becomes the template for liberal politics. It defines the political good to be achieved by the state.

This should strike us as ironic. How can the view that any and all political order is unnatural—a fall from our original apolitical blissful and natural condition—be the inspiration and template for creating a new political order? Rousseau recognized the contradiction, without resolving it, and so that contradiction remains at the heart of liberalism. The state is seen as unnatural (that is, purely artificial), something that, like culture itself, represses our original spontaneity. Yet it is the state that, insofar as is possible, must create the situation whereby individuals can act like Rousseau's natural man and woman.

Rousseau's alternative Eden is ultimately the source of the various positions, ideas, and aims for which liberalism employs political power. And we should note that those aims are not positive goals. They are defined by the negative aspiration of *freeing us from* Christianity. Remember, liberalism comes from *liber*, "free" in Latin. The purpose of Rousseau's anti-Genesis account is to make us *free from* the Genesis account, and liberal politics aim for the same goal.

Thus, following Rousseau, liberalism regards the good of sexuality to be the satisfaction of individual desire, not the generation of offspring. Thus homosexuality is as licit as heterosexuality—satisfaction is satisfaction, however it occurs. The aim of sexual liberation is freeing sexual desires from any limits on spontaneous sexual satisfaction.

"Sexual education" by the liberal state therefore focuses on the satisfaction of desire however it may occur, and the state both encourages and provides contraception and abortion to remove the unintended side-effects (for so the biological purpose of sex has now been redefined) of heterosexual sexuality, so as to re-create the supposed original condition of sexual freedom. The aim is to convince women that it is natural for them—it once was natural for them and it can become so again—to pursue spontaneous sexual gratification.

Since the aim of sexuality is only sexual satisfaction, heterosexuality has no privileged position. State-sponsored sex education must lead the way in remolding sexuality back into its "original" state. Needless to say, all legal barriers that protect heterosexual privilege must be removed, and educators spend their efforts in inculcating in the young the belief that sexual freedom is a *right* that the state must protect and extend.

Precisely because marriage is artificial, it must be dissolved. It isn't just that marriage inhibits our spontaneous sexuality. Also, marriage and the family have always involved a real differentiation of the sexes, thereby causing inequality between men and women. Women must be taken out of the home and encouraged to perform exactly the same functions as men, so as to recapture the original, natural equality of the sexes. Women must be made like men, and moreover, men must be made like women. Therefore, the liberal state actively supports the liberation of women from the bonds of marriage and the family.

Furthermore, since it is natural to enjoy sexual pleasure, and unnatural to care for children, the liberal state will do everything it can to relieve individuals of the burden of children and childrearing. If children are permitted to be born, the state will take over their care, both in regard to the funds necessary to provide for them but also in the labor of actually taking care of them. For Rousseau, the father was originally entirely free of the burden to provide for his offspring. The liberal state, with its welfare programs, allows men once again to have the freedom of the original Rousseauian anti-Adam.

Since the family is artificial, the destruction of the family is liberating. The focus of the state's care is the individual—the isolated and pleasure-loving individual who emerges from the destruction of the family. That individual is free from all restrictions on sexuality, free from all duties of fatherhood or motherhood, free from the moral and legal entanglements and burdens of marriage and the family, free from all constraints of gender. This liberated individual, governed only by his desires, will displace the family as the founding unit of society and the aim of the state's ministrations.

According to Rousseau, good and evil only developed within the artificial confines of society, as did the distinction between virtue and vice. Since the pursuit of pleasure is, in and of itself, entirely innocent, the radical liberal state protects the pursuit of any pleasure, without making any distinction between good and evil, and without asking whether such pleasures promote or destroy virtue. The main reason that liberals want the church to be separated from the state is that they want to erase Christianity's moral code from the public sphere.

Therefore, the liberal state does not define law in terms of the promotion of virtue and the prohibition of vice, but in terms of the protection and promotion of individuals' private pleasures, which—since all such pleasures are natural—are declared to be *rights*. Any limitation of these "rights" is considered unjust; that is, justice is redefined to mean everyone getting as much of whatever he or she wants as long as he or she doesn't infringe on anyone else's pursuit of pleasure.

Of course, liberal politics tends toward socialism, welfare-statism, and radical egalitarianism. We have seen the sources of all these in Rousseau's account of human origins. Socialists, and even more, communists, aim to recreate the original condition in which there was no private property, and everyone had everything he needed or wanted without labor. They also hope to erase the differences caused by the application of differing natural talents and abilities, either literally—by the forcible redistribution of wealth—or through spreading the belief that actual differences have artificial (that is, social) or even evil causes, such as private property.

Since labor is unnatural, the liberal state will, insofar as it can, reduce the need for individuals to work. Everything that comes from labor—private property, wealth, privilege, esteem, greater capacity for comforts and enjoyments—must be redistributed by the state so that it can be equally enjoyed, since such equality best represents the original natural state envisioned in Rousseau's anti-Eden.

Finally, the state will be overtly or covertly secular, that is, it will either enforce a secular viewpoint or else co-opt religious language for purely secular purposes. Hard liberals, the most radical disciples of Rousseau, want God removed from any role in public affairs, and they are unafraid to use force to effect that goal. Soft secularists are gentler in their methods, but no less intent on excluding a real, transcendent God from the public square. They are more inclined to claim that Jesus Christ preached tolerance than that he was a fraud.

Hard and Soft Liberalism

Hard and soft liberalism both have their roots in Rousseau. As we shall see, the difference between them arises from the above-mentioned contradiction in Rousseau's thought—the notion that the state is on the one hand unnatural but on the other necessary for the re-creation of our original natural Edenic condition.

While Rousseau painted an Edenic picture of our unfallen, natural and animal-like condition, he also made it clear that humanity had irredeemably fallen from that condition. That is, we now live in highly developed societies with families, morality, private property and laws that protect it, vices that come with luxury, and virtues that are made necessary by the fact that we are no longer simple animals. According to Rousseau, our "fall" is this: we have become social, moral, cultural, artistic, rational, political animals— and that is why we are so miserable. We have lost our natural simplicity, trading it for a thousand artificial and destructive superfluities that come with advanced civilization (all of which were especially in evidence among the upper levels of eighteenth-century French society). The question Rousseau asked was, What can we do to ameliorate this fallen—in other words, civilized—condition?

Enter hard liberalism. Against the debauched luxury of his own age, Rousseau preached the severities of ancient Sparta, of the primitive Teutonic peoples, and especially of republican Rome. All three of these political regimes were defined by a simplicity of life and manners and by the rough equality of citizen-soldiers. And all of them aimed at military virtue rather than artistic, economic, or intellectual development.[17] This was a condition at least closer to our natural origins.

Of course, Rousseau's praise of the Roman Republic and its military courage should remind us of Machiavelli and his praise for the manly vigor of republican Rome in contrast to the softness and effeminacy brought in by Christian other-worldliness. No wonder Rousseau decided to preach a different gospel—a new "civil religion" that explicitly rejected Christianity, and took Roman republicanism as its model.

We'll examine Rousseau's civil religion below, but before doing so we must bring out some important implications of Rousseau's praise of Roman republicanism for the development of later liberalism. Rousseau's admiration of the pagan Roman Republic, brought forward from Machiavelli, provided the intellectual inspiration for the Jacobins of the French Revolution, with their stress on virtue against the debauched upper classes and the church. By taking upon themselves the name "republicans" and setting up a French Republic they meant to reject Christianity as well as depraved eighteenth-century notions of nobility. Their return to pagan virtue allowed them to maintain the high moral ground, at least in their own minds, and vindicated their purifying brutality. Thus the figure of Robespierre, at once austerely virtuous and entirely savage.

The hard liberalism of the French Revolution was a child of Rousseau (and a grandchild of Machiavelli), as was the Romantic nationalism of both Fascism and Nazism, rooted in the primitive religio-mythic origins of, respectively, ancient Italy and Germany—pre-Christian cultures that Rousseau himself praised.

But what is the origin of soft liberalism, whose proponents rightly recoil from the horrors of Fascism and Nazism? How can hard and soft liberalism be related, when they seem so contradictory?

The contrast originates in the contradiction we have already seen in the philosophy of Rousseau himself. While hard liberalism embraces Rousseau's praise of Sparta, the Teutonic tribes, and republican Rome, soft liberalism embraces Rousseau's Eden. Both strains of liberalism are inspired by Rousseau, and both represent a rejection of Christianity. And the horrifying excesses of hard liberalism in the first half of the twentieth century have led to the victory of soft liberalism in France and Britain, and now in the United States. The goal of liberal politics today is not the creation of Spartan or Roman warriors. Instead, liberalism is creating a kind of soft techno-political paradise where Rousseau's Adams and Eves can enjoy pleasure in peace.

But both hard and soft liberalism are anti-Christian. To understand the hostility of both kinds of liberalism to the Christian church, we need to look at Rousseau's proposed "civil religion" in some detail. We need to understand why he believed that civil society needed a new religion of its own.

Rousseau's Civil Religion

In a sense, when it comes to Rousseau's "civil religion" we are right back with Machiavelli. Rousseau's belief that society needed religion was not really any more pious than Machiavelli's; it was simply a matter of political prudence. Rousseau, too, saw that religion is helpful in controlling the masses. But while Machiavelli had advised the prince to co-opt the Christian church for political purposes, Rousseau realized (perhaps more clearly than any liberal thinker before him) that Christianity ultimately cannot be tamed by the state because it is essentially directed toward the next world, not this one. So Rousseau wanted the state to have *nothing* to do with Christianity. Try to domesticate the Christian religion, once let it into the secular house, and it will show its true supernatural colors and inexorably pull citizens away from obedience to the secular sovereign. Therefore, for Rousseau, there can be no "church and state." As long as there is a church, there cannot truly be a state, at least, not of the kind that Rousseau wanted (again following Machiavelli, who had invented the very concept of "state").

We should not be misled by Rousseau's high-flown talk against despots and his trumpeting of the "General Will" to believe that he is fundamentally at odds with Machiavelli. A key clue to Rousseau's fundamental approval of Machiavelli's aims is his pretense that Machiavelli was really a man of the people, rather than of the prince. As Rousseau remarked of Machiavelli in his *Social Contract*, "While pretending to give lessons to kings, he gave great ones to the people. Machiavelli's *The Prince* is the book of republicans."[18] Rousseau pretended that Machiavelli was just fooling, so to speak, when he gave his ruthless advice to the prince—he really meant it for the people. Actually, Rousseau was taking over Machiavelli's advice for his own purposes, with the result that the radical secular "republicans" of the French Revolution would act with the ruthlessness of Machiavellian princes, openly rejecting Christianity, pitilessly slaughtering priests and nuns, desecrating churches, and setting up a "religion of reason" in place of Christianity. The French revolutionaries didn't have to hide the brutality because there was no longer any need to hide one's animosity to Christianity; another religion, a civil religion, had taken its place.

It is, in fact, in Rousseau's *Social Contract* that we get the broad outlines of the kind of "civil religion" that the French revolutionaries established. Rousseau begins this work by praising ancient pagan religions precisely because religion and political power were fused in one man, one imperium, and the gods served their kingdoms. In this situation, all gods were national gods—"each State had its cult and its Gods"—and there were consequently "as many Gods as there were peoples." For this reason, "there were no wars of religion" because there were no rival religions competing within any pagan state. When one nation conquered another, it simultaneously imposed its religion upon the subjugated peoples and absorbed the alien gods of the conquered into its own political pantheon. The height of paganism was the Roman Empire, which subjugated the known world under its political-theological rule.[19]

And then, according to Rousseau, things took a wrong turn: "It was under these circumstances that Jesus came to establish a spiritual kingdom on earth. By separating the theological system from the political system, this brought about the end of the unity of the State, and caused the internal divisions that have never ceased to stir up Christian people."[20] We must be clear about what Rousseau means here. Like Machiavelli, Rousseau saw that Christianity causes a division of power within society. Both secular philosophers were bent on eradicating the division that the church had invented between church and political power, and firmly subordinating religion to the political regime. Accordingly, Rousseau bemoans the fact that the "Spirit of Christianity has won over everything." Despite attempts to tame it, to use it, to subordinate it to the state, the "sacred cult has always remained, or again become independent of the sovereign, and without a necessary bond with the body of the State." (Here Rousseau pauses to praise Islam for contriving a full unity of political and theological power.)[21]

The key problem is that "Wherever the clergy constitute a 'body,' it is master and legislator in its domain."[22] Rousseau is, of course, quite correct here. We have seen that it was precisely the distinction between the functions of the priest and that of the king—rooted in the distinction between the next world and this one—that was at the root of the invention of the Christian distinction between church and state. And we must not miss Rousseau's use of the word "body," given St. Paul's description of the church as the "Body of Christ." For Rousseau there can only be one body—the body politic—and Christ cannot be its head. (It is also no accident that Rousseau declares sacramental power to be the root cause of Christianity's power: "Communion and excommunication are the social compact of the clergy, a compact by means of which it will always be master of peoples and kings.")[23]

So Rousseau sets out to re-paganize the state. He argues for an absolute "separation" of the church from the state—for removal and replacement by another religion.

Like Machiavelli, Hobbes, and Spinoza, Rousseau realized that the secular state cannot do without religion altogether, for "a State has never been founded without religion serving at its base." But he rejects the attempt to use a reformulated version of Christianity for this purpose because, "Christian law is fundamentally more harmful than useful to the strong constitution of the State."[24]

Rousseau damns Christianity with faint praise as "the saintly, sublime, true religion" that leads people to "acknowledge one another as brothers," even while pointing out that "Christianity is a totally spiritual religion, uniquely concerned with heavenly matters. The Christian's homeland is not of this world." Then Rousseau echoes Machiavelli's criticisms of Christianity, and lets us know what he *really* thinks. "As long as [a Christian] has nothing to reproach himself for, it matters little to him whether things go well or badly here on earth." There cannot therefore be a "Christian republic," for "these two words"—"Christian" and "republic," are "mutually exclusive." This is a lesson that should be learned from Christianity's beginnings: "when the cross chased out the eagle, all Roman valor disappeared." People preoccupied with the next world will not fight for the state in this one. And then, sounding not just like Machiavelli before him, but like Nietzsche after, Rousseau declares, "Christianity preaches nothing but servitude and dependence. Its spirit is so favorable to tyranny that tyranny always profits from it. True Christians are made to be slaves. They know it and are scarcely moved thereby; this brief life is of too little worth in their view."[25]

So in Rousseau's view what is needed is a "civil religion," one "that causes [the citizen] to love his duties" in this world, the duties that support the state. Rousseau's "purely civil profession of faith" will have few dogmas, and those are "for the sovereign to establish" by law: "The existence of a powerful, intelligent, beneficent, foresighted, and providential divinity; the afterlife; the happiness of the just; the punishment of the wicked; the sanctity of the social contract and the laws." Rousseau adds, "These are the positive dogmas. As for the negative ones, I limit them to a single one: intolerance. It belongs with the cults we have excluded." The reason offered by Rousseau:

"It is impossible to live in peace with people whom one believes are damned."[26]

We are familiar with liberalism's affirmation of tolerance as the one virtue. In the creed of the religion of liberalism, intolerance is the greatest and only vice (though of course Christianity cannot be tolerated by the liberal state because it turns citizens' loyalties to the next world and even worse, claims that its dogmatic beliefs are objectively true, and the only way to happiness in the next world). But what about Rousseau's positive dogmas? What connection do they have with liberalism? We don't recognize these beliefs from the liberalism that we know today.

Perhaps the quickest and most accurate way to explain what Rousseau was offering in the way of positive religious dogma for his "civil religion" is to point out that it would become the Deist creed, a belief system that appears to be a watered down version of Christianity but was actually meant to displace Christianity, serving as a political-theological control for the masses. Here it has to be admitted that this is the Deism that many of our Founding Fathers shared, and that it is in great part because they shared it that even these few positive dogmas they believed have since given way to the religion of liberalism, characterized by only the negative dogma, Thou shalt not be intolerant.

Historically, Rousseau's Deism was reduced to no-intolerance liberalism as the arguments in Rousseau's *Discourse on the Origin and Foundations of Inequality* overtook and transformed the arguments in his *Social Contract*. Thus the real "civil religion" of the liberal state came to be defined by the aspiration for re-creating a world where Rousseau's Adams and Eves can live in something like man's original state. Liberalism therefore drives toward a kind of primitivism, even while it applies the most advanced technology and the greatest political power to recreating an Edenic condition in which plenty frees us from the necessity of labor, sexuality is liberated from any restraint, and each individual is free to do as he or she wishes without worrying about the morrow (much less eternity). If you do not agree with the sovereign will—which Rousseau, interestingly calls the "General Will," so that it appeals to the greatest number and seems to represent them—then, in his immortal words, "whoever refuses to obey the General Will shall be constrained to do so by the entire body; which means only that he will be forced to be free."[27]

Rousseau, Marriage, and Liberal Theocracy

Rousseau ends his *Social Contract* with a stab and then a flourish of his rhetorical sword.

As for the stab—one with a point relevant to our current dispute over who will define marriage, the church or the state—Rousseau makes it clear that the clergy cannot retain power over marriage. That is, there must be civil marriage, marriage redefined as a "civil contract." If the priests retain power to make marriages, they retain the power to define marriage—a significant power that would not be in the hands of the civil sovereign.[28] With Rousseau, as with the proponents of gay marriage (and even "civil unions") today, the aim is to drive the Christian understanding of marriage into extinction. The Christian view of marriage is the product of what Rousseau calls an "intolerant religion," and therefore it violates his civil religion's one negative dogma: thou shalt not be intolerant.

As for the flourish of Rousseau's rhetorical sword—"whoever dares to say *there is no salvation outside of the church* should be chased out of the State, *unless the State is the church*, and the prince is the pontiff" [emphasis added].[29] Unless, indeed.

Note that Rousseau is not opposed to theocracy—as long as it's a theocracy of the religion of the liberal state. Rousseau's state requires complete devotion. That's why he cannot allow the existence of any other church.

PART IV

THE NEW BIG PICTURE

CHAPTER 10

═══════

LIBERALISM TRIUMPHS IN THE MODERN WORLD

W e've been looking at some great theoretical shifts that occurred in Western thought between the time of Machiavelli and Rousseau, that is, between the 1500s and mid-1700s. Now we're going to take a look at the implications of those theoretical shifts for modern Western culture—political, intellectual, and moral. We're going to see how contemporary secular liberalism is the culmination of the intellectual attack on Christianity originally launched by Machiavelli and Hobbes, and radicalized by Spinoza and Rousseau.

There are different strains of liberalism running through modernity. The philosophy of a nineteenth-century "liberal" such as Tocqueville seems like conservatism to us today. We'll have something to say about that strain of liberalism in the next chapter. But here our focus is specifically the liberalism of Machiavelli, Hobbes, Spinoza, and Rousseau, flowing through the French Revolution into the radical thought of the nineteenth century, which informs the thought, culture, morality, and political aims of the Left today. That is the liberalism that concerns us at this point.

To help illuminate the secular liberalism that dominates the mainstream today, let's consider the question. "What do liberals believe about the world?" Or, to put it another way, "What would the world have to be like for the liberal worldview to be true?"

World without Ends (Amen)

The great liberal thinker Isaiah Berlin rightly noted,

> Most modern liberals, at their most consistent, want a situation in which as many individuals as possible can realise as many of their ends as possible, without assessment of the value of these ends as such, save in so far as they may frustrate the purposes of others. They wish the frontiers between individuals or groups of men to be drawn solely with a view to preventing collisions between human purposes, all of which must be considered to be equally ultimate, uncriticisable ends in themselves.[1]

This is quite a startling way of looking at human affairs. What would the world have to be like for such a view to make sense? In other words, what cosmological support does liberalism demand?

For liberalism to make sense, we would have to live in a world without ends—to put it in technical philosophical terms, in a *non-teleological* universe (*telos* means "goal" or "end" in Greek), where, since there are no ends written into nature (including human nature) by God, we are free to create them ourselves.

But what exactly does a non-teleological universe look like? It looks like Hobbesian materialism—the cosmology that, as we've seen, Hobbes adopted from the materialist pagan thinkers that Christianity had rejected. Hobbes put us on the path to a blind, purposeless universe, and later materialists in the eighteenth and nineteenth centuries filled in the details.

Imagine that there is nothing else in the universe but empty space and material atoms eternally jostling about. Everything we see—stars, planets, water, grass, trees, pigs, cows, salamanders, human beings—it's all nothing more than the result of the different configurations of the atoms that have randomly shuffled out different combinations over the endless eons. These atoms are, quite literally, imagined so as to make belief in God unnecessary—they are themselves eternal, and they've been jostling around eternally.[2]

Each thing, whatever it is, is only a result of endless, blind material processes—endless in two senses. As with the atoms themselves, the universe itself is eternal, that is, without beginning or end, and so it has no need of a creator. And nothing in the universe has an end or intrinsic goal built into it. Each thing, whether planet, rock, bird, cat, bee, or tree—is just a momentary configuration of matter that will soon enough pass away, resolving back into its fundamental constituent atoms in the endless atomic flux.

On this view, the universe isn't trying to produce anything. Things just happen to be produced, by accident. You can't read any kind of intention into what you find in nature. Everything has been created by chance and mindless material processes, and so all things in nature are ultimately pointless and meaningless. Whatever meaning we might happen to impose upon them, or upon ourselves, is arbitrary—that is, any meaning or purpose we happen to impose has no support whatsoever in the nature of the cosmos.

Why would liberals embrace such a worldview? Notice that if there is no cosmological support whatsoever for anyone's chosen end, then no goal or end is any better than any other. All goals are all equal because they are all equally arbitrary. None is any better or worse than any other.

This kind of purposeless universe fits the modern liberal desire to create a situation in which everyone's individual pursuits must be, to quote Berlin, "considered to be equally ultimate, uncriticisable ends in themselves," a situation in which individuals are free to "realise as many of their ends as possible, without assessment of the value of these ends as such, save in so far as they may frustrate the purposes of others."

The non-teleological universe justifies each individual's pursuit of whatever he chooses to pursue. Liberal politics require a liberal cosmology—and that's the historical order in which they appeared, too. Men did not find themselves in a purposeless material cosmos and then figure out what political regime would best suit that universe. On the contrary, as we've seen in Machiavelli and Hobbes, the desire to rid the universe of Christianity led to the embrace of a materialist view of the universe, a cosmology that would help accomplish the desired liberation.

The liberal desire to escape the constraints of Christianity was the original reason for the modern embrace of a world without ends, beginning as far back as the Renaissance. And the same impulse was behind the nineteenth-century enthusiasm for scientific materialism.

We now see why liberalism needs for science itself to be materialist. Only thus defined does science provide support for cosmic moral relativism. And so materialist science is the kind of science that liberalism preaches, and it does so with real evangelical fervor. Think of men such as Thomas Huxley, Ernst Haeckel, and Karl Vogt, who enthusiastically spread the Darwinian evolutionary dogma of a world without ends.

But the liberation promised by liberalism is twofold: we are to be freed not just from God, but also from nature. The doctrine of materialism achieves the first kind of liberation quite handily, by destroying the natural foundations of Christianity and positing an entirely secular cosmos that purports to explain itself without any need for God.

But materialism also frees the human will from the restrictions of nature itself. If no God stands behind the order of nature, including human nature, then human beings are free to manipulate nature, and especially their own nature, without fear of transgressing any moral limit or inviting divine retribution. And, in a kind of vicious circle, the successful manipulation of our nature in turn becomes an argument for the materialist cosmology that justified it in the first place. Continually overcoming the restrictions of nature "proves" that the limits being transgressed were not laid down by an omnipotent God. (In our own time, to use an obvious example, genetic manipulation "proves" that human nature is not definite, but malleable, and new reproductive technologies "prove" that the union of male and female does not define sexual morality.)

In the twentieth century, the secular state took an increasingly active role in evangelizing for the materialist worldview. Think of the *Scopes* trial, and the establishment of non-theistic, materialist Darwinism as the only account of evolution allowed to be taught in the public schools. The liberal state also, by its concentration of political, economic, and technical power, creates and sustains the conditions "in which as many individuals as possible can realise as many of their ends as possible"—with no questions asked about the worthiness or goodness or morality of anyone's arbitrary choice of ends. As the state increasingly takes over space formerly occupied by the church, it allows fewer moral challenges to individuals' choices, even while the limits that nature had imposed on the human will in the past are continually being overcome by state-sponsored technology. Today, the sphere in which the arbitrary will can choose seems to be ever-expanding.

A World without Ends Gives Us Endless Rights

In the liberal account, we live in a purposeless universe, so that each person has just as much right as anyone else to pursue his or her arbitrarily defined goals or ends. Notice how desires are given moral weight by being categorized as exercises of "rights." And there is ultimately no other justification given for the existence of such rights than the one originally offered by Thomas Hobbes—the assertion that there are no intrinsic ends, natural goals, or moral standards written into nature. As a result, in our liberal world today, there is no real difference between "having a desire" to do something (anything!) and "having a right" to do it.

The full implications of liberal "natural rights" philosophy became clear only in the closing decades of the twentieth century. Think of the Supreme Court ruling in *Planned Parenthood v. Casey* quoted above, which justified the right to abortion with the liberal axiom, "At the heart of liberty is the right to define one's own concept of existence, of meaning, of the universe, and of the mystery of human life." As we have seen, the groundwork for the liberal justices' understanding of natural rights was laid by Thomas Hobbes.

Hobbes designed his "natural rights" philosophy to displace the Christian understanding of the *natural law*. It's a typical case of a liberal thinker using the pagan thought that Christianity had rejected against the pagan thought Christianity had accepted. The Christian understanding of the natural law was largely based on the pagan philosophy of Cicero and the Stoics, who in their turn had learned from Plato and Aristotle. The materialism espoused by Hobbes and embraced by liberalism is indebted to the pagan Greek philosopher Epicurus and his Roman disciple Lucretius instead. Epicurus and Lucretius designed their materialist atomism for the precise purpose of eliminating religion and leaving human beings free to define their own earthly ends, liberated from fear of the gods and the afterlife. Hobbes and his disciples used that same materialism as a weapon against Christianity—to posit a world into which Christianity could not fit.

Elsewhere I have given a more detailed account of how this Epicurean materialist revolution took place.[3] Our goal here is to understand the implications of replacing "natural law" with "natural rights."

On the "natural law" understanding, human nature comes already defined by a wise and loving God. Our God-given nature defines what is good and evil for us, moral and immoral, and hence what should be lawful and unlawful. We perfect, or destroy, our God-given nature through our actions, moral and immoral.

To take one obvious example of natural law reasoning, human nature is divided into male and female, whose union brings forth new human life, which is good. Therefore, marriage between a man and a woman is the natural standard. Marriage defines sexual morality. Marital chastity is the perfection of our sexual nature; sexual promiscuity and perversion destroy it.

In Christian morality, the natural law is not the last word, however. Christianity went beyond this natural law foundation to a demand for supernatural holiness. Christ declared that lust is equivalent to adultery (Matthew 5:27–28). St. Paul said that a husband must sacrifice himself for his wife as Christ did for the church (Ephesians 5:25).

But liberalism tore down not only supernatural holiness but the natural law as well—to rebuild on a foundation of cosmic relativism. With no intrinsic moral order built into nature, we are free to impose whatever order we wish. Indeed, we have a "right" to.

Turning back to the example above, liberalism will assume with Rousseau that sexual passion freed from all restriction is natural, and marriage is unnatural. Thus "natural" comes to mean "spontaneous," that is, an act of arbitrary will undefined either by God or nature, by tradition or law, by one's previous acts of will or by anyone else's choices.

In the twenty-first century, the liberal state takes upon itself the task of removing all moral restrictions on sexuality, dissolving the Christian understanding of marriage, providing the technological and socio-economic means to free sexuality from restraint, and re-educating the citizenry accordingly. To restate the obvious implications, the liberal state thereby sets itself up directly against the church, wrenching Christianity out of its culturally-defining position and putting the secularizing state in the church's place as the definer of marriage and the defender of sexual rights (versus sexual morality).

The Re-Paganization of Morality, and the Triumph of Liberal Rights

With the triumph of rights-based liberalism over Christianity and natural law morality, we have the effective re-paganization of morality. Abortion, infanticide, contraception, euthanasia, easy divorce, sexual promiscuity, pornography, homosexuality, and pedophilia, all of which were part of pagan Rome's accepted way of life, reappear and are affirmed by the liberal state.

But there are two important differences between our situation today and that of the first Christians. First, in ancient Rome, the pagan moral view was already established before Christianity arrived on the scene. The original pagan morality was not specifically designed as an attack on Christianity. Because the liberalism of today did originate as a challenge to Christianity, the modern re-paganization of morality defines itself specifically *against* Christianity. Thus liberals today relish pushing explicitly anti-Christian acts and agendas. They aim not just at reestablishing paganism but at profaning Christianity. And because the Christian moral understanding rests on natural law, liberalism tends more and more to embrace the anti-natural in sexuality (just as it adopts the anti-natural and the grotesque in art), so as to entirely negate any connection between human nature and God.

Second, and perhaps even more destructive, Christians themselves have largely adopted the "natural rights" language of Hobbes. They continually attempt to reframe Christian moral arguments in terms of rights, and thereby continually undermine their own efforts.

Thus Christians defending "the right to life" are surprised to find themselves confronted with equally fervent claims that a woman has a "right to choose" or a "right to control her own body." The rights of Christian churches to recognize only traditional marriage is trumped by the right of others to marry whomever they wish. Christians assert the right to practice their religion free from the state's interference, but then find that the same right is claimed by atheists, pantheists, neo-druids, worshipers of a revivified pagan Roman pantheon, and even Satanists.

Christians never get anywhere with this rights language adopted from Hobbes because Hobbes's natural rights were built upon a foundation of complete moral relativism, which was designed precisely to replace Christianity's exclusive moral claims. Once the liberal understanding of rights is adopted, all views are equalized, and the secular state assumes the power to ensure that all views can be equally expressed and represented. This is not, however, a victory for neutrality, but a kind of strategy by which the fundamental liberal premise that there is no moral truth is ensconced as the default position of the state, and a paganized, anti-natural morality can be imposed by the state through "tolerance."

The Passion for Extreme Democracy

This notion of equality built upon complete moral relativism is the source of liberalism's extreme passion for democracy (or, we might more accurately say, with Plato, its passion for extreme democracy).[4] Liberals don't just believe in equal political representation or even equal incomes. They believe that no principle or belief is any better or worse than any other—all are equally unfounded, equally arbitrary. So, to quote Isaiah Berlin once again, all ends "must be considered to be equally ultimate, uncriticisable ... in themselves." They are "uncriticisable" because there is no standard built into nature by a creator God by which to judge them; there is nothing above the human will.

This kind of extreme democracy entails the belief that any notion of higher or lower, better or worse, noble or base, is entirely unfounded. All instances of hierarchy, restriction, or limit are suspect—as being based merely upon someone else's arbitrary will. All that is higher, or considered better or more noble, must be unmasked, torn down, and humiliated in the name of equality. This is both a political passion, expressed most vividly in the violent leveling egalitarianism of the French Revolutionary Jacobins and the Soviet Communists, and a cultural impulse, expressed in many Western liberals' complete disdain for the past, for academic intellectual standards, for Christian moral standards, for artistic or literary standards, and even for good manners. It is a passion for destruction, for tearing down, and for profanation.

Materialist, extreme democratic liberalism is therefore *reductionist*. It assumes that any higher motives or capacities expressed by human beings must be reducible to something lower and even ignoble. Aspirations to truth can be reduced to the will to power (Friedrich Nietzsche); the glories of religion and morality can be reduced to a primitive desire for incest with one's mother and murderous jealousy of one's father (Sigmund Freud); all the greatest thoughts and aesthetic productions of a culture are mere epiphenomena of the modes of economic production and class conflict (Karl Marx); everything we previously attributed to the soul, from the desire for truth to love and morality, can be reduced to the results of blind natural selection (Charles Darwin); all of the achievements of human beings, their noblest thoughts, their great designs, their valiant struggles to choose the good, their everyday love of each other, their endlessly intricate activities, can be reduced to the randomly contrived patterns of their DNA (Richard Dawkins).

All these reductionist views, including even the seemingly anti-democratic ones, such as Nietzsche's, have a leveling effect. They destroy any natural hierarchy, undermine any notion that there is anything better or worse than anything else in our purposeless cosmos. All these views are therefore helpful to liberalism as tending to level any standard or limit that might infringe on our "right" to pursue any end we desire. Liberalism thus embraces a version of democracy, a notion of equality, that ultimately rests on nihilism. All notions of intrinsic order or nobility that would define and limit the human will are considered to be tyrannical, dismissed as hypocritical masks for self-interest. At bottom, there is nothing but the self-interested will.

This passion for destruction of all that is higher characterizes liberalism precisely because from the beginning liberalism has defined itself directly against Christianity, and even against all the pagan natural law philosophy that was compatible with Christianity. In affirming God as both Creator and Redeemer, Christianity teaches that the wonderful order of nature—including the human soul with its aspiration to virtue, all human nobility, and all human achievement—point upward. Everything fine and noble on the natural level (even among pagans) is an indicator of supernatural goodness and truth. Nature itself is a kind of ladder that allows us to climb toward supernatural truth (although grace is required to direct and purify our ascent).

For liberalism to triumph, any cosmic ladder leading up to God must be kicked away. This kicking away of all ladders, of all notions of higher, better, more noble, wiser, more virtuous, more holy, characterizes liberal egalitarianism. This extreme egalitarianism can take many forms: the political destruction of the noble class, the slaughtering of priests, the desecration of altars, the mockery of virtue, the humiliation of crucifixes, the destruction of churches, endless cynicism and skepticism, the representation of Christians as hypocritical and of Christian morality as the result of various neuroses, the turn in art from the noble and beautiful to the ugly and profane, the academic humiliation of Great Books by deconstructionism, the reduction of all the greatest thoughts to the crudest desires for sex and power, the turn from the natural to the unnatural and even to the antinatural in sex itself, the elevation of nihilism as the greatest achievement of human philosophy.

All of these developments—from the passions of the French Revolution to the passions of our current intelligentsia—are results of the deeply anti-Christian origins of modern liberalism. The liberal impulse is not only to reject Christianity itself, but to destroy anything that could lead to it. All that is high and could lead higher must be brought low. That's the characteristic passion of extreme democratic liberalism.

This radical egalitarian rebellion, of course, is ultimately waged against God, the supreme thing above us. Cosmic nihilism—belief in a God-less, purposeless cosmos—is an essential aspect of the advance of liberalism from the 1750s up to the present day. The most extreme form of this democracy takes two forms.

The first, we've seen in Spinoza: pantheism, the belief that God *is* nature, and hence, we are god. Pantheism first took political form in the French Revolution's official civil religion of the Supreme Being, in which nature replaced the Creator God of Christianity, a substitution that ended in the worship of the revolutionary state itself.

The second is outright atheism, the removal of God from the cosmos, and hence from all aspects, political, cultural, and moral, of the secularized world. The imposition of atheism by force characterized Soviet Russia and Maoist China. But atheism is also characteristic of the soft liberalism that "boils the Christian frog," so to speak, by removing Christianity from our own society by degrees.

Both pantheism and atheism have the effect of divinizing man since in the absence of God, man imagines himself to be the only source of rational, purposeful order in the world. Both kinds of anti-theism are antithetical to Christianity, even while they are themselves animated by religious zeal. That is a key point illuminating the essentially religious nature of liberalism: the religious passion that would naturally be directed to God is directed toward humanity itself, toward the creation of the conditions that would maximize our freedom from all limitations, natural or otherwise.

Again, the state plays an essential role in creating those conditions, because it can marshal the greatest power and resources in service of the ongoing evolution of freedom. I use the term "evolution" purposely, because the notion of purposeless evolution is essential to liberalism's cosmos and its political progressivism.

The Endless Evolution of Everything

Liberalism draws significant support from the Darwinian doctrine of biological evolution, a doctrine that assumes that the development of life is driven by entirely random, material processes. In this view, the human species is an accident. Darwinism has demoted man from being made in the image of God, to being made by meandering and mindless nature.

Let's pause here to note that the materialistic view of evolution, the one championed by Darwin, did not have to be the one that took historical hold. There were viable theistic alternatives in Darwin's day—an important point I've argued elsewhere.[5] But these other evolutionary approaches were quashed by a kind of propaganda campaign waged with great religious zeal by the likes of Thomas Huxley in England and Ernst Haeckel in Germany, and continued in our own day by the infamous Richard Dawkins and his ilk. Darwin's apologists are determined that evolution will serve secularism. It is the "Genesis account" of their materialist faith.

In the materialist version of evolution that is now generally accepted, human beings suffer a kind of egalitarian demotion from their position above the other animals, to being just another animal. This radical egalitarianism serves liberalism. The significant advance for secularism in this Darwinism—as opposed to a theistic understanding of the development of life, where purposeful evolution guided by a Creator culminates in the development of a rational animal as the pinnacle of creation—is that blind, purposeless evolution means human beings are freed from any natural moral absolutes or God-given commands. In this endless (and pointless) evolutionary "development," human nature itself is essentially malleable, that is, able to be molded and remolded at will. Human beings are only clay. And there is no divine Potter. So by default the clay becomes the potter.

The Clay Becomes the Potter, the Creature Becomes a Self-Creator and Self-Redeemer

We can understand more clearly what is at stake, if we recall what liberalism wants to replace. The Christian natural law understanding, in contrast, recognizes that human nature is definite and designed. Christian moral reasoning is built into our nature as beings made in the image of God. As, for example, on the questions of human sexuality we discussed above—the Christian understanding of marriage is rooted in the natural complementarity of the sexes.

But the materialist evolutionary view assumes that our nature is in flux, a mere epiphenomenon of the ebb and flow of matter. That's good news for liberalism. It means that we are free to manipulate, to re-create, ourselves. Just as we human beings can take other species—pigeons, say, or peas—and actively re-form them by breeding and genetic manipulation according to our will, so also we can take our *own* nature into our own hands, and as both potter and clay, remake ourselves according to whatever we wish, in the ultimate liberation of liberalism.

Our future is then quite literally open-ended. We don't know what we'll make of ourselves. Living in a God-less biological world without ends, we are free to re-make ourselves in the image of whatever we imagine. The human species is a work in progress, bounded only by the present state of technology and the supply of money to support its advance.

Since, as we have seen, the state is the institution that can gather the greatest political, technological, and economic resources for this progressive improvement of human nature, the secular state becomes the great vehicle for refashioning human beings. The liberal improvement project displaces the church as a vehicle for *regenerating* human beings.

This is the new understanding of history that liberalism proposes. The state replaces the church, becoming the instrument of this-worldly human regeneration and salvation, the great god-like demiurge with the power to transform, to perfect, and (most ominously) to correct matter, including human matter.

The passion for correction was famously embraced by the state religion of Nazism with the elimination of "defective" human beings and "inferior" races. Negative eugenics, though in a milder form, is also warmly embraced by liberal democratic regimes in their support of the prevention and elimination of "defective" and "unwanted" human beings through birth control, sterilization, abortion, infanticide, and euthanasia.

And implicit in negative eugenics is positive eugenics—the notion that we can remake human nature by successfully breeding or creating something better, something that rises *above* human nature. This new supernatural goal ("super" is Latin for *above*) displaces the supernatural goal offered by the church. In the place of the Resurrection of the Body, liberalism proposes physical perfection in this world through the ministrations of breeding or genetic manipulation. Spiritual transformation through the ministrations of grace in preparation for the next world is no longer necessary. We can have it all in the here and now.

Hence the doctrine of racial salvation by eugenics that so enthralled English, French, German, *and* American intellectuals in the late nineteenth and first half of the twentieth century. But hence also the passion for social engineering in the late twentieth and early twenty-first century. Hence the impulse to improve the moiling mass of humanity in a great political experiment carried on by the elite who are mercifully constructing—so they maintain—a world without tears, without sorrow, without pain, and quite possibly without death. And hence the fascination today with what's been dubbed "transhumanism" among the zealous advocates of transforming human beings by means of, and even by fusion with, machines.

Such is the "new man," a concept taken over from Christianity, but now imagined as the product of an entirely this-worldly salvation. The new man has no end defined by God or nature. He is capable of endless transformation and re-creation. Thus progress itself, framed as continual self-transformation, rather than arrival at any particular goal, becomes the aim. And the pursuit of progress for its own sake creates a fundamentally revolutionary dynamic in history.

The Doctrine of Historical Progress

This notion of "progress" deserves our closer attention. Many are aware of the general contours of Progressivism narrowly defined. As a political movement arising in late nineteenth- and early twentieth-century America, it was originally concerned with the protection of laborers, the abolition of child labor, education reform, and cleaning up governmental corruption. Progressivism has since converged with liberalism.

But we are concerned not just with the Progressive movement of a century ago, but with progressivism in the broader and deeper sense. The cult of "progress" in history is intimately connected with liberal secularization—the liberation of society from Christianity.

On this view, progress is understood as the steady removal of Christianity from the center of culture, whether it is achieved by intellectuals, at the behest of the state, or by the two working in concert. In fact, this secularizing liberation is most likely to occur when intellectuals control the state.

Machiavelli considered it progress for princes to throw off the shackles of Christianity and return to the noble pagan days of Republican Rome. Rousseau's civil religion was modeled on Machiavelli's return to pagan

Rome; that return was a step forward (progress!) out of Christian darkness. That same idea of progress was behind Voltaire's famous motto, which became the battle cry of the eighteenth-century Enlightenment—*écrasez l'infâme* (destroy the infamous thing)—the "thing" ostensibly being the Catholic Church in France. But as historian Peter Gay rightly notes, it was a cry directed not just at French Catholicism, but "against Christianity itself, against Christian dogma in all its forms, Christian institutions, Christian ethics, and the Christian view of man."[6] Voltaire meant this battle cry as a call for history to move forward. The same view of progress defined the French Revolution, which was heavily indebted to both Rousseau and Voltaire. That Revolution had a pivotal role in the liberal understanding of historical progress, and it foreshadows what that progress will mean.

The French Revolution

As we've noted, the radical revolutionaries in France were not interested in reforming the church, but rather in replacing it with a religion of reason, the cult of the Supreme Being—a religion largely based upon Rousseau's outline of civil religion and explicitly meant to replace Christianity. Removing Christianity and establishing the new civil religion thereby represented historical progress.

Given that the utopian results promised for the future were contingent upon removal of Christianity in the present, the revolutionaries were inflamed by a self-righteous passion to exterminate Christianity in the name of liberty, equality, and brotherhood. Precisely because the new civil religion was defined against Christianity, its establishment as the state religion of revolutionary France meant the state-sponsored extermination of priests, monks, and nuns, and other enemies of liberty who still clung to Christian beliefs. Such was the horror of the Reign of Terror (1793–1794), and in particular the horror of the Vendée (1793), the crowning achievement of the Terror.

It is essential to understand that the Reign of Terror, when the passions for liberty and equality were at their height, was not a mere civil war in

France, or a war of one class against another. It was a real religious war waged to ensure a decisive break with the past and define the subsequent march of history. The anticlericalism of the revolutionaries in France, as of Voltaire before them, was not just directed at corrupt bishops, but against believers as such. That is why revolutionaries butchered aristocratic bishops and simple believers alike in the Terror. Christianity was being purposely destroyed and a new civil religion was being imposed in its place by force. The Terror therefore included *both* the slaughter of priests and nuns, the beating of women on their way to mass, the confiscation of church property, the stripping of altars and profanation of churches and sacred vessels, *and* the declaration of a kind of new natural pantheistic religion, the imposition of a new secular calendar, the renaming of public streets from saints to revolutionaries and revolutionary abstractions, and the actual worship of those great and horribly destructive abstract deities, Liberty and Equality. Both the destruction and the reconstruction were understood by the "patriots" and "citizens" of the Revolution to be necessary elements of the progress of humanity.[7]

That progress could be so monumentally barbaric has always been a puzzle for later liberals. The facts of the French Revolution do not fit in with their belief that religion in general and Christianity in particular are the real causes of epic slaughter throughout history. Liberal historians therefore dwell on the St. Bartholomew's Day massacre that took place in Catholic France in 1572, when somewhere between five and ten thousand were killed, as a sign of the fundamental rot at the heart of Christian belief. But they pass over completely, treat lightly, or misrepresent the carnage that occurred during the Reign of Terror in the Vendée where upwards of 250,000 were slaughtered by the French Revolution's Jacobins in their effort to eradicate both Christianity and Christians as enemies of the newly established secular state.

That liberal scholars have been skeptical of the enormity of the destruction—downgrading the numbers killed,[8] and explaining the horrors of the Vendée in terms of class conflict rather than recognizing it as an anti-Christian program of extermination—is not surprising. The skepticism about the historical crimes of secularism is essential to maintaining liberals' belief that historical progress is essentially secular.

But as historian Michael Burleigh has rightly pointed out, we must understand the Vendée as a secular atrocity that foreshadowed even worse to come: "This was the first occasion in history when an 'anticlerical' and self-styled 'non-religious' state embarked on a programme of mass murder that anticipated many twentieth-century horrors." The horrors of the Vendée proved that "the secular state was just as capable of unimaginable barbarity as any inspired by religion, eclipsing such limited atrocities as the Inquisition or the Massacre of St Bartholomew's Day, a modest affair when set alongside rampaging mobs of sans-culottes, in what was tantamount to genocide."[9] But, as Burleigh goes on to show, the French Revolution actually was animated by a political religion, one of many that would darken the following two centuries.

As the first attempt to incarnate the new liberal political order in a great secularized state, the French Revolution is iconic for liberalism. With all its passionate speeches about liberty, equality, and fraternity; its ruthlessness in achieving its goals; and its embrace of the austere pagan Roman Republic as its model; and even a revised pagan religion of its own, the French Revolution is an obvious example of what we've called hard liberalism. Later secularizing attempts to eliminate Christianity from history have not all been equally bloody. (Some have been even more so, as for example in the Soviet Union; some less so, as for example soft liberalism's continual pressure to secularize the public sphere in twenty-first-century England and America.) But all share the same passion and the same goal. They all define historical progress in terms of secularization, the elimination of Christianity, and the substitution of some version of secular political religion.

Salvation History According to the Religion of Soft Liberalism

In Europe and America today, our concern is with soft liberalism. While the secular religion in the ascendant in our society today is related to the civil religion put forward in the French Revolution, it presents a much different face. In this version of the secular religion of liberalism, sociology replaces theology. Social scientists become the functional equivalent of the church hierarchy, directing humanity towards a this-worldly Edenic utopia.

The founding prophet of sociology was Auguste Comte (1798–1857). Comte was born in the midst of the turmoil of revolutionary France. By the age of fourteen he had rejected his parents' Catholicism and declared himself an atheist. He would later go on to invent a new religion to take the place of Christianity. Comte's "Religion of Humanity" scooped the original content out of Catholicism and re-filled its eviscerated form with entirely secular content, including devotion to secular "saints" on secular saints' days and elaborate secular liturgies celebrating human beings as self-creating and self-redeeming gods.

Comte's sacralization of the secular was undergirded by his famous view of historical progress, which he promoted as a great fundamental "law of history." The notion that progress was a "law" gave it the air of both scientific certainty and historical inevitability. In Comte's telling of the story, history moves—must move—from the early, infantile or primitive theological stage (the stage of ignorance), through the metaphysical stage (the stage of unscientific philosophic abstraction), and finally, as the culmination of history, to the positive stage (the stage where utilitarian, materialistic science defines everything, especially human beings).[10]

Comte's "positive" stage, which he presents as the ultimate goal of history, is the era in which Christianity has been decisively left behind, and all of humanity has embraced a thoroughgoing secular view of reality, buttressed by materialist science. The materialism of Comte's "positive" stage most definitely applies to human nature itself, which will be studied and manipulated like any other physical reality. Thus for Comte, the progress of history culminates in what he dubbed "social physics."[11]

Sociology is the science by which the state—through a small cadre of experts in social physics—understands and manipulates its citizenry as "matter" for the sake of ushering in the culmination of history in the "positive" stage. Comte's experts are recognizable as a new iteration of the

experts of Spinoza's social pyramid, the middlemen who take the philosophic ideas handed down from the enlightened few at the top of the social
pyramid and apply them to the ignorant masses at the bottom. Social physics is not democratic, but elitist; that is, it follows Spinoza in pushing an
elite revolution even while appealing to seemingly democratic ideas and
goals. Progress is defined by the liberal elite and imposed by bureaucratic
experts using state power. Even while it rests on an ultimate democratization
of the cosmos, where all wills are equal because all wills are equally arbitrary,
it turns out that only some wills should count.

One might think that Comte would have heralded his third and final
"positive" stage of history as an age of atheism. But Comte firmly believed
that this final stage necessitated the creation of the Religion of Humanity
for exactly the same reason that Machiavelli advised his prince to appear
religious: crowd control. But also for another reason: Comte believed that
we *all* need to worship something. Thus religion can't be left behind, but
must be transformed into worship of ourselves. In Comte's Religion of
Humanity we worship ourselves through the state, which substitutes for
the church.

Comte's "Religion of Humanity" is even more artificial and bizarre than
the French Revolution's Religion of Reason. In deference to the French
Revolution, the new calendar would begin in 1789. (The Revolution displaces the Incarnation as the pivotal event in history.) Secular saints would
replace Christian saints for the feast days. There would be endless festivals,
as in the French Revolution, dedicated to, among others, mothers, fathers,
children, capitalists, and workers. And Comte planned for nine sacraments
(taking the place of the Catholic Church's seven) to mark all the significant
transitions of a person's life from infancy up through retirement at age
sixty-two (now you know why today's French are so touchy about their
retirement age). There was a final sacrament of transformation after death
to ensure one's memory in the temple of humanity. Even more bizarre,
Comte himself engaged in cultic adoration of a young woman named
Clotilde de Vaux, who had spurned his advances, and whom, after her death,

he idealized to the point of worship, meditating before the chair in which she had sat and uttering effusions to her immortal womanhood three times a day.[12]

Despite Comte's personal oddities—and, we must note, he spent a fair amount of time in mental hospitals (not touring, but as a patient)—his three-stage view of history and his vision of sociology as social physics were immensely influential first in Europe and then in the United States. Sociology as a discipline assumed Comte's view that religion in general and Christianity in particular had to give way to the welcome advance of secularism, a secularism that was, paradoxically, fundamentally religious.[13]

The essence of "social physics" consists in the belief that (as in physics and chemistry) the laws of human behavior and social interaction can be discovered, and that once they are discovered, society can be rationally reconstructed by experts to eliminate the problems Christianity ascribed to a fallen world, and to create the kind of conditions in this world that Christians had dreamed of enjoying in the next. We'll soon see how the social physicists came to power in American liberalism.

In this chapter we've gotten an overview of modern liberalism as shaped by Machiavelli, Hobbes, Spinoza, Rousseau, and Comte. But this account raises quite a few questions. If liberalism is essentially anti-Christian, then what about liberal Christianity? And how are nineteenth-century economic liberalism and the free market economics of conservatism today related to our contemporary liberalism? In the next two chapters we'll be focusing on these and other points of confusion in the history of liberalism. As we'll see, the confusion can be cleared up if we distinguish different and sometimes competing strains of liberalism—and confront the ambiguous legacy of John Locke.

CHAPTER 11

SORTING OUT
SOME CONFUSIONS

From the eighteenth through the twentieth centuries, the secular state ascended triumphantly while the Christian church receded. But that "progress" doesn't look like a straight line. Nineteenth-century Europe was characterized by alliances of "throne and altar"—that is, of the state and the church—and hence by what would appear to be political conservatism, rather than liberalism.

If that weren't confusing enough, we've got a problem with the term "liberal" itself. As I've mentioned, some nineteenth-century "liberals" sound like twentieth-century "conservatives." Alexis de Tocqueville, a self-identified liberal, is the darling of twentieth- and twenty-first-century conservatives. Friedrich Hayek, the great twentieth-century conservative economist, identified himself explicitly as an heir to nineteenth-century liberalism.[1]

This ambiguity is often dealt with by calling nineteenth-century liberals who sound like twentieth- and twenty-first-century conservatives "classical liberals," so as to distinguish them from twenty-first-century liberals who seem to hold opposite opinions.

But why are they both called "liberal" then? Is there some kind of identifiable lineage between what we call liberalism and conservatism today? Are they both species of a liberal genus—*liberalis classicus* and *liberalis liberalissimus*? If they are, what do they have in common? How can the same term describe both a philosophy that favors limited government and at the same time a belief that there should be an all-encompassing state that attends to our every need? How can those who favor the negative freedom of the individual to worship without state interference or coercion and those who push a program of positive secularization and even worship of the nation-state itself, both be called "liberals"?

We've obviously got some sorting out to do. We'll focus on the question of "throne and altar" conservatism in this chapter, and of "classical" liberalism in the next.

The Long Shadow of the French Revolution

Let's begin by reminding ourselves of the shadow cast upon the nineteenth century by the carnage of the French Revolution. To many Europeans of the early nineteenth century, the horrors of the French Revolution—especially its vicious attack upon the church in the name of an alleged Religion of Reason, and the release of the lower orders of society from all constraints in a barbaric free-for-all of violent political fanaticism—meant a new appreciation of the value of the church for keeping latent social mayhem at bay. This appreciation was only deepened every time the revolutionary spirit pushed itself to the surface again, as in the revolutions of 1848.

The result was a kind of "conservative" reaction in which some European states re-embraced the church as a buttress to political order, and some churches re-embraced the state for protection. This double embrace was in a certain sense a rollback or even repudiation of the general secular advances that had taken place during the previous century, the century of Enlightenment. But the reaction to the French Revolution was actually quite complex, containing three distinct strains.

First there were Christians who had been suspicious of the Enlightenment all along. They had been warning that human beings were not essentially good, as Rousseau had claimed, but rather deeply wounded by sin. They had even predicted political apocalypse if the moral order of Christianity were destroyed by its secular critics. These Christians were not surprised at the Revolution's hellish Reign of Terror. They could say, sadly enough, "I told you so"—the state that rejects the church will soon devour its own citizens in an orgiastic banquet of bloodshed.

There were also people (and governments) in the middle who might never have questioned the progress of liberalism if not for the horrors of the French Revolution. These were essentially frightened into conservatism by the excesses of the Revolution.

But there was also a third apparently "conservative" reaction from *within* liberal secularism. It was an "I told you so" from Machiavelli and especially Hobbes, to the more radical Spinoza and Rousseau. Both Machiavelli and Hobbes were "conservative" in one sense. Atheism in their view was not for the masses; it belonged only to the rulers, and should be their secret. The infamous infidel Voltaire, the great wit of the eighteenth-century Enlightenment, firmly adhered to the Machiavellian view. Atheism could be discussed among the philosophes, but not in front of anyone else—that would undermine the morality of the common people. "I want my lawyer, tailor, valets, even my wife, to believe in God," remarked Voltaire candidly, "I think that if they do I shall be robbed less and cheated less."[2] Voltaire preached the need for the religion he didn't believe in, not its elimination: "Why take away from the common people a salutary yoke, a fear which is needed because only thus can secret crime be stopped? Belief in future rewards and punishments is a check which the people needs."[3]

The people, not the Enlightened few. Religion was necessary to rule the masses, and as Machiavelli had made clear, *the prince or king should use the very religion the masses actually believe in* to control them—rather than, as the French revolutionaries had done, concocting some kind of arbitrary civil religion out of thin air. The clever ruler must co-opt Christianity, not try to destroy it and replace it by force with something entirely new and thus obviously artificial. Hence Machiavelli's counsel on the necessity for the prince to appear to be a very pious, religious Christian. Hence Hobbes's advice to the sovereign on subtly reconstructing Christianity from within, rather than creating some cerebral new state religion out of whole cloth. After the French Revolution it appeared that Spinoza, in creating a severely liberalized form of Christianity, and Rousseau, in repudiating Christianity entirely and replacing it with a civil religion, had gone too far and unleashed the fury and chaotic passions of the masses that Christianity had been so useful in containing. So a third reason to be a nineteenth-century "conservative" was to be a more Machiavellian liberal.

Throne and Altar

We can see then how a "conservative" nineteenth-century political figure might embrace Christianity sincerely, or for Machiavellian reasons. In the latter case, an attempt to restore the old order after the French Revolution might simply mean a bid for absolute liberal sovereignty of the kind touted by Hobbes.

The phrase "throne and altar" describes the pact among European governments after the defeat of Napoleon to ensure that rabble-rousing revolutionaries would be kept firmly under the control of their respective states. The alliance was forged at the Congress of Vienna in 1814, even before Napoleon's final defeat, by Great Britain, Austria, Prussia, and Russia, guided by Klemens von Metternich, the Austrian foreign minister.

The "throne and altar" policy aimed to restore order by restoring monarchs to power and balancing the various European powers against one another so that no one of them would be too strong, and all of them could keep France under control. Part of the strategy—an obvious one, given the anti-Christian fury of the French revolutionaries—was to reseat Christianity firmly as the official state religion across the continent. Since there were now different Christian churches, rather than a single church, the alliances of thrones and altars amounted to something like a reaffirmation of *cuius regio, euis religio*, but with no questions asked about the sincerity of the ruler's religion.

Did such alliances represent a genuine repudiation of liberalism and an authentic return to Christianity? Or were they politically calculating? One suspects that motives were very often mixed, even within the same breast.

After all, the situation *prior to* the French Revolution had been ambiguous enough. What did a return to the old order really mean? Recall that Machiavellianism and the rise of nationalism, sometimes operating together and sometimes independently, had already been at work from the sixteenth through the eighteenth centuries. Established state churches with the church firmly under the control of the state had become the norm, especially given the multiplication of Christian denominations after the Reformation and the weakening of the papacy.

The Anglican Church is a case in point. Since the time of Henry VIII and his Machiavellian policies (or at least policy-makers), the Anglican Church was the Church *of* England, the church of, by, and for the government of England and the classes in political control. That was the very state of affairs that drove the Puritans out of England to America's shores in the early seventeenth century.

The Catholic Church in France, the one so hated by the French Revolutionaries, was really France's Catholic Church, the so-called Gallican Church, firmly under control of the French monarch and nobles. That, of course, is why there was so much corruption among the French bishops. They were by and large appointees of the monarch from the loyal noble class. No one would suspect Cardinal Richelieu (d. 1642) of sincere piety, but in his service to France's Louis XIII he certainly did a splendid job of exercising Machiavellian control of the church for state purposes. The same can be said of Richelieu's successor, Cardinal Mazarin (d. 1661). Louis XIV's motto, "One king, one law, one faith" was a very exact description of the order of the priorities in pre-Revolutionary France, with the faith firmly supporting the king and his law—exactly what Hobbes had prescribed.

So in both England and France the church was already entirely subordinate to the state long before the French Revolution. The same was largely true of the various state churches and their hierarchies, Protestant or Catholic, in the patchwork of German states or principalities in a yet-to-be-united Germany. Not long after Luther helped throw off the yoke of Rome, for example, Lutheran pastors had become civil servants in the pay of—and controlled by—the state. This occurred, as historians R. W. Scribner and C. Scott Dixon make clear, because "From the very beginning... *the institutionalization of reform was an erastian phenomenon*: that is, the church was subjected to the control of secular authority" [emphasis in the original].[4] As Scribner and others argue elsewhere, "A major goal of German politics at all levels well before the Reformation was to submit the church and its agencies to secular control."[5]

So in truth the alliances of "throne and altar" in the nineteenth century were very often politically motivated reaffirmations of the established state churches that had been in place before the French Revolution. The apparent return from liberalism to Christianity was often the result of calculation rather than sincere piety.

The insincerity is obvious enough in someone like Napoleon himself. One can hardly believe that Napoleon's reestablishing the Catholic Church after the Revolution was motivated by his personal piety. He had none. But he was an astute observer of the damage that the direct attack on the church had caused the Revolution. Napoleon therefore sought to reestablish a renewed form of the Gallican church in the home-nation of his empire.

And one cannot be surprised to find the Catholic Church in France, and even the pope himself, happy enough to welcome the insincere embrace of Napoleon as a relief from the policy of extermination in the Terror.

With the fall of Napoleon and the restoration of the Bourbon monarchy under Louis XVIII in 1814, the old noble class and the monarchists won a temporary victory in France. Napoleon III, declared Emperor of France in 1852, was no more religious than Napoleon I. But he was just as convinced as the first Napoleon of the social utility of Catholicism.

Nor did the upper class in England experience a renewed piety after viewing the destruction to the French state caused by the Jacobins over the channel. They simply had a renewed appreciation of the value of their own state Anglicanism for keeping the lower orders both ordered and lower. It became characteristic of the English upper classes to be personally skeptical, but heartily affirmative of the church in public.

The true believer—the truly devout Catholic in France or the truly pious Anglican in England—was entangled in this ambiguity. Fearing the release of the barbarism and ruthless attack on Christianity that had characterized the Reign of Terror, sincere Christians held tightly to the state church for safety as an anchor in an impending storm, and very naturally they often gave that church their uncritical loyalty. But partly for this reason, the various churches risked being seen as mere props for the powers that be, the old order. They seemed more devoted to saving the necks of the rich and powerful than to saving souls.

So whatever sincere piety there was in the nineteenth-century alliance of throne and altar, in no case did it represent a return to the original Christian arrangement hammered out by the church in the period from Augustine to the High Middle Ages, in which the religious power and the political power were distinct and yet complementary, and the church was functionally independent and universal in scope.

The Religion of Nationalism

One sign that the original complementary relationship between the church and the political power had been lost was that in the nineteenth century, nationalism itself became a religion.

Religious devotion to the nation was not invented in the nineteenth century. National messianic tendencies had already emerged centuries earlier in England, France, and Germany, wherein each nation, taking on the mantle of the new Israel, held itself to be *the* bearer of Christianity's universal claims and dominion over all nations.[6]

What was new in the nineteenth century was that the nation itself now appeared as the divine bearer of this-worldly salvation. The Christian aspects of each nation's messianism faded and finally disappeared as the church's doctrines became secularized and its functions were absorbed into the state. The earlier messianic nationalism that had been fueled by Christianity slid all too easily into secular messianic nationalism, as more radical liberal ideas permeated the intellectual culture, dissolving the hold Christianity had on the minds of the intelligentsia and redirecting religious energy to the state's secular programs. Liberalism and nationalism often went hand in hand in the nineteenth century.

There were, of course, transitional schemes that seemed to have feet in both sacred and secular camps. The German philosopher Georg Hegel (1770–1831), famous for declaring that "Man must...venerate the state as a secular deity,"[7] saw the state as a kind of Spinozan pantheistic fusion of God and the church. He arrived at this conclusion from the assumption that the Spirit revealed himself through and in history—as if human history were God successively incarnating himself, with his ultimate self-revelation being the modern state (the Prussian state, to be exact). But Hegel meant all of this, somehow, to be the ultimate realized goal of Christianity, rather than its repudiation.

The great proponent of German nationalism, Ernst Arndt (1769–1860), was a liberal who had originally welcomed the French Revolution, then repudiated it as Napoleon ran roughshod over Europe. At that point Arndt became a passionate nationalist, declaring, "To be a nation...is the religion of our time. Leave all the little religions and perform the great duty to the single highest, and unite yourselves in it to one belief high above the Pope or Luther. That is the ultimate religion...."[8] It was zeal for this liberal national ideal that led to the unification of Germany.

The unification of Italy, too, was fueled by nationalism that crossed over into a religion (which is why it ended in the triumphant takeover of Rome itself, the pope's domain, in 1870). The quasi-religious flavor of Italian nationalism is clearly seen in the Young Italy movement started by hyper-patriot Giuseppe Mazzini in the first half of the nineteenth century. For Mazzini, as for the ancient pagan Romans, religion was secondary to the nation and should serve it, and the nation itself took on the form and con-tent of the church. Young Italy morphed into Young Europe, which united like-minded nationalists in a kind of trans-national religion. Mazzini declared Young Europe to be "a religious party," and proclaimed a new vision in which "all the altars of the old world have fallen," and "two altars shall be raised upon this soil that the divine Word has made fruitful; and the finger of the herald-people shall inscribe upon one Fatherland, and upon the other Humanity."[9]

And the divine Word? One suspects that Mazzini considered Christian-ity to be at best a kind of precursor of the newly revealed secular truth, at worst a useful source of slogans. However that may be, it is certain that Mazzini yoked the religion of nationalism to something like Comte's Reli-gion of Humanity. True to the perennial aspirations of more radical liber-als, Mazzini thought his union of nationalism and universal brotherhood would result in a utopia. "Like sons of the same mother, like brothers who will not be parted, the people shall gather around these two altars and offer sacrifice in peace and love."[10] Mazzini died about a year and a half after the capture of Rome in 1870, in the humiliation of the papacy that left it stripped of any territorial holdings other than Vatican City, and about forty years before nationalism nearly incinerated Europe in World War I.

From such beginnings in the early nineteenth century it is not difficult to see why any mention of God could soon be skipped, so that in the next century, the human achievements of the state would be worshipped in a kind of human self-divinization as nationalism increasingly became a kind of religion. As historian Michael Burleigh rightly notes, "for the elite minor-ities of nationalists their patriotic faith became analogous, depending on the depth and intensity of their commitment, to membership of an alterna-tive Church, or in extreme cases worship of the nation as a God," so that, in their schemes "the power of the state...replicated that earlier deployed by the Church."[11]

"Nationalism," as Burleigh rightly points out "was the most pervasive and potent Church to emerge during the nineteenth century."[12] The established

Christian state churches that existed at the beginning of the nineteenth century became, in both form and function, increasingly absorbed into the state itself, as the state became the means of this-worldly salvation and the object of the people's highest devotion.

This absorption was aided immensely by pounding waves of anti-clericalism and also by various movements to disestablish different Christian state churches.

Very Strange Anti-Clerical Bedfellows

In the renewed fusion of states and churches after the French Revolution, those on the outs could in many cases rightly accuse the established state church of being simply a prop for the politically and economically powerful—at worst, a tool of oppression, at best a sop to keep the moiling masses now heaped together in squalid cities satisfied with their miserable lot.

Could either very sincere Christians *or* very sincere secularists be blamed for seeing the church in that way? Honest Christians realized that the supernatural, supra-national call to holiness of the Gospel was incompatible with the church's absorption into the interests of the nation-state. Meanwhile secularists saw a church being used for Machiavellian control of the masses. They were ready to re-embrace the radical Enlightenment—going beyond even Rousseau—to lead an atheist revolt of the masses against the church and the state it supported. Looking at the nineteenth century situation from this angle, we can even have some (but only some) sympathy with Karl Marx. Perhaps the church he saw really did merely reflect the interests of the most powerful classes. Perhaps that church really was handing out opium at the door. Small wonder that both sincere Christians and sincere secularists were deeply anti-clerical in the nineteenth century. The church hierarchies seemed to many to be deeply hypocritical. Sincere Christians wanted major reform. Secularists wanted to be rid of the church, period.

The alliance of convenience between Christian reformers and radical secularists explains the strange dynamic in the nineteenth-century movement to disestablish the state churches. The two anti-clerical factions united, but with two quite different ends. Christians desired reform of the church and secularists wanted its complete and final removal from history. In this alliance, secularists were very happy to use reform-minded Christians for their purposes—and just as happy to dispose of them when they were no longer needed.

Disestablishing the Churches, Establishing Secularism

Thus in the end, disestablishment helped usher in state secular liberalism, despite the fact that many who worked for it were motivated by sincere Christian zeal. Christians—especially those not represented by the state church, such as the non-Conformists in England—seeing all the problems that the state establishment of the church caused, pushed hard for disestablishment. But so did the secularists. And the secularists used the zeal and force of Christians rightfully trying to reform the church to bring about their own aim: an entirely secular state.

"To the extent that political structure was secularized during the nineteenth century," notes historian Owen Chadwick, "it was secularized, for the most part, by men without desire to make society more secular; and in some part by men who had the opposite aim."[13] A secular or liberal minority in the disestablishment movement got what it wanted using a well-intentioned Christian majority. Ironically, sincere Christians contributed to the establishment of secular liberalism in place of the church.

For example, consider the 1905 Law of Separation in France that removed Catholicism as the favored state religion in France's Third Republic. Different factions were pushing for disestablishment of the Catholic Church in France in the latter half of the nineteenth century. Moderate republicans campaigned for disestablishment so as to be fair to non-Catholics, Protestants wanted disestablishment because they chafed under state support of Catholicism, and radical republicans and other freethinkers wanted to be rid of Christianity altogether, just as radicals had wanted in the original French Revolution. The greatest push came from those furthest left. "The separation of church and state," historian Hugh McLeod notes, "had come to have great symbolic significance for many French Radicals and Socialists, for whom it symbolized the liberation of the French state."[14] Liberation from Christianity, that is, and the dawn of a new secular age.

So in late nineteenth-century France we see something quite familiar to Americans today: the attempt by the Left, using the banner of "separation of church and state," to strip all vestiges of Christianity from public view, thereby creating what Richard Neuhaus called "the naked public square." Crucifixes and statues of saints were removed from public places, religious processions were officially outlawed, streets named after saints were renamed after Enlightenment heroes, and so on.

But the very heart of the secular revolution in France was, just as it has been in America, the secular takeover of education. French schools had largely been funded by the state but staffed by Catholic priests and religious. The empowered Left of the Third Republic was now able to replace religion-based education with secular education, creating a state education system staffed almost exclusively by lay teachers who embraced the radical republican cause. Obviously this had a direct effect on the substance of what was taught. History was now taught from the secular liberal view. Christianity was cast as an obstacle to real human progress and progress toward secularism as inevitable and wholly salutary. Moreover, a secular view of morality was substituted for one rooted in the Catholic understanding of the natural law.[15] Secular liberalism thereby became established in France and was taught as gospel in mandatory public education to young, unformed minds.

One cannot overestimate how significant it was in France (and is in America) for liberals to have gained complete state control of education, and for that education to be mandatory. Mandatory public education under control of the state allows for a top-down revolution wherein a relatively small minority may impose its worldview upon the entire population using state power. And the education establishment in our own country, as was the case in France, is dominated by radicals and socialists from the Left, from the universities right down to the elementary schools.

So the nineteenth-century restoration of "throne and altar," while it may look like a setback for liberalism, was really no more than a bump in the road the liberal juggernaut was rolling over. The throne's support for the altar was too often merely cynical, and the alliance of convenience was doomed to failure.

It's fair to say, then, that "throne and altar" in the nineteenth century was not really (or at least, not simply) an instance of a reverse in the fortunes of triumphant liberalism. But what about "classical liberalism"? Many modern conservatives trace their intellectual ancestry to eighteenth- and nineteenth-century "economic," "free market," or "classical" liberals such as Adam Smith. What is classical liberalism? And can strength to resist the triumph of secular liberalism be found in the thought of such conservatives as Smith and Tocqueville? To crack the riddle of "classical liberalism" we need to take a close look at the thought of John Locke, a figure remarkable for his ambiguity, and for his influence on America.

CHAPTER 12

JOHN LOCKE AND THE TWO FACES OF LIBERALISM

I t is really very difficult to trace a coherent history of liberalism. Setting aside for the moment "classical liberalism," which may or may not be a species of the liberal genus, liberalism has two faces. There is an inherently cautious or cynical (we might even call it "conservative") strain of liberalism in competition with a more ambitious and utopian strain (what we might call "radical" liberalism). Thus, as we have already seen from the fallout of the French Revolution, the more cynical disciples of Machiavelli and Hobbes tend to come into conflict with the hopeful or optimistic disciples of the more utopian Spinoza and Rousseau. Locke, as we'll see, is a key figure standing somewhere in the middle, facing both ways.

As we begin sorting things out, let's remember that the more "conservative" liberalism (the cautious and cynical sort) is ultimately just as radical as "radical" liberalism (the more obviously ambitious sort), perhaps even more so, at its core. But it plays its cards closer to the chest. For "conservative" liberals, the radical core of liberalism—the complete liberation from

Christianity, the embrace of a totally secular worldview—is meant only for the rulers and the Enlightened few. (In our day, with the mass publication of classic texts like Machiavelli's *The Prince* and Hobbes's *Leviathan*, it's hard to remember that neither book was meant for consumption by the common people.) "Conservative" liberals didn't want to abolish Christianity. They wanted to keep the Christian church around—as an effective instrument for state control of the masses.

Radical liberalism, on the other hand, aimed to enlighten the masses, and to secularize and democratize the political order. Thus Rousseau's political program culminated in baptizing the "General Will" as the new absolute sovereign, the will of the masses replacing the will of the prince or king or nobles. He ejected Christianity altogether and put a new, secular religion in its place (hence, the French Revolution's Religion of Reason, and following it, Comte's Religion of Humanity). When we say "in its place" we are speaking very exactly: radical secular liberalism self-consciously takes the form and fills the entire space of the church. In Rousseau's democratized civil religion and its descendants a kind of secular anti-church fulfills all the functions of the church. And this "church" is bent on ushering in a this-worldly utopia, one largely built upon the idyllic hedonistic primitivism of Rousseau's Eden, even if in practice the hedonism is achieved using the latest technology.

Spinoza, too, must be considered a radical liberal. While he had nothing but contempt for the masses, his radical reconstruction of Christianity was only a thinly disguised pantheistic materialism. And Spinoza's disciples were largely responsible for broadcasting the seeds of radical liberalism to all kinds and conditions of people. Spinoza's inner circle, no doubt with the blessing of the master himself, made ingenious arrangements for smuggling his banned works all over Europe after his death. Thus the radical Enlightenment spread all over Europe in the eighteenth century by means of a ready army of radical liberals ever prepared to break forth and spread the secular gospel to everyone.[1]

But then the bloody chaos of the French Revolution convinced even some radical liberals that the conservative branch of the family had been correct, and they re-embraced the kind of royal absolutism championed by Hobbes. So the nineteenth century, the century of "throne and altar," can be characterized as in no small part a struggle *within* liberalism—a disagreement between more cynical and more utopian or obviously radical liberals, not just about the pace of secularization but about whether popular secularization should take place at all.

The tension between the two poles of liberal thought was sustained throughout the 1800s, with the more obviously radical strain breaking out periodically not only in political revolutions (such as the political upheavals that swept across Europe in 1848), but in intellectual revolutions as well. Thus the century of "throne and altar" conservatism is also the century of radicals such as Feuerbach, Marx, Comte, Darwin, Huxley, and of secular socialism, a new religio-political movement that we'll explore below.

To understand this tension most fully, especially as it impacts America, we have to explore the one figure who has been conspicuously absent from our discussion of modern liberalism so far, the man often taken to be the founder of "classical liberalism," John Locke, the quintessential "conservative" liberal.

Locke has always been a man hard to pin down, causing controversy right from the beginning. The reason is that he often seems to have a foot in two opposing camps. Or, to change the metaphor, Locke appears to show two different faces depending on what angle he's viewed from, sometimes speaking as if he were heir to the Christian natural law tradition that stretches back to the Middle Ages and into antiquity, and at other times coming across as Hobbes's somewhat sweeter younger brother and fellow champion of purely secular natural rights.[2] So, for example in his *Second Treatise of Civil Government*, Locke begins with an appeal to the Biblical Adam. But then he launches immediately into an account of the origin of society in terms of Hobbes's fictional "state of nature." Locke can speak in one breath about "men being all the workmanship of one omnipotent and infinitely wise Maker," who would seem to be in moral control of his creation, and then, in the next breath, make the very Hobbesian claim that each individual in the state of nature is the judge and executioner of any and every perceived transgression.[3]

Locke was more of a popularizer than Machiavelli or Hobbes, in two senses: His political arguments were pitched to a far larger audience, not just to the rulers. And he wrote extensive Biblical commentaries meant to re-present Christianity as supportive of his political arguments. But in all his work, political, Biblical, or philosophical, there runs a deep ambiguity. Locke was a kind of conservative revolutionary. Because he was so immensely influential in Europe (the eighteenth century is often referred to as "Locke's century") and even more so in America (Locke is rightly credited with being one of the great influences on our founders), that ambiguity traveled far and wide.

As I've already suggested, the ambiguity in Locke's thought is seen especially clearly in his account of the "state of nature."[4] To begin with, the very pretense that there was a pre-social state of nature in which every individual was free to do what he liked is antithetical both to the Christian natural law tradition and to the commonsense notion that the first society was and is the family. As we've seen, the "state of nature" was invented by Hobbes as an antithesis to the Christian account in Genesis and it is clear from Locke's account that he knew Hobbes's very well.

In his version of the "state of nature" Locke affirms the Hobbesian right of self-preservation. At first that right seems to be limited —Locke writes of "bounds of the law of nature"—but we soon find out that according to Locke each individual is himself the "executor" of the law of nature, the policeman, judge, and executioner of any infractions,[5] something no Christian natural law thinker would ever allow. The ultimate result of everyone exercising this absolute right is, exactly as it was in Hobbes, a natural state of war.[6]

The twist that Locke puts on Hobbes's account is his extension of the natural right of self-preservation to include the right to property—in fact, the limitless accumulation of property.[7] So in escaping the chaotic state of nature for civil society, we put ourselves under a civil sovereign to save our lives *and* preserve our property. Hence, in Locke's famous words, "The great and chief end…of men's uniting into commonwealths and putting themselves under government is the preservation of their property."[8]

In defining the sole end of government as the preservation of our bodily life and our material property, Locke made a definitive break with the Christian natural law tradition, in which the goal of government had been the preservation of life, the administration of justice, and the inculcation of virtue—all in the context of the understanding that this world is a stepping stone to the next. And this makes Locke definitively liberal: *in cutting off any higher goal than the preservation of life and property, Locke was siding with Machiavelli and Hobbes in defining the state as purely secular and concerned with the body alone.* (And as we shall see, he was also siding with the new rising propertied class against the old noble-monarchical order.)

So Locke joined Hobbes and Machiavelli in rejecting the complementary relationship between church and state that had been carefully worked out over the first thirteen centuries of Christianity's history and opted for a secular state defined in terms of bodily needs alone.

The Classical Liberal State: Property Takes Center Stage

Locke was thus the inventor of the "classical liberal" state, concerned with protecting property rights, especially the property rights of the new commercial class, that is, the merchants and money-men who were displacing the old noble class. That is the stratum of society that Locke identified with in England's Glorious Revolution in 1688, the moneyed class that wrested control from the king and nobles and placed political power in the hands of the Parliament, which better represented its own interests.

And in the nineteenth century there was yet another wave of newly rich because of the immense wealth gained in the various enterprises of the industrial revolution. They used Locke against the established order (who, ironically, were the heirs of the winners in the Revolution of 1688, who had displaced the established order of that day). Locke became the (classical) liberal guide for these newly prosperous Englishmen.

While Locke was a liberal, he was no friend of the moiling masses. He had lived through the English Civil Wars at mid-seventeenth century, and he had nothing but disdain for the lower-class radicals tearing up the social fabric and calling for the equal and common distribution of property in the name of God.[9] His contempt for the common people put him in the "conservative" liberal camp with Machiavelli and Hobbes.

But Locke had ties to radical liberalism, too. As a member of the anti-royalist party he spent time on the continent as a political exile (1683–1689). And there he became well-acquainted with the circle of Spinozan radicals. While Locke himself was at the time considered a political radical,[10] he was wary of where radical views might lead if unleashed upon society as a whole. We might even say that Locke foresaw the dangers of Rousseau more than a half-century before Rousseau wrote, and more than a century before the French Revolution.

It was that fear that made Locke a "conservative" liberal, a proponent of moderate rather than radical Enlightenment. Thus he was far more inclined to lean on Christianity as a moral prop for society than were the more radical liberals who came after him. What he wanted was a "reasonable" Christianity—in fact the title of one of his works was *The Reasonableness of Christianity* (1695)—a tolerant and tepid Christianity, a Christianity with minimal reliance on creeds and maximal reliance on the morality so useful for controlling the masses. It was that kind of Christianity that Locke espoused in his extraordinarily influential Biblical commentaries.[11]

Agreeing with Spinoza, Locke asserted that the multitude was not capable of using reason to arrive at moral conclusions; therefore, the masses need Christianity. As he wrote with uncharacteristic bluntness, "The greatest part of mankind want leisure or capacity for [rational] demonstration, nor can carry a train of proofs....And you may as soon hope to have all the day-laborers and tradesmen, the spinsters and dairymaids, perfect mathematicians, as to have them perfect in ethics this way. Hearing plain commands is the sure and only course to bring them to obedience and practice. The greatest part cannot *know*, and therefore they must *believe*." Teaching morality by rational demonstration is "proper only for a few, who had much leisure, improved understandings, and were used to abstract reasonings. But the instruction of the people were best still to be left to the precepts and principles of the gospel."[12]

In Locke we find something like Spinoza's pyramid, with the rational, secular philosophers at the top realizing that they need to rule the common people at the bottom through Christianity, the religion of the masses. As with Spinoza, Locke's version of Christianity is a liberalized one, in which Jesus is reduced to a moral teacher. But Locke differed from Spinoza in this: the more radical Spinoza denied miracles, but Locke thought that belief in miracles was necessary for "the bulk of mankind" to adhere to Christ's moral commands.[13]

Locke's approach of eliminating or severely limiting all doctrine to reduce Christianity to a moral core backed up by a few miracles would soon lead to liberal Protestant Christianity or mild Deism, both of which affirmed Jesus as a great moral teacher, jettisoned the notion that he performed miracles, and politely declined to affirm his divinity—a religion, most likely, close to what Locke actually believed.

Locke's connection to liberal Christianity, and even to Spinoza's radical revision of Christianity, can be seen in his plea for toleration (his *Epistola de Tolerantia*, or *Letter on Toleration*, was published anonymously in 1689), in which he took the unorthodox position we've already seen in Spinoza—that "Toleration" was "the chief Characteristical Mark of the True Church."[14] That's quite a step from the orthodoxy of the Nicene Creed, the central revealed truths about God the Father, the nature of Christ as fully human and fully divine, and the Holy Trinity. (Locke was, at best, a Socinian, i.e., in our parlance, a Unitarian, so he had a personal interest in promoting toleration of heretical brands of Christianity.)

Like Spinoza, Locke claimed that toleration was necessary because everyone has his own ideas about what is orthodox—witness the splintering of all kinds of Christian sects—and these ideas cannot be rationally sorted out since they are the result of subjective causes. Therefore, all beliefs must be tolerated *as long as the believer is law-abiding*.[15] Hence the basic dogmas of liberal Christianity: doctrine is inconsequential; one is free to believe whatever one wants, as long as one is a good person; and essential to goodness is tolerance of everyone believing whatever he or she wants.

This reasonable Christianity could well serve as the unofficial religion of the liberal state Locke had in mind. The kind of state Locke wanted was liberal, but it was not a democratic state. Liberty for the new propertied class was good, but liberty for the unpropertied mob running riot was not; therefore, religion was needed to keep the unpropertied class from bursting forth as it had done during the English Civil Wars. Religious dissent from state Anglicanism could and should be tolerated as long as the dissenters were law-abiding (and after the Glorious Revolution, Locke was very law-abiding).

The state should be indifferent to the multitude of beliefs because the state was only concerned with bodily preservation and comfort; that is, the state should be entirely secular, liberated from entanglements in questions about the next world. In his *Letter on Toleration* Locke defined the "Commonwealth…to be a Society of Men constituted only for the procuring, preserving, and advancing of their own *Civil Interests*," where civil interests were limited to "Life, Liberty, Health, and Indolency of Body; and the Possession of outward things, such as Money, Lands, Houses, Furniture, and the like." In short, government was for no other purpose than the preservation of one's body and property, and the freedom to do with them as one likes. To realize the depth of Locke's revolution against the Christian understanding of political power as defined during the first twelve centuries of

Christianity, we need to pay attention to how very materialistic (that is, soulless) these "Civil Interests" are.

The highest goal of Locke's secular state—what we know as the classical liberal state—is economic. It is liberal in two senses, a negative and positive: negative in that economic liberty frees the individual from state interference to pursue his happiness by the accumulation of material possessions, and positive in that personal religious liberty allows the individual to believe whatever he wants as long as he is law-abiding. With Locke's revolution, one is freed *from* the Christian worry about the ill effects of riches on the soul, and freed *to* passionately pursue the endless accumulation of goods for the body. These two senses of "free" are embedded in Locke's particular form of liberalism.

For Locke's version of the liberal state to work, religion must be entirely privatized—that is, made a matter of the soul alone. To this end, Locke declared that "true and saving Religion" *only* concerns "the inward perswasion of the Mind, without which nothing can be acceptable to God."[16] No one can compel "inward perswasion," so "the Magistrate's Power extends not to the establishing of any Articles of Faith, or Forms of Worship, by the force of Laws."[17] The "power of Civil Government relates only to Men's Civil Interests," that is, it "is confined to the care of the things of this World, and hath nothing to do with the World to come."[18]

Locke's is a soulless political order.

This subtraction of the soul from politics is extraordinarily significant. We recall that in the arrangement that was reached in the church's first twelve centuries, the religious and political power were institutionally and functionally distinct but not entirely separate. While the church primarily took care of the soul and the government looked after the body, the soul and body were essentially united. A sign of this connection is that the state had to care for the souls of citizens as well as their bodies, that is, it had to be concerned about *virtue*, about moral excellence. It is of the greatest consequence that Locke drops any mention of the state's care of the soul, and likewise says nothing of virtue. His state is entirely this-worldly, entirely secular, as if, somehow, the economic pursuit of material prosperity could take the place of the need for virtue. Insofar as that can happen, the state has less and less need for the church, and perhaps even for privatized religion.

We should be very clear about the kind of liberty entailed in Locke's privatizing of religious belief. It is not just that government should *allow* religion to be privatized, but that the government must *ensure* that religion is privatized so that the political order will remain secular. To achieve this privatization, Locke flatters the multitude, we might say, by utterly democratizing religious belief, declaring that in regard to religion, "Every man...has the supreme and absolute Authority of judging for himself."[19] Against the orthodox view that Christ's very person and what he revealed to his apostles and the church through the Bible define what must be believed, Locke affirmed the *right* of each person to believe anything he wants (again, as long as he is law-abiding).

Obviously, with "supreme and absolute Authority of judging for himself" placed in the individual, there is no need for a church, except insofar as individuals gather together in a voluntary association with those who happen to believe the same thing.

The result of embracing the individual's right to believe whatever he or she wants is that the church as the Body of Christ is atomized, dissolved into a multitude of unconnected individuals. The church no longer stands in any real distinction from or opposition to the state. The delicate balance of church and state has been swept away. The church is no longer a viable intermediate institution, standing independent of the political power and protecting the individual from the state. Rather, we are left with the individual believer, secure, at least for the time being, in his right to believe anything he wants, *but facing the state alone.*

On Locke's plan, then, we arrive at a kind of liberal political order that may rightly be called "conservative" liberalism, in which the state is entirely secular, its aims defined completely by material economic considerations. As in the schemes of Machiavelli and Hobbes, there may be an established state religion—Locke opted for affirmation of a liberalized Anglican Church after the Glorious Revolution—but the established church won't have any teeth because ultimately faith is an entirely subjective matter. In Locke's scheme the whole point of religion, whether in an established liberal church or in wholly privatized Christianity, is to be a moral support for the political stability of the state and the economic prosperity it fosters. (We note that while England still has an established state Anglicanism, it is entirely formed by the doctrines of liberalism, and so presents no threat to the increasingly radical liberal secular state.)

The Radical Revolution against Classical Liberalism

The process we still see going on in England and America today is the final collapse of Locke's classical liberal order (often understood as "conservative") at the hands of more radical liberals. We are seeing the endgame of a process that began in the eighteenth century and really heated up in the nineteenth: classical liberalism is challenged by radical liberalism, and gives way.

What moves things from conservative liberalism to radical liberalism, *liberalis classicus* to *liberalis liberalissimus*? In great part, the recognition that Christianity in the classical liberal state really is a prop for the political-economic elite that control the government.

Thus classical liberalism prepares the way for radical liberalism. The radical liberal Rousseau, writing over fifty years after Locke, took Locke at his word that "The great and chief end...of men's uniting into commonwealths and putting themselves under government is the preservation of their property." Civil society and its laws really *are* all aimed at the preservation of the property of the few (a notion Marx later took over from Rousseau). But against Locke, Rousseau asserted that this legal appropriation by the few rich of the goods of nature that belonged to everyone was unjust.[20]

Here Rousseau doesn't so much reject Locke as democratize him. Radical liberalism aims at redistributing the property of the few to the many, so that *all* can enjoy (in Locke's words again) "Life, Liberty, Health, and Indolency of Body; and the Possession of outward things, such as Money, Lands, Houses, Furniture, and the like." And moreover, *all* should be able to believe whatever they want, not just the elite. So everyone has the right to be completely skeptical of religion, and see it as a ruse invented by the few haves in power to manipulate the many have nots.

The democratic radicalism of Rousseau led to the destruction of the wealthy nobles by the French Revolutionaries, and beyond that, to the various socialist and atheistic movements against the capitalists (the classical liberals) in the nineteenth and twentieth centuries.

We can now see much of the turmoil of the nineteenth century as a kind of internecine battle between the two strains of liberalism, classical liberalism and radical liberalism, with classical liberalism (looking behind at the carnage of the French Revolution, and forward to the new revolutions bubbling up on the horizon) holding ever more dearly onto some form of modified, liberalized Christianity as a barrier against the advance of atheist radicalism.

But the irony is that the "conservative" liberals actually affirmed the same set of radical ideas as the radical liberals—but only in private and for the few. Meanwhile the radicals were busy evangelizing the whole of society with those ideas. Liberalism was becoming a mass movement. The central doctrines of liberalism were being preached to all the nations as a kind of universal religion displacing Christianity. Nowhere is this seen more clearly than in socialism.

Socialism, the New Religion of Humanity

In socialism we approach another area of confusion, or at least significant ambiguity. Besides being the era of "throne and altar," the nineteenth century also saw, it would seem, a kind of rebirth of Christianity in the Social Gospel—an outpouring of Christian concern about gross injustices by industrialists against workers, and for the heart-wrenching plight of the poor, especially in inner cities. There seemed to be a renewed awareness of the seriousness of Christ's warnings about dividing the sheep and goats, allowing the former into heaven and casting the latter into hell according to whether they had fed the hungry, clothed the naked, and cared for the sick, the widow, and the orphan.

What causes significant ambiguity is a kind of fusion or confusion of purposes in the nineteenth century between, on the one hand, well-intentioned Christians trying to recapture Christ's call to holiness in concern for the poor and downtrodden and in recognition that purely personal piety was not enough and, on the other, socialists and communists, who while also deeply moved by concerns for the poor and downtrodden, saw Christianity as part of the problem and believed it needed to be superseded. Oddly, the two camps often made common cause against what they perceived to be the common enemy: the propertied industrial elites who seemed smugly unconcerned about the plight of the poor, even while mouthing Christian platitudes.

This same phenomenon had occurred during the French Revolution itself. In the earlier part of the Revolution poor parish priests, well acquainted with the trials and sufferings of the poor, united with Jacobin revolutionaries who had nothing but inner contempt for Christianity, in an effort to unseat the unworthy bishops who were so obviously using Christianity and the power of the Gallican state church to feather their ecclesial nests at the expense of the poor. Both sincere Christians and sincere secularists were, therefore, sincerely anti-clerical. But the anti-clerical animus of the Christians was bent on reform; they shared the same zeal as was found in the reforming popes of the eleventh century, whereas the anti-clerical animus of the Jacobins was aimed at the destruction of Christianity itself.

Much the same thing held true in the nineteenth century as well, when a renewed anti-clerical spirit swept in waves across Europe. This anti-clerical animus was expressed by orthodox Christians who cringed at the tepid religiosity of the various established state churches and at the tendency of the established church hierarchy, who were political appointees of the state, to shepherd the flock as the state demanded (rather than as good shepherds of Christ and his church). This anti-clerical animus was also expressed by Christian non-Conformists, generally Christians of the more liberal persuasion, who were barred from full participation in civil life because they were not members of the state's established church. This anti-clerical animus was even expressed by classical liberals who cringed at the increasingly tight bond between the state and one particular Christian confession or another, and wanted to go back to something like what Locke or Spinoza had imagined. And finally, this anti-clerical animus was expressed by radical liberals, who wanted Christianity entirely flushed out of the system and replaced by a purely secular worldview, with a new politics devoted to maximizing our happiness in this world.

Unfortunately for the Christians involved, these alliances, built upon shared goals and shared hatreds, were only momentary: the secularists were happy to use reform-minded Christians and then dispose of them when they were no longer needed. This familiar pattern in the nineteenth century, repeated in the twentieth, illustrates the insight that the enemy of my enemy is not necessarily my friend.

The existence, however temporary, of these alliances led to the confusion of Christianity with socialism. For some reformers, it also led to the zealous embrace of socialism as itself a religion, as the purified core of Christianity once one got rid of the dross of doctrine and other otherworldly distractions.

The new gospel—a message often preached by secularists in an attractive form—was that *the church was bad but Jesus was good*. Jesus was, after all, concerned with the poor and had snapped at the rich. He would have had no more truck with an elegant bishop or a state-supported preacher than he would with a Pharisee or Sadducee. This was a gospel that could be preached by the most radical of secularists, as in fact occurred in the case of the communist Rosa Luxemburg and the Social Democrat movement.[21]

For secular socialism to make any headway, it *had* to be preached this way. Otherwise the many Christian believers it was attempting to reach, and ultimately to convert, would have immediately recoiled from the radical secular core and re-embraced the church. But they didn't notice the wolf beneath the sheep's clothing, and so this secularism in the guise of liberalized Christianity was quite successful. The secularizing socialist Social Democrat movement in the latter half of the nineteenth century could boast many clergy within its fold, as well as many sincere lay believers tired of the hypocrisy of an established state church that merely served to buttress an economic order pressing down upon them with crushing weight.

The approach of the "moderate" socialist revolutionaries was Machiavellian: "Don't preach atheism to the masses. You'll only scare them off. Warmly affirm Jesus's concern for the poor, and the right of each party member to believe as he likes *privately*." Such was the position on religion laid out in the Gotha Program adopted in 1875 by the German Social Democratic Party at its party congress: religion is a man's private concern, as long as he supports the socialist goals of the Party.[22] Thus the most radical atheists could march together with the most dedicated Christian reformers, at least until the success of the secular socialist revolution made the Christian element in the alliance no longer necessary. Radical atheists who refused to mask their animosity for Christianity, such as Marx, became communists. But the more Machiavellian socialists taught that atheism must be kept in the closet—at least for the time being. The term "secular," interestingly enough, was invented in the mid-nineteenth century by the radical atheist George Holyoake, a follower of Auguste Comte. He thought it sounded less jarring, and far more neutral, than "atheist," a term that tended to spook the poor among whom he preached his gospel of social revolution.[23]

A religion of progress mouthing the moral verities of Christianity was born. It was, at its heart, Comte's Religion of Humanity, the religion of a socialist society guided by technocratic elites, manipulating those they were saving, to create a real, material heaven on earth.

Utopian Robert Owen (1771–1858) was the first person to use the term socialism.[24] His connection to more radical liberalism is obvious enough.

Owen was a devout secularist and looked upon all religions, Christianity especially, as sources of ruin. He didn't believe in the Fall of Man. But he didn't believe human beings were naturally good either. Instead, they were neither good nor evil, but molded entirely by forces outside themselves.

This doctrine fit perfectly into the materialism saturating Europe in the nineteenth century. Materialism assumes that all matter (including human matter) is essentially inert. Its more complex conglomerations are merely the result of external causes—so many billiard balls being hit by other billiard balls. Any particular arrangement of atoms is simply the result of the sum total of material actions and reactions occurring up to that point in time. Human beings are like billiard balls. An individual's current "nature," so to speak, is entirely the result of the history and environment—the material causes—impacting him. We are what has been done to us. People turn out "bad" only because the "wrong" material conditions have exerted the "wrong" material forces on them. Change the material conditions, and you may re-form the human material rationally and purposely (rather than as nature had, randomly and without purpose, or as badly designed society had, to the detriment of its members).

Liberal socialism as practiced by Owen in his various utopian communities, with its emphasis on social engineering and reconstruction and its exclusion of notions of the soul, free will, and sin, was very clearly grounded in the materialist worldview. Owen asserted in his famous essay "A New View of Society" (1813) that there was no real difference between a machine and a man, except that we take care of and improve our machines, and foolishly neglect the upkeep and re-engineering of men. "Experience has also shown you the difference of the results between mechanism which is neat, clean, well-arranged, and always in a high state of repair," explained Owen, "and that which is allowed to be dirty, in disorder, without the means of preventing unnecessary friction, and which therefore becomes, and works, much out of repair":

> In the first case the whole economy and management are good; every operation proceeds with ease, order, and success. In the

last, the reverse must follow, and a scene be presented of coun-
teraction, confusion, and dissatisfaction among all the agents
and instruments interested or occupied in the general process,
which cannot fail to create great loss.

If, then, due care as to the state of your inanimate machines
can produce such beneficial results, what may not be expected
if you devote equal attention to your vital machines, which are
far more wonderfully constructed?[25]

Letting loose a thought that would come into its own in twentieth-century
liberalism, Owen declared, "Here, then, is an object which truly deserves
your attention; and, instead of devoting all your faculties to invent improved
inanimate mechanism, let your thoughts be, at least in part, directed to
discover how to combine the more excellent materials of body and mind
which, by a well-devised experiment, will be found capable of *progressive
improvement*" [emphasis added].[26]

Owen's socialist utopian communities, including one in New Harmony,
Indiana, were experiments carried out upon their members. He imagined
that social engineering of the human machines under the community's care
would lead to the greatest amelioration of human misery—perhaps even
to its cure.

Although Owen himself was an unbeliever, he was astute enough to
understand the need to dress out socialism in Christian garb, likening his
new social doctrines to "the second coming of Christ" and promising that
socialism would usher in "the foretold millennium," but with Owen's own
Book of the New Moral World (1836–1844) taking the place of the Bible.[27]
Imagine singing the following inspiring hymn (or perhaps you don't need
to imagine it because you've recently heard something like it at your church):

Community! The joyful sound
That cheers the social band,
And spreads a holy zeal around
To dwell upon the land.[28]

There can be no doubt of Owen's sincerity in trying to lessen the horrible conditions of the working-class poor in Britain, and then in America. One also suspects that his use of Christian phrases and symbols was not exactly Machiavellian, but inspired by something like Comte's view that Christianity was not so much something that was wrong, but something that needed to be surpassed, with socialism carrying forward the gold purified of the dross of superstitious doctrine. Whatever his motives, Christians latched onto his schemes because they sounded familiar.

As the nineteenth century progressed, the fusion and confusion between secularism and reform-minded Christianity continued. Among the Chartists in Britain there was a deeply sincere anguish at the established Anglican church's alliance with the economic and social powers that were weighing down on the poor, and a deeply felt understanding that—contrary to the notion that the church should foster a merely private devotion, and leave this world to this-worldly powers—Jesus really did mean what he said when he commanded his believers to care directly for the poor and oppressed.

So we can see why Christian Chartists called for disestablishment of the church, even while their own meetings resembled church revivals. As with the great reformers of the Dark and Middle Ages, they knew that a worldly church was no church at all. Chartism faded soon after mid-nineteenth-century, but its influence flowed into the mainstream of socialism, including into self-avowedly secular socialist societies.

As Owen Chadwick wryly notes, these secular societies dotting the landscape in the nineteenth century looked and acted a whole lot like the churches they meant to displace:

> Though chapels and churches regarded them as enemies, their structure, outlook organization and philosophy resembled nothing so much as a loose structure of independent chapels. They ministered to much the same personal needs and to much the same social groups. They served the want of private

friendships, a moral cause, a common work for good and instincts of religion.

Indeed, the infamous atheist and evangelist for socialism Charles Bradlaugh (1833–1891) "always dressed so that he could be mistaken for a nonconformist minister, or even a Roman Catholic priest."[29]

Socialism was not just a political program, but a way of defining all of life. The extent of the ground that socialism was intended to cover was equal to the previous extent of Christendom. As Burleigh notes, "Socialist meetings followed a liturgy that unconsciously mimicked that of the Churches, with choral singing of alternative words to the tune of Christian hymns, together with cheers and toasts to socialism."[30] Turning our gaze from England to Germany, the Social Democrats adapted "for socialist purpose.... Protestant hymns, including most frequently the most famous and popular of them all, Luther's '*Ein Feste Burg*,'"—"A Mighty Fortress Is Our God," but without the "God" part.[31]

We must be clear about why socialism became a religion, and more particularly why it wrapped itself in Christian language and ritual and the Christian scheme of salvation, even while it more and more came to attack Christianity explicitly. Secularist socialism was in great part an outgrowth of de-supernaturalized Christianity. And its adherents believed that it could completely replace Christianity, filling every nook and cranny occupied by the church and Christian culture with an entirely this-worldly religion. "In the case of Socialists," McLeod points out, "rejection of older religious traditions was partly based on the conviction that Socialism contained within it all that was necessary for human salvation, and that anyone who retained older loyalties was trying to serve two masters, and must therefore be less than wholly loyal to the Socialist cause."[32]

So in France, following Comte's lead, "the 1880s French Freethinkers, including many socialists, were devising new rituals, designed to cut their members off from the old Catholic world." And in Germany, this tendency went even further with the creation, in the 1890s, of "an elaborate network of Social Democratic institutions and accompanying celebrations and rites...designed to embrace every area of the comrade's life."[33]

To recapitulate, the nineteenth century witnessed a struggle between the two kinds of liberalism, conservative and radical. On one side was classical or "conservative" liberalism, representing the capitalists or new industrialists, and beholden to Locke. Classical liberals were inclined to see the state religion as a support for the capitalist economic order or else to assume that a disestablished Christianity should support that order morally. In either case, the Christian religion was meant to control the unpropertied laboring masses. On the other side was radical liberalism, stemming from Rousseau. Radical liberals pushed for reform and wanted to do away with the Christianity that supported the haves against the have nots. Radical liberalism tended toward socialism. But to make matters even muddier, socialism also had its own brand of liberalized Christianity. Confusingly, both kinds of liberals claimed Christ, at least publicly; both sides preached a merely moral Christ unconcerned with doctrines and only vaguely concerned with the next world. For Lockean classical liberals, the merely moral Christ served to shore up the established order; for radical liberals, he was a moral revolutionary who challenged it. But how exactly did Jesus become merely a great moral teacher—whether of conventional or of revolutionary morality—rather than the Son of God?

How Jesus Was Demoted to a Great Moral Teacher: the Revolution in Scriptural Scholarship

From the earlier chapters above on the church's first centuries, we recall how important the Bible itself, as a source of divine authority, was for defining the church and its distinction from the state, or more properly, the political power. The church authorized the Bible, declaring what writings counted as Holy Scripture. And the authority of Holy Scripture in turn determined the orthodox boundaries of the church.

The Bible proclaimed that Jesus was divine, the incarnation of the God above nature, and that he came to draw members of the church to a supernatural, trans-historical kingdom, leaving behind the kingdoms of this world. All such kingdoms, whatever their merits, could not ultimately fix what was broken in humanity. Our happiness, our salvation awaited us on the other side of death. The church and political power were, therefore, distinct yet complementary, the church aiming at an eternal kingdom and the political power concerning itself with good order in this fallen world.

But again since the eternal kingdom dwarfed the temporal kingdom in its promise of both reward and punishment, and since the goods of the soul were more noble than those of the body, the church's authority overshadowed that of any merely this-worldly political kingdom.

From Machiavelli forward, liberalism tried every means to draw this world out of the shadow of the next. And that meant the Bible had to be dealt with—tamed, declawed, rendered submissive. That is why, from Machiavelli to the nineteenth century, liberalism had to bring Scripture itself under secular control.[34] We've already seen how Hobbes asserted that the political sovereign controlled both the canon and interpretation of the Bible. But even more influential was the liberalization of Scripture that started with Spinoza, the real father of modern scriptural scholarship.

Spinoza's aim, we recall, was to set up a method of approaching the study of scripture that systematically purged the Biblical text of miracles and reduced the theological or dogmatic content to harmless moral platitudes. The scholars that used this method, or one of its many variations, would act as scriptural "experts" in the middle of Spinoza's pyramid, dictating what the great mass of humanity at the bottom of the pyramid were allowed to take from the Bible—and more importantly, what they were not. The scripture scholars' approach was deemed "scientific," giving it the status it needed to prevail in a society that was increasingly offering scientists the kind of deferential respect once given to clergy.

By the nineteenth century, this secularizing approach to Scripture was deeply entrenched among the intelligentsia and had made great headway in European universities. The aim was "de-mythologizing," removing from the Biblical text (just as Spinoza had dictated) all of the miracles, and hence undermining all the doctrinal claims related to Christ's divinity, so that readers were left with, at best, Jesus the very admirable moral man who was misunderstood to be divine by his wishful disciples. Christianity—so the Scripture scholarship seemed to establish—was built upon a case of mistaken identity. But the moral core could be salvaged.

The "demythologizing" enterprise depended upon the scripture scholars' acceptance of a materialist worldview. Immaterial causes were ruled out of court and everything about the visible, material world was assumed to be ultimately reducible to the movements of inert matter and the laws that governed those movements. Thus the new scholars approached the text with a great winnowing fork, removing all that did not accord with the allegedly iron laws of nature.

While a Deist God was allowed a short stint as the master clockmaker of the material-mechanical world, it soon became obvious (it had already been to Hobbes) that no deity was needed. So as the eighteenth century gave way to the nineteenth, scripture scholars moved from Deism to atheism.

Typical of the adherents of the latter view—and certainly its most influential proponent among scripture scholars in the nineteenth century—was the German D. F. Strauss, a left-wing disciple of Hegel. In his most influential work, *The Life of Jesus Critically Examined*, Strauss declared that real history must be distinguished from mere unhistorical myth. A Biblical "account is not historical," and hence "the matter related could not have taken place in the manner described" if "the narration is irreconcilable with the known and universal laws which govern the course of events. Now according to these laws, agreeing with all just philosophical conceptions and all credible experience, the absolute cause never disturbs the chain of secondary causes by single arbitrary actions of interposition."[35] In short, all miracles reported in the Bible are false, from the miraculous creation of the world to the resurrection of Christ. "Scientific" scholarship must separate the mythological from the factual, and then see what was left of the Bible (if anything).

Strauss completed in the nineteenth century the long demotion of Jesus from God to mere man that had been actively pushed from the advent of Socinianism in the sixteenth century, and through the heyday of Deism in the seventeenth and eighteenth centuries. Jesus the merely moral man was no threat to political power. A merely moral man could not serve as the mystical head of the church, binding its members together in a supernatural union transcending temporal existence and stretching into eternity. The church, bereft of the belief in Christ's divinity, collapsed in a heap. Or, to put it less dramatically, the churches that drank deeply from the well of modern scripture scholarship became mere organizations of individuals dedicated to idiosyncratic personal spirituality, or else this-worldly social or political groups. The focus shifted decisively from God to ourselves and this world.

Strauss himself is a case in point, and a very important one, given the extraordinary influence Strauss's work had in the nineteenth and twentieth centuries. Having spent hundreds of pages dismantling the Gospel, Strauss ended his *Life of Jesus* by transferring the central doctrines that had previously been applied to Christ and our supernatural redemption, to human beings themselves, thereby divinizing this-worldly political "progress" with all the borrowed glory he had wrenched from Christianity. His encomium to humanity's self-salvation is remarkable enough to quote at length. The notion that God could become a man is, Strauss proclaimed, a contradiction. But, he asserted, one may speak of the divinization of the human race itself insofar as we, by progressively conquering nature—even human nature—through technological science become our own deified saviors and the creators of heaven on earth by conquering matter with our minds:

> Humanity is the union of two natures—God become man, the infinite manifesting itself in the finite, and the finite spirit remembering its infinitude; it is the child of the visible Mother

and the invisible Father, Nature and Spirit; it is the worker of miracles, in so far as in the course of human history the spirit more and more completely subjugates nature, both within and around man, until it lies before him as the inert matter on which he exercises his active power; it is the sinless existence, for the course of its development is a blameless one, pollution cleaves to the individual only, and does not touch the race or its history. It is Humanity that dies, rises, and ascends to heaven, for from the negation of its phenomenal life there ever proceeds a higher spiritual life; from the suppression of its mortality as a personal, national, and terrestrial spirit, arises its union with the infinite spirit of the heavens. By faith in this Christ, especially in his death and resurrection, man is justified before God; that is, by the kindling within him of the idea of Humanity, the individual man participates in the divinely human life of the species.[36]

We note Strauss's proclamation that humanity itself, marching forward in progress, does not—cannot—sin. Since we are now gods, or will be soon, we are "blameless," and since humanity's march forward takes place through the concentrated power of humanity wielded by the state, the state, in pursuing progress, cannot sin. No more dangerous idea is imaginable.

Meanwhile, what was the significance of the de-divinized person of Jesus himself? At best he could function as a kind of moral exemplar, a really good person. But what was now defined as "good" had to correspond to liberal progressive notions of goodness.

That brings us to our final area of confusion: What exactly is the content of the morality that the merely moral Jesus—the one stripped of his divinity—is supposed to teach?

The Moral Bait and Switch

To make a long story short—and it would be a very long story, worthy of a book—liberals originally pretended, sometimes even to themselves, that while they rejected the doctrines of Christianity, they retained the moral core. The pitch liberals made to Christians was something like this: "Don't worry. We're not dangerous. See!—we all hold the same morality, even if we cannot agree on the more abstruse, abstract doctrinal issues (and, neither can you Christians, by the way). So let's leave all the speculation aside, and agree to disagree about that, because the Good News is that we agree about morality. And isn't that all that really matters anyway? Wasn't Christ himself passionately concerned about our being good? Well, since we can agree on the importance of moral goodness, then there's nothing to worry about."

But ultimately, this peace offering was a bait and switch. Liberals baited Christians with a purportedly common morality and then, when the Christians were doctrinally disarmed, switched to full-bore liberalism, which has a radically different moral worldview—the one it now wants to impose by force on Christians.

It's not difficult to see why this happened. The materialism at the very heart of liberalism ultimately had to lead to a morality in which good was reduced to physical pleasure and evil to physical pain. That ultimately meant embracing hedonistic utilitarianism, a moral system that aims only at the greatest pleasure for the greatest number. This is in fact the ethical view that prevails in all liberal democracies and that forms the basis of both their frantic consumerism and their swelling welfare-statism. Maximizing the physical pleasures of the electorate and minimizing their pains becomes the great guiding vision of politics and liberal humanitarianism.

Hedonistic utilitarianism is entirely incompatible with Christianity's severe moral code rooted in the affirmation of the immortal soul as the fundamental locus of moral goodness. Thus any overlap between the ethic of hedonistic materialism and that of Christianity is spurious, and only hides the actual abyss which separates them.

For example, Jesus did in fact say that the rich were going to have more than a bit of trouble squeezing into heaven and that we'd be judged by our treatment of the poor, oppressed, hungry, naked, and incarcerated. And liberals embrace socialism and the welfare state because they are truly concerned with alleviating poverty, oppression, hunger, and so forth. But the apparent moral overlap is deceiving. The deception becomes clear when we see what else radical liberalism pushes as part of the humanitarian package: contraception, abortion, infanticide, sexual libertinism, homosexuality, easy divorce, homosexual marriage—in short, all the things that elevate sexual pleasure and remove any restrictions on or pains attendant upon that liberation. So liberal morality isn't just about feeding the poor; it's also about liberating them, spreading pleasure to the greatest number.

That the state is essential to the moral revolution unseating Christianity should be obvious. The courts and state-mandated education have been the main engines driving the replacement of Christian morality with the hedonistic utilitarianism of liberalism. The revolution has been imposed from above.

In overview, that is what has occurred in the West, especially in Europe over the course of the last two centuries. But there is one wrinkle we must note, so that we may clear up another potential confusion. While we find materialist hedonism in Hobbes and Locke, and of course in later liberals like Jeremy Bentham and the arch-liberal John Stuart Mill, there is also, we may recall, the appeal that Rousseau made to something like pagan Stoicism—the sturdy, manly virtue of the most noble of the pre-Christian pagan Romans.

Many of the Deists of the eighteenth century appealed to something like Stoicism as well, which they believed could serve as a common moral foundation of society. They asserted that there was a natural religion that could be held in common between believers and non-believers, one that had, in fact, predated Christianity, and formed in great part the Christian formulation of the natural moral law, rooted largely in Stoicism. The theory was that we could agree to disagree about Christian doctrine precisely because we could rely on this common, natural morality, rooted in something like a natural theology. After all, Jesus was very concerned with our being good in this world, whatever we may or may not believe about the next.

On this theory, "nature and nature's God" was enough of a foundation to allow us to live together in earthly peace, whatever we might happen to believe about Jesus privately. And this peace had some obvious merit. It seemed to allow Deists who had rejected Christ's divinity to share common ground with Christians who passionately affirmed it. If Christian morality was in fact built upon pagan formulations of the natural law, then why not agree on this pagan foundation, and agree to disagree about the Christian part?

But the new world, the endless world of materialism, the world as defined by the new science, ultimately undermined the natural law, both the Christian version and the Deist attempt to revive the Stoic version. Both Christian and Stoic morality require the soul because both focus on virtue. Materialism, in killing the soul, kills both.

Locke is, as we noted above, studiously and strangely ambiguous. He seems to speak at one and the same time as if he's a proponent of something like the Christian natural law tradition and as if he accepts the materialistic natural rights position set out by Hobbes. Locke seems to have a foot in each camp. He seems to belong with the Deists who looked back on pagan virtue with admiration, and also to the utilitarians who look forward to a hedonistic paradise.

But where Locke *really* stands, what foot he really puts his weight on, should be clear from the fact that he shifts the goal of government from virtue to the limitless accumulation of material goods. And it is now crystal clear where Lockean liberalism leads. Today all liberals, whether classical or radical, speak in terms of Hobbesian *natural rights*, not natural law.

And so liberal governments of the classical sort, in focusing primarily on economic production and consumption, end up creating a citizenry absorbed in the passionate pursuit of material gratification. Whatever the citizens may privately believe about the soul and its destiny, the pursuit of material gratifications "enervates" their souls, to borrow the famous language of Tocqueville. They do not so much rebel against Christianity as allow it to fade to a still, very small, and whispery voice. With their religion in this condition, it is easier for them to fall comfortably into the arms of the welfare state, which takes away their anxieties and efforts, and spreads out gentle pleasures with utilitarian equality. Why expend much individual effort in making your life in this world comfortable, when the state can do it for you?

That helps explain why, historically, the classical liberal regimes have ended in something very like socialism. Locke has yielded to Rousseau, and the family dispute within modern liberalism has ended, after much argument, with a kind of reconciliation that has established radical liberalism as the state worldview. That worldview is as comprehensive as the Christian worldview was in Christendom. It is the *de facto* religion of Western culture, defining its entire approach to politics and morality.

But we've been looking mostly at European thinkers and the effect of their ideas on European culture. America is a special case. And Locke is a big part of the American story. Now we turn to the question of how it was that liberalism came to our shores.

PART V

LIBERALISM
COMES TO AMERICA

CHAPTER 13

―――

THE FIRST WAVE: LOCKE, DEISM, AND THE FOUNDERS

Quite obviously, the first wave of liberalism did not hit our shores with the Pilgrims, whose notions of how to govern a society came almost directly from the Old and New Testament. Nor was the American Revolution merely another version of the French Revolution inspired by Rousseau, or the American Constitution a palimpsest of Spinoza's *Tractatus*. Liberalism had come to our shores by the time our Constitution was drafted and ratified, but it was a moderate brand of liberalism inspired largely by Locke, a "conservative" liberal, who, as we have seen, sometimes didn't look like a liberal at all.

If Locke is the most important liberal influence on the founders—and who can deny the impact of his writings on Jefferson and Madison?—then the first wave carried with it considerable ambiguity. To better understand the influence of liberalism on the founding generation, let's look at one of the most influential men at the time of our revolution, the Deist Thomas Paine, who even today is held in honor by many religious conservatives.

Paine at Our Founding

Thomas Paine (1737–1809), who was born in England but emigrated to America, was the author of one of the most stirring and widely read pamphlets in American history, *Common Sense* (1776), which made the case for a definitive break with Britain. But this same Thomas Paine also wrote the *Rights of Man* (1791), making the case for the French Revolution against its critics. Far more telling, Paine was the author of *The Age of Reason* (1793–1794) advocating Deism *against* Christianity. In it, he takes up the free-thinker's cane to beat institutionalized Christianity, Christian doctrine, and the Bible itself.

The Age of Reason, like *Common Sense*, was a bestseller in America, and it did much for the Deist cause on our shores, especially among our educated elite. Many accused him of atheism, but Paine was not an atheist. He believed in a creator God, as long as it was the Deist divine clockmaker. And so he could cheerfully affirm "nature and nature's God" even while giving Christianity a good public flogging. For the sake of human progress, Paine urged, we must advance to an "age of reason." That means being freed from Christianity, leaving the church and irrational superstitions behind. This was pretty standard fare from the trove of eighteenth-century European Enlightenment thought that would form the background of Comte's formulation of the three stages of history.

On the spectrum of liberal thought from Machiavelli to Rousseau, Paine is well to the left of Locke, but perhaps not quite as far in the radical direction as Spinoza and Rousseau—although the influence of Spinoza's *Tractatus* on Paine is undeniable. And no one can doubt the influence of Paine, any more than that of Locke, on Jefferson, Franklin, Madison, or any of a number of lesser luminaries at our founding.

Paine was in no way an original thinker, but merely a conduit for the more radical Enlightenment liberalism that had already been circulating in

Europe for some time. He was not the only Enlightenment thinker being avidly read in America at the end of the eighteenth century, but he was certainly one of the most influential.

The influence of Paine and other anti-Christian Enlightenment figures on America was soon muted, however, by a kind of religious counterattack in the form of the Second Great Awakening, a Protestant religious revival that began to pick up steam at the very end of the eighteenth century and helped define the religious temper of America in the first half of the nineteenth century. (The influence of the Second Awakening on American culture faded only with the second, far more radical wave of liberalism that reached our shores in the nineteenth century. We'll get to that in the next chapter.)

Jefferson and *Everson*

Jefferson was greatly influenced by both Locke and Paine. Recall the famous Supreme Court case *Everson v. Board of Education* (1947), which we looked at briefly in the very first chapter above. In that landmark case the Supreme Court decided two things, both with momentous consequences: (1) the First Amendment's Establishment Clause demanded the erection of "a wall of separation between church and State," and (2) the Establishment Clause could be applied by the federal government to the states through the Fourteenth Amendment (and, therefore, the federal government could use all its powers to enforce this separation).

We should note a very curious thing. The famous "wall of separation" phrase is not from the First Amendment. Justice Hugo Black, writing the Court's majority opinion in *Everson*, was the one who created the connection between that phrase and the First Amendment, asserting that "the clause against establishment of religion by law was intended to erect 'a wall of separation between church and State,'"[1] But the famous phrase itself actually comes from Thomas Jefferson's letter to the Danbury Baptist Association" on January 1, 1802.

Justice Black quite literally inserted Jefferson's views into the First Amendment—so effectively that, as Daniel Dreisbach, a historian of

American law, points out, "the Jeffersonian metaphor has eclipsed and supplanted [the] constitutional text in the minds of many jurists, scholars, and the American public." The result is that Jefferson's "architectural metaphor" of a wall of separation between church and state "has achieved virtual canonical status and become more familiar to the American people than the actual text of the First Amendment."[2]

It was only at mid-twentieth century, through this Supreme Court case, that Jefferson's views about the separation of church and state became so immensely influential, empowering the federal government to strip Christianity from our culture in a manner reminiscent of the secularizing that occurred in French culture with France's radical secularists' enactment of the French Law of Separation a half-century earlier.

It didn't have to turn out that way. Before *Everson* in 1947, Jefferson's famous phrase "a wall of separation between church and state" was all but unheard of in jurisprudence (the exception was *Reynolds v. United States*, an 1878 case.[3] Again, the First Amendment says nothing about a wall, or separation, and it does not mention either church or state. Literally all it says on the subject of religion is that "Congress shall make no law respecting an establishment of religion, or prohibiting the free exercise thereof."[4]

We've seen how Jefferson's views on church and state became so influential, but just what were they? Unsurprisingly, his thoughts on the subject were much like those of Thomas Paine, moderated by deep reflection on John Locke.

As is well known—I've seen it myself—Jefferson had a bust of Locke at Monticello, and fully admitted his influence. (He also had the works of Spinoza in his library, but we don't know whether he read them.) Because Locke seemed so moderate, spoke so warmly of Christianity, and wrote such popular Biblical commentaries, deep appreciation of Locke in the late eighteenth century was not definitive evidence of secular liberalism. But like Locke, Jefferson was not a Christian, but an Enlightenment Deist.

Jefferson, the Moderate Deist

The moderate Deists of the Enlightenment worshipped "nature's God." As we've seen, they considered Deism to be "natural religion"—the set of religious beliefs we can arrive at through reason alone (not revelation), the religion that nature itself supports. Deists thought the notion of supernatural or revealed religion to be essentially irrational and divisive. In fact, revealed religions were divisive *because* they were essentially irrational.

Whatever valuable role revealed religion had played in the past could be far better filled in the future by a religion of reason. Thus Deists hoped that the hold Christianity had on society would, as a matter of historical progress, yield to natural reason and natural religion.

Whereas the radical Enlightenment was quite often hostile to Jesus—the infamous and influential *Treatise of the Three Impostors*, declaring Moses, Jesus, and Mohammed to be impostors, was written in Spinoza's intellectual circle, published in 1719, and circulated widely in Europe—moderate Deists tended to view Christianity as a religion of corrupted priests and superstition, but asserted that Jesus himself was an excellent human being, a moral exemplar. He was not divine, but he was a great, if not the greatest, moral teacher.

Deism therefore rejects the doctrine of the Trinity, and hence Christianity, even while admiring its alleged moral message. That seems to have been Jefferson's position from very early on, as early as 1776.[5] It is quite evident in the now famous *Jefferson Bible* from later in the great man's life. Jefferson simply cut out—literally cut out, with a razor—all the parts of the Bible that didn't fit his belief that Jesus was a great but very merely human moral teacher. He titled what was left *The Life and Morals of Jesus of Nazareth*.[6] Death ends this life, as it does in any biography; resurrection has been cut out of the story, along with all other miracles that violate the laws of nature.

Estimating the Merits of Jesus

In 1803 Jefferson also wrote what he called a "Syllabus of an Estimate of the Merit of the Doctrines of Jesus, Compared with Those of Others"

(April 21, 1803). He sent it first of all to Dr. Benjamin Rush, noting that he had promised to give Rush his "views" of the Christian religion:

> They are the result of a life of inquiry & reflection, and very different from that Anti-Christian system imputed to me by those who know nothing of my opinions. To the corruptions of Christianity I am indeed opposed; but not to the genuine precepts of Jesus himself. I am a Christian, in the only sense he [i.e., Jesus] wished any one to be; sincerely attached to his doctrines, in preference to all others; *ascribing to himself every human excellence; & believing he never claimed any other.*[7] [emphasis added]

In Jefferson's "Syllabus" we find that Jesus is indeed the greatest moral teacher—though merely a human teacher—going beyond all the ancient philosophers and also beyond the Jews. The best of the pagan philosophers (Pythagoras, Socrates, Epicurus, Cicero, Epictetus, and Seneca) "were really great," but defective insofar as they were focused more on individual virtue than on duty to others or benevolence to "the whole family of mankind," a defect Jesus would remedy.[8] The Jews fell short as well. Their religious "system was Deism; that is, the belief of one only God." While their Deism was correct, the Jews' religion was defective because their ideas of God "& of his attributes were degrading & injurious." Furthermore, "Their Ethics were not only imperfect, but often irreconcilable with the sound dictates of reason & morality...."[9] Jesus was a moral advance over both the Jews and the Greeks. His main aim was to purify Jewish Deism. He did not come to proclaim his own divinity as part of the Holy Trinity—the foundational claim of Christianity.

How came the mix-up, then, the one that resulted in Christianity? Like Socrates, Jesus didn't write anything. So, Jefferson maintained, "the committing to writing [of] his life & doctrines fell on the most unlettered & ignorant men; who wrote, too, from memory, & not till long after the transactions had passed."[10] These "unlettered & ignorant" men are otherwise known as Matthew, Mark, Luke, and John.

Thus "the doctrines which [Jesus] really delivered were defective as a whole, and fragments only of what he did deliver have come to us mutilated, misstated, & often unintelligible." Yet, given all these "disadvantages," a "system of morals is presented to us, which, if filled up in the true style and spirit of the rich fragments he left us, would be the most perfect and sublime that has ever been taught by man."[11]

Would be. Even Jesus could stand improvement, Jefferson implies. Interestingly, and condescendingly, Jefferson notes that Jesus's life was cut short "at about 33 years of age, his reason having not yet attained the maximum of its energy...." Given the short length of his ministry, he didn't have sufficient "occasions for developing a complete system of morals."[12] Mankind's reason has had much time to develop since then, and so a more complete system can now be constructed by those whose reason—in the Age of Reason—has attained maximum energy.

Jesus' moral system can be surpassed by the more Enlightened precisely because he was just a man. On his being mortal, Jefferson was quite clear, at least in private. As Jefferson explained to Dr. Rush, in regard to the "question of his being a member of the god-head, or in direct communication with it, claimed for him by some of his followers, and denied by others, [that] is foreign to the present view...."[13] That is, to Jefferson's own view, a view he still held in 1820, noting in another private letter, "That Jesus did not mean to impose himself on mankind as the son of god physically speaking I have been convinced by the writings of men more learned than myself in that lore."[14]

The Need to Separate the Church from the State

From what Jefferson maintains about the Bible, it is not a stretch to infer that Jefferson was against an established church because all Christian churches are based on Biblical revelation and on doctrines derived from faith in the divinity of Jesus Christ. Jefferson thought these doctrines were without rational foundation. Christians' fundamental error was taking the Bible to be revealed by God when in fact it was cobbled together by those "most unlettered & ignorant men" who wrongly believed Jesus to be God. (But, as we shall see, that does not preclude a rational *Deist* foundation for government.)

Nor is it difficult to tease out how Jefferson's beliefs (or lack of them) informed his support for separation of the Christian churches from the state. From Jefferson's point of view, the attempt to build religion on the Bible—a defective foundation—must necessarily end in conflicts among a multitude of equally irrational churches, each of which spins off all sorts of doctrines based upon the erroneous assumption of Christ's divinity. Irrational conflict must not be allowed to undermine civil peace. Therefore all churches must be separated from the political power of the state by a wall, the same one that divides the irrational from the rational, and revealed religion from a natural Deist religion based upon reason.

In another private letter, Jefferson hints that promoting a diversity of sects through religious freedom—that is, promoting maximum Christian disunity—actually benefits the state. As he wrote to Jacob de la Motta in 1820, "religious freedom is the most effectual anodyne against religious dissention: the maxim of civil government being reversed in that of religion, where its true form is 'divided we stand, united, we fall.'"[15] The best, most stable situation is state and churches, for then no one church can gain enough power to cast its influence over the government, and each church is willing to accept a secular government in order to keep other churches from gaining control.

James Madison's warnings in the *Federalist Papers* about the dangers of factions sound a similar note. The question was not what denomination of Christianity was true, but how to prevent any one "faction" of Christianity from gaining control. The remedy, as with all factions, was to divide and conquer—split them up so as to make each smaller and weaker. So, reasons Madison, "a religious sect may degenerate into a political faction in a part of the confederacy; but the variety of sects dispersed over the entire face of it, must secure the national councils against any danger from that source...."[16] From a certain angle, the value of promoting religious liberty—the right to believe as one wills—is that it is the surest means of creating the maximum disunity among churches and therefore the maximum freedom for the secular state from any interference from Christianity.

The Civil Religion of Deism

But "secular" isn't quite the right word, at least in regard to Jefferson. Jefferson was not looking for an atheistic government, for he wasn't an atheist himself. Jefferson can speak about the Creator, about nature and nature's God, and even about the sublimity of Jesus' moral teaching, and mean what he says. That doesn't mean that he was a Christian or that he had any desire to set up a Christian nation. As he revealed in a private letter to John Adams, Jefferson believed that our history must move beyond Christianity:

> And the day will come when the mystical generation of Jesus, by the Supreme Being as His Father, in the womb of a virgin, will be classed with the fable of the generation of Minerva in the brain of Jupiter. But may we hope that the dawn of reason, and freedom of thought in these United States, will do away with this artificial scaffolding, and restore to us the primitive and genuine doctrines of this most venerated Reformer of human errors.[17]

Jesus, the moral teacher, the sublime Deist, yes; Christianity, no.

With all due respect, we can say that Jefferson was not above using the conflicts between rival Christian sects to achieve his true goals—the removal of the doctrinal influence of Christianity as a revealed religion, and its eventual replacement by a Deistic natural religion functioning as a civil religion.

This Deistic civil religion could look very much like Christianity, including notions of an afterlife. Even the radical Rousseau, who explicitly rejected

Christianity, incorporated the afterlife among the dogmas of his civil religion, not because he himself believed in it, but because it was necessary to control the masses even in a civil religion. As Rousseau explains in his *Social Contract*:

> The dogmas of the civil religion ought to be simple, few in number, stated with precision, without explanations or commentaries. The existence of a powerful, intelligent, beneficent, foresighted, and providential divinity; the afterlife; the happiness of the just; the punishment of the wicked; the sanctity of the social contract and the laws. These are the positive dogmas. As for the negative ones, I limit them to a single one: intolerance. It belongs with the cults we have excluded.[18]

And for less radical Deism, too, civil religion was also a good thing, and it did have its dogmas, including that great negative dogma, Thou shalt be tolerant. For Rousseau civil religion meant the exclusion of Christianity, period. For Jefferson, it meant the removal of the Christian churches from access to state power, which amounted to excluding them by privatization rather than by banishment.

Separation as Strategy

But given the diversity of Christian sects, separation of church and state could be put forward as in the best interests of Christians themselves. So, in Virginia, Jefferson could stir up fear among the Baptists (and other religious minorities) that the Anglican Church could be (re-) established as the state church of Virginia, and that that would lead to the same kind of religious persecution experienced by Anabaptists and Puritans in sixteenth- and seventeenth-century England.

The ultimate goal, it would seem, was to get the various Christian denominations to accept a secular (seemingly neutral) government, a state in which Christian doctrine played no part, but in which Christians were free to worship as long as they didn't disturb the peace.

The state could affirm the uncontested ground, the moral fundamentals that were left over when the doctrine was subtracted. Thus natural Deism could become the state civil religion by simple subtraction of supernatural Trinitarian doctrines.

Separation as Shield

Moreover—and this was no small concern, given the real, public animosity of those who suspected Jefferson of atheism at the time—a secular state protected Deists themselves from persecution.

As Jefferson himself pointed out in his *Notes on the State of Virginia*, in the Virginia "act of assembly of 1705…a person brought up in the Christian religion [who] denies the being of a God, or the Trinity…or the scriptures to be of divine authority…is punishable on the first offence by incapacity to hold any office or employment ecclesiastical, civil, or military; on the second by…three years imprisonment, without bail."[19] But progress had been made since then, reflected Jefferson, "I doubt whether the people of this country would [now] suffer an execution for heresy, or a three years imprisonment for not comprehending the mysteries of the Trinity."[20]

Jefferson was not being irreligious here. Deism is a religion. And Jefferson believed it to be the only rational one, the religion ideally capable of functioning as a kind of civil religion.

So, Jefferson seems genuinely to have been a Deist, not an atheist—though it must be admitted that he did not always make his own motives clear, and he was suspected during his lifetime of being a secret atheist and devotee of the radical Enlightenment. Now and then he did let a more radical streak show; Jefferson can even seem to be faintly reminiscent of Spinoza. As we recall, Spinozan atheists often argued that the state shouldn't care anything about what any citizens did or did not believe, as long as they were moral. Spinoza himself was put forward by his disciples as the perfect example, an upright citizen and an atheist, an atheist much more moral than a lot of Christians. The lesson: if an atheist can be more moral than most Christians, then atheists should not be persecuted for their private beliefs.

That, I submit, is what was behind Jefferson's infamous quip: "The legitimate powers of government extend to such acts only as are injurious to others. But it does me no injury for my neighbor to say there are twenty gods, or no god. It neither picks my pocket nor breaks my leg."[21] But generally Jefferson spoke in such a way that his Deism sounded genuine, and very close to Christianity, as for example in his Inaugural Addresses.[22]

In his First Inaugural, for example, Jefferson espoused a more moderate form of Enlightenment thought, speaking of the United States as "enlightened by a benign religion, professed, indeed, and practiced in various forms, yet all of them inculcating honesty, truth, temperance, gratitude, and the love of man; acknowledging and adoring an overruling Providence, which by all its dispensations proves that it delights in the happiness of man here and his greater happiness hereafter...." These are the tenets that Deism shared with revealed religions. Deists believed that revealed religions such as Christianity had truth in them insofar as they were in conformity to Deism. And so Jefferson ended his First Inaugural with a typical Enlightenment flourish: "And may that Infinite Power which rules the destinies of the universe lead our councils to what is best, and give them a favorable issue for your peace and prosperity."

Jefferson ended his Second Inaugural Address with a prayer that seems to imply his reverence for, even his acceptance of, the Bible:

> I shall need, too, the favor of that Being in whose hands we are, who led our fathers, as Israel of old, from their native land and planted them in a country flowing with all the necessaries and comforts of life; who has covered our infancy with His providence and our riper years with His wisdom and power, and to

whose goodness I ask you to join in supplications with me that
He will so enlighten the minds of your servants, guide their
councils, and prosper their measures that whatsoever they do
shall result in your good, and shall secure to you the peace,
friendship, and approbation of all nations.

Yet even this passage can be read in a Deist sense. Revealed religion represents the youth of humankind; we progress from needing to be taught moral truths and general truths about God through the Bible in a confused way to understanding them clearly by reason alone.

Deism, the *de Facto* Established Religion

Jefferson, therefore, did affirm a place for the Deist God in public affairs. It was Bible-based Christianity, not Deism, that Jefferson wanted to wall off from the state. After all, according to Deism, natural reason confirms the natural religion of Deism, and natural reason, natural religion, and natural morality provide the true foundation of the state, so that Deistic natural religion can and should function as the civil religion. Jefferson had therefore found it entirely appropriate to ground the Declaration of Independence in "the Laws of Nature and Nature's God." But the various Christian churches, being essentially irrational because they are based on confused notions from the Bible, could only bring chaos into public life if they were in any way sanctioned or aided by the power of the state. Therefore the Christian churches had to be separated off by a wall.

So we have Jefferson's famous words from his letter to the Danbury Baptist Association: "I contemplate with sovereign reverence that act of the whole American people which declared that their legislature should 'make no law respecting an establishment of religion, or prohibiting the free exercise thereof,' thus building a wall of separation between Church & State."[23] But here Jefferson is reading his own unique views, which we've explored at length above, into the First Amendment.

As we have seen, Jefferson's words were what Justice Black quoted in *Everson v. Board of Education*, thereby fusing the First Amendment (which says nothing about separation, church and state, or building walls) with Jefferson's views. *Everson* thus became the landmark case used for disestablishing Christianity from our culture. But liberalism in America had changed in the century and a half since Jefferson. So the religion that was established in Christianity's place was not the moderate Deism of Jefferson, but radical liberalism.

To understand why it was radical liberalism rather than Deism that replaced Christianity as the new foundation for American culture, we'll need to take a look at the second wave of liberalism to hit our shores, which is the subject of the next chapter. But first we need to see what exactly in the first, moderate wave of liberalism in the eighteenth century made America especially susceptible to the next, radical wave of liberalism in the nineteenth century.

How the First Wave Prepared for the Second

That second wave, as I mentioned above, hit America in the last quarter of the nineteenth century. It involved the import of the most radical Enlightenment (and even post-Enlightenment) thought from European universities. But it didn't find America unprepared. Moderate liberalism, which had been warmly embraced by Jefferson and so many other prominent American intellectuals, had readied Americans for the radical rejection of Christianity.

This preparation had taken the form of a kind of undercurrent running beneath the surface of nineteenth-century American life, as the Second Great Awakening had fairly successfully submerged the Deism that had exercised such an influence among so many prominent Americans at the end of the eighteenth century. After the Second Great Awakening, Evangelical Protestantism came to dominate American culture, and Deism receded into a religion practiced in the private chapels of New England Unitarians.

Deism receded, but it remained as a strong undercurrent, its proponents generally preferring to keep quiet rather than challenge Protestant cultural hegemony directly. While no particular Protestant denomination could assert public control of the national culture—there were too many different churches, and significant doctrinal disagreements existed among them—Bible-based Protestantism defined American culture for the first three-quarters of the nineteenth century.

That included defining American education, even college education. Colleges in early nineteenth-century America were not hotbeds of radicalism. They were almost entirely denomination-based intellectual supports for a Protestant American culture. With a few exceptions—Jefferson's University of Virginia was founded as an explicitly secular institution—American colleges existed for the training of the Christian mind, especially the minds of the pastors who were understood to be the intellectual leaders of Christian culture.

America appeared to be an unambiguously Christian nation, but in reality there existed considerable ambiguity in the situation. Moderate Deism had not been eliminated, but suppressed. And suppressed dissidents often become more radical as they await liberation. So—to take a bit of historical license to make a point—America had a kind of Jacobin class bubbling away underneath its Protestant surface, plotting its own version of a radical cultural revolution.

Locke's America

America was also vulnerable to radical liberalism for another reason. Evangelical Protestantism and the American character itself had fused, more or less happily, with elements of Locke's liberal philosophy. Locke, as we recall, was a studiously ambiguous figure in the history of liberal thought, with one foot in the moderate and the other in the radical camp. Locke's ambiguity made his liberalism more palatable to Americans and at the same time made Lockeanism a kind of gateway drug to radical liberalism.

American readers found Locke, unlike Paine, speaking of the Bible in approving terms, affirming the need for Christianity as a moral foundation for society, and inserting references to the natural law and its divine source in his arguments. Locke's extensive Biblical commentaries were widely read in America, and had a gentle but pervasive and deep liberalizing effect on American Christianity.[24]

Yet, as we've seen, this same gentle and seemingly innocuous Locke had one foot very firmly planted in Hobbes's account of secular natural rights grounded in the decidedly anti-Biblical "state of nature." Locke had set out a purely secular, this-worldly political philosophy. He had rejected any but an economic aim for politics and embraced a secular state unconcerned with the virtue of the soul, or its eternal fate.

Locke's radicalism was largely overlooked by Americans. His Biblical posturing made his philosophy seem, well, all very Biblical, or at least not anti-Biblical. By comparison with many Enlightenment skeptics, Locke seemed downright pious.

But that wasn't the only reason Locke, the moderate liberal, was attractive to Americans. Americans embraced Locke because the conditions in America matched up so neatly with Locke's account of the state of nature and the origins of society and even more with the economic emphasis of American political life.

Just like Locke's state of nature, America was largely undeveloped "waste"[25] that Americans had to overcome by their very hard labor just to provide the necessities of food, clothing, and shelter. Just as in Locke's account of labor as the key factor creating private ownership, this common land (or Indian land) was turned into private property largely by that hard labor—the man who worked the soil and made it productive could claim it as his own.[26] Just as in Locke, individuals joined together in political-civil unions, expecting the laws to protect them and their property.[27] Property was the most important condition of participation in political life at our country's founding and for much of the first half of the nineteenth century. If there would be no taxation without representation, there would also be no representation of those whose material possessions were too meager to tax.

Having to spend so much energy in creating a civilization quite literally from scratch, building up its material foundations bit by laborious bit, Americans tended to define themselves in economic terms, thereby inviting into American culture a kind of "virtuous materialism," to crib from Alexis de Tocqueville.

Americans did not become materialists because they rejected the soul, as the European intelligentsia had, but because they focused so assiduously on providing for the needs of the body.

To understand American materialism and its effects, let's turn to Alexis de Tocqueville, that most insightful analyst of early nineteenth century American culture, whose *Democracy in America* is still the single most profound, accurate, and enlightening portrait of our American character.

The Passion for Material Well-Being and the Eclipse of the Soul

From the very beginning, Americans were drawn almost exclusively from Europe's middle and lower classes. Landed nobles cannot take their land with them, and the land Americans found waiting for them was almost entirely undeveloped. At first the main focus for those taming the land was survival, and building up the basics of an economy.

Since America was a land of opportunity, and no entrenched noble class stood in the way of men's efforts to better themselves, Americans were extremely industrious, always working their way up the ladder, always seeking to better their material conditions. Thus Tocqueville found Americans animated by "the passion for material well-being." As a result of this passion, "The care of satisfying the least needs of the body and of providing the smallest comforts of life preoccupies minds universally" in America, he reported. The "Love of [material] well-being has become the national and dominant taste; the great current of human passions bears from this direction; it carried everything along in its course."[28]

The preoccupation with providing for our material necessities and enjoying the material comforts and conveniences of this life has a very dangerous effect on us, Tocqueville warns. We all too easily become *de facto* materialists:

> Materialism is a dangerous malady of the human mind in all nations; but one must dread it particularly in a democratic people because it combines marvelously with the most familiar vice of the heart in these people.
>
> Democracy favors the taste for material enjoyments. This taste, if it becomes excessive, soon disposes men to believe that all is nothing but matter; and materialism in its turn serves to carry them toward those enjoyments with an insane ardor. Such is the fatal circle into which democratic nations are propelled. It is good for them to see the peril and restrain themselves.[29]

This isn't radical materialism based upon an explicit and thoroughly reasoned philosophical account of the cosmos that reduces everything to mere matter in motion, such as is found at the core of European liberalism from Machiavelli and Hobbes to Spinoza and Rousseau. The soul is not rejected, but rather just fades from view. Higher, ennobling, spiritual realities are not reduced to ignoble material causes, but instead gather dust from neglect. Americans are consumed by consuming small pleasures:

> adding a few toises [a toise was about forty square feet] to one's fields, planting an orchard, enlarging a residence, making life easier and more comfortable at each instant, preventing inconvenience, and satisfying the least needs without effort and almost without cost. These objects are small, but the [American] soul clings to them: it considers them every day and from very close; in the end they hide the rest of the world from it, and they sometimes come to place themselves between it and God.[30]

Virtue was not rejected, but downgraded to serving the pursuit of physical well-being. American materialists did not scorn Christianity as incompatible with this-worldly material happiness, as Machiavelli and other like-minded liberals had. Instead, Christianity was made into something entirely compatible with pursuing the most comfortable material happiness in this world.

This aspect of Tocqueville's assessment of our democracy is well worth quoting at length. He explains, "The particular taste that men of democratic centuries conceive for material enjoyments is not naturally opposed to order," as the radicalism of the French Revolution proved to be, because this taste "often needs order to be satisfied. Nor is it the enemy of regular mores [morals and manners]; for good mores are useful to public tranquility and favor industry. Often, indeed, it comes to be combined with a sort of religious morality; one wishes to be the best possible in this world without renouncing one's chances in the other." One can have one's this-worldly cake and eat it in eternity as well. The tension between this world and the next dissolves.

That doesn't mean that nineteenth-century Americans were notorious debauchees. "Among material goods," continues Tocqueville, "there are some whose possession is criminal; one takes care to abstain from them. There are others the use of which is permitted by religion and morality; to these one's heart, one's imagination, one's life are delivered without reserve." But, as Tocqueville warns, "in striving to seize them, one loses sight of the more precious goods that make the glory and greatness of the human species."

"What I reproach equality for," explains Tocqueville, "is not that it carries men away in the pursuit of forbidden enjoyments; it is for absorbing them entirely in the search for permitted enjoyments." Uttering a kind of prophecy about democracy in general and America in particular, Tocqueville remarks that "there could well be established in the world a sort of honest materialism that does not corrupt souls, but softens them and in the end quietly loosens all their tensions," or as another translation memorably puts it, "a kind of virtuous materialism…which would not corrupt, but enervate the soul and noiselessly unbend its springs of action."[31]

The Key to American Liberalism

This uniquely American brand of materialism made Americans particularly susceptible to Locke's apparently moderate liberalism. Locke didn't attack the soul or Christianity directly as the more radical liberals did. But he focused exclusively on physical self-preservation and liberated the human passion for accumulating wealth from moral and religious restrictions. By this strategy Locke achieved the same ultimate aim as the more radical materialists, only using far gentler means. The Lockean moderate liberal revolution made men materialists by absorbing their interests entirely in the worldly pursuit of material things. Eventually, men would be creatures entirely formed by material considerations, producers and consumers who had no time for the soul and no desire for heaven except the one that could be produced on earth. At that point, the political order would be freed from Christianity. Arguments would be unnecessary.

Unfortunately Tocqueville found Americans to be very inclined to follow Locke, both in theory and in practice, and hence already well on our way to allowing the soul and heaven to fade away. Christianity was often quite fervent in America, but it was subtly reconstructed to be compatible with passionately this-worldly material pursuits. It was not a Christianity that could produce martyrs or even severe judges of the fallen secular order. It was not the Christianity that had originally insisted on the sharp distinction between religious and political power, the next world and this one, heaven and earth.

As the nineteenth century wore on and the engines of industrialization gained steam, Americans became ever more prepared, consciously or unconsciously, for the more radical liberal materialist ideas that would crash upon our shores in the second great wave of liberalism in the last quarter of the century. To that wave we now turn.

CHAPTER 14

THE SECOND WAVE: RADICALS AT THE UNIVERSITIES

W e are used to seeing the 1960s as the great era of radicalization at American universities, the watershed time when radical students rebelled against their conservative teachers, a tie-dye revolution by long-haired *sans culottes* against the staid coat-and-tie university professors. Then, so the story goes, these student radicals became professors themselves, and so began the reign of "tenured radicals" at our nation's universities in the latter half of the twentieth century.

This popular portrait of the revolution is off by a century. If we want to find the real origins of the campus radicalism in America, we must go back to the 1860s, and even beyond.

Here's the simple story. In the first half of the nineteenth century, almost all American colleges were denominational Protestant institutions, headed or controlled by Protestant clergy. What America lacked were graduate schools, that is, universities that could grant advanced degrees. An American student wishing to earn a Ph.D. had to travel to Europe, whose universities had been granting master's and doctoral degrees since their origins in the Middle Ages.

The favored destination was Germany, because Germany's universities were the most renowned in Europe. As historian George Marsden notes, "Americans stood in awe of the German universities. Eighteenth-century Germany universities had taken the lead on the European continent and, especially after the establishment of the University of Berlin by Prussia in 1810, had moved to world preeminence."[1] By the nineteenth century German scholarship defined scholarship. Thoroughness and rigor made the German university *the* academic model—in structure, in underlying assumptions, and in intellectual substance. Unfortunately, that intellectual substance was liberal—permeated with extreme liberalism of the latest, most radical kind.

That's what those innocents abroad—the American doctoral students who studied in Europe in the nineteenth century—got for their money. They may have packed their Bibles when they left our shores. But they came back packed with Spinoza, Rousseau, Darwin, Huxley, Comte, Herbert Spencer, D. F. Strauss, and Marx.

How many students were involved, and how early did this process begin?

Prior to 1850, about a quarter of the students going overseas "studied with the Protestant theological faculties of the leading German universities,"[2] where they would have imbibed the very latest in German historical-critical scholarship, studying something along the lines of D. F. Strauss's reduction of the Bible to a set of myths and moral platitudes. By the end of the Civil War, "the advanced German theological views" had become "commonplace in American education circles.,.,"[3]

The first attempt at creating a German-style university in America occurred at the University of Michigan under the chancellorship of Henry Tappen (1852–1863). Tappen was fired for his liberal views, but one of his protégés, Andrew Dickson White, went on to found Cornell University.

Money to found Cornell in Ithaca, New York, in 1865 came from one Ezra Cornell, a rich Unitarian who had nothing but scorn for Protestant sectarianism. Like Jefferson, he believed that all the doctrinal squabbles among Christians were based upon the false assumption that the Bible was revealed and Jesus was divine. Cornell was all for casting away "the dead and putrid carcass of 'the Church,'" believing firmly that technology could replace it. "The steam engine, the railroad and the electric telegraph [Cornell was the founder of Western Union] are the great engines of reformation, and by the time we enter upon the twentieth century the present will be looked back to as we now look back to the dark ages." In a Comtean flourish, Cornell proclaimed "A new era in religion and humanity will have arrived."[4]

Andrew White's views about Christianity were similar. He was a great admirer of Jefferson. And White, like Cornell, was strongly dyed with the secular liberal view that science was inevitably displacing theology. His strategy as Cornell's first president was to publicly affirm a kind of general morally defined Christianity, but vehemently oppose any sectarian views—that is, any form of Christianity that extended beyond the moral principles everyone could agree on. White is famous not just for founding Cornell as America's first university explicitly based on the German model, but even more for penning the Comtean *A History of the Warfare of Science with Theology in Christendom*, published in its final form in 1896. As the title makes crystal clear, White saw theology as entirely opposed to the advance of science. By theology White meant Bible-based Christian theology, and by science he meant materialist science. That secular salvation history was precisely what White taught as a member of Cornell's history faculty.

Beginning with Cornell, many explicitly secular universities were created, in large part—and here is an interesting connection between Locke and the more radical liberals—with the money of the great capitalist tycoons: Johns Hopkins at Johns Hopkins University (1876), Leland Stanford at Stanford University (1891), John D. Rockefeller at the University of

Chicago (1890), Cornelius Vanderbilt at Vanderbilt University (1873). These schools either were explicitly secular from the beginning or soon shed their denominational loyalties. And older colleges began to fall into line with the secularizing trend as well. Harvard, taken over by New England Unitarians at the very beginning of the 1800s, was completely at home with the infusion of liberalism into American higher education.

So it was that major universities in the U.S. were increasingly defined by the German model and German standards, whatever their origins or the intentions of their founders. And as more German-educated Ph.D.s entered American institutions of higher learning as professors in the latter half of the 1800s and the early 1900s, scholars no longer had to travel to Europe to receive instruction in the radical Enlightenment.

Establishing the Liberal Secular Revolution, from the Top Down

Meanwhile, American higher education was growing by leaps and bounds. The number of university professors in America grew from something over 5,500 in 1870 to almost 24,000 in 1900, and to over 82,000 in 1930. In 1870 there were about 52,000 students in American colleges and universities; in 1890, about 157,000; in 1900, over 284,000; and by 1930, over 1,178,000.[5]

By 1870 the liberal intellectual makeover of American higher education had passed the tipping point. Secular liberalism was firmly entrenched in the universities by 1930. Thus the scene was set for a top-down, liberal intellectual-cultural makeover of American society. As sociologist Christian Smith explains, "the number of Americans who were being exposed to Europe's secular Enlightenment ideology through higher education and going into knowledge-elite professions was reaching a critical mass and forming into self-conscious communities."[6]

The numbers of Americans attending colleges and universities jumped with inflows of federal funds under FDR in the 1930s, again with the G. I. Bill for veterans of World War II, and most dramatically with Lyndon

Johnson's Higher Education Act of 1964 providing our current federally funded student loan and grant program. As a consequence, the number of students leapt from one million in 1930 to over fifteen million by the end of the twentieth century. Millions of students in every discipline from theology and biblical studies, philosophy, political science, literature, and history, to law, sociology, psychology, and any of a number of sub-disciplines were formed intellectually by European-born radical liberalism of one kind or another. So liberalism came to dominate the upper levels of society.

That's how our universities became the citadels of the liberal revolution that they still are—and how liberals come to associate being educated with being liberal. Even "conservative" reactions in academia are, with notable exceptions, only calls for a return to moderate liberalism—to Locke against Spinoza, Rousseau, and their even more radical progeny.

The radical liberal revolution at the top intellectual echelons began a century before the 1960s. The bursting forth of Spinoza's and Rousseau's radical children in the 1960s was a change in scale, not substance. The enormous leap in numbers attending colleges and universities caused by the massive federal funding injected into the system allowed for liberalism to become a mass movement. But this movement was led by the elite that was already well established in our universities. With the enormous influx of dollars, radical liberalism was democratized, preached to the masses flowing through these universities and out into the wider culture. Radical liberalism was thereby established in our culture with a pervasiveness that rivaled what Christianity had achieved in Christendom a millennium before.

The radical liberal revolution only became visible in the 1960s; it had already been going on for a very long time. The liberal knowledge elites, just as Spinoza had planned, had been in place at the top of the societal pyramid for several generations. There was very little in the agenda of the 1960s radicals and flower children that wasn't also, at least in embryo, in the pages of Rousseau. In reacting against the "capitalist establishment," the sixties radicals were merely repeating Rousseau's criticisms of Locke (here we recall Marx's great indebtedness to Rousseau in this regard). And in tuning out, turning on, and staging love-ins, they were merely following in Rousseau's footsteps back to his hedonistic, carefree, labor-free Eden. The moral relativism, the reduction of reason to irrational will, the hedonism, the rejection of God, the charges against Christianity—all these cutting-edge ideas had already been set forth by Machiavelli and Hobbes, the original liberals. But now they were democratized, openly declared to the many.

We must understand how important the state was for this revolution. Massive federal funding was essential right from the beginning in establishing liberalism firmly as the elite worldview. Cornell University was only partially funded by the largesse of Ezra Cornell. The bulk of the money came from the Morrill Land Grant, signed into law by Abraham Lincoln in 1862, which allowed money from the sale of federal land to be used for "the endowment, support, and maintenance of at least one college where the leading object shall be, without excluding other scientific and classical studies and including military tactics, to teach such branches of learning as are related to agriculture and the mechanic arts, in such manner as the legislatures of the States may respectively prescribe, in order to promote the liberal and practical education of the industrial classes in the several pursuits and professions in life."[7] This was a very Lockean project in aid of the technological mastery of nature for the sake of agricultural and industrial economic enterprises.

Educationalists with liberal views were able to take that very practical this-worldly money and yoke the technological-industrial (Lockean) education the state was paying for to their (Spinozan and Rousseauian) liberal-theoretical radicalism from Germany. The result was the federal *establishment* of very powerful scientific and academic research institutions guided entirely by liberal theoretical views.

Enormous infusions of federal funds into higher education under FDR and LBJ intensified this connection. In establishing liberalism—as against the Christian view—in American intellectual life, the federal government ensured that liberalism would be the worldview defining how our ever-increasing technological power would be used. An entirely materialist view of human nature would control an ever-expanding increase in power over nature, including human nature.

The Rise of the Expert: Spinoza's Elite

The rise and ever-increasing authority of the "expert," too came from the German model of university education, wherein academic study was divided up into ever smaller numbers of distinct disciplines, each focusing on a narrowly defined area.

As historian Lenore O'Boyle notes, this model resulted in the "growing acceptance of the idea that only those with certain stipulated academic credentials had a legitimate right to judge in certain areas of knowledge." The "experts" pushed themselves forward in the university system, and hence in the wider society, as the new leaders of society, and "their claims to leadership rested on certified, specialized training. In their own minds…the experts believed themselves to be the means of redeeming the democratic system, albeit by the undemocratic substitution of their own judgment for that of the mass of the people."[8]

These experts became the intellectual elite, the middle layer in Spinoza's social pyramid, the useful middlemen putting the liberal views of the philosophers at the top of the pyramid into effect, and molding the great mass of humanity at the bottom of the pyramid in accordance with the secular liberal vision. The notion of accredited academic "expertise" gave the "experts" the aura of intellectual eminence and neutrality, even though in reality they were thoroughly committed to liberalism.

Thus, the new "experts" in academic religious studies departments, using the latest research from German universities, declared what could and could not be believed about the Bible according to the scientific study of scripture in which they—and only they—had "expertise." Their historical-critical science had been defined by Spinoza and those like him precisely for the sake of establishing liberal intellectual and political control of the Bible (a point that I've argued in greater depth in my *Politicizing the Bible*, written with biblical scholar Scott Hahn).[9] The new "experts" in psychology departments declared what could be believed about the mind and the "soul," but in accordance with the father of modern psychology, Thomas Hobbes, who first set out a thorough-going materialist version of the human psyche.

The new "experts" of sexology, such as Alfred Kinsey, declared what could be believed about sex, but behind Kinsey's purportedly neutral account was Rousseau's campaign for the complete liberation of sexuality from its Christian moral framework. (And behind Kinsey's stern scientific façade there bubbled a cauldron of sexual perversity that would have made even Rousseau blush.)[10]

In discipline after discipline, we find the same pattern: an allegedly neutral expertise that is actually defined against some aspect of Christianity. But sociology is a special case. Let's take a closer look at the experts on humanity itself, who were self-consciously replacing Christianity with a religion of their own making.

The Science—or Is It the Religion—of Human Physics?

We recall that sociology was defined by its founder Comte as "social physics." Comte set out the framework for secular salvation history, wherein the human race moves historically, inevitably, progressively from childhood attachment to religion to the mature adult acceptance of a materialist world without ends, a godless cosmos that leaves us alone to worship ourselves as we become the scientific gods controlling nature—including human nature. With the triumph of liberalism, sociology would take the place of theology as the queen of the sciences.

In Comte's scheme, historical progress means inevitable secularization. And secularization means the disestablishment of Christianity and the establishment of the liberal secular worldview. While he may have put it in a very clear and influential form, Comte was simply crystallizing the main ideas of liberalism going all the way back to Machiavelli. The Christian church had to go, and the church of the religion of humanity must take its place. Comte's "social physics,"—sociology, the science of human nature—was to be *the* guide in this new religion's drama of self-redemption. Sociology became liberalism's guiding science, first in academia (where minds were changed), and then through the influence of sociological "experts" on politics (where political power put social physics into action).[11]

Comtean positivism came to America with the waves of radical liberalism hitting our shores in the latter half of the 1800s. It was during that period that sociologists argued that their not-yet-established science should be added to the curriculum of higher education. "The early American sociologists," explains Christian Smith, "staked their claim" on their belief that "American society" was "undergoing such rapid social transformation and confronting so many new social problems," that it "desperately needed a true science of society to discover the fundamental properties and laws of social life in order to provide the knowledge necessary for the *management of social order* and for the *making of progressive social reform*" [emphasis added].[12]

To put it less politely, the sociologists were claiming that their "science" qualified them to manage the lives of their fellow human beings. They were not neutral "experts" at all. As Smith goes on to show in great detail,

> Nearly all of the leading academic sociologists in America during the discipline's establishment were personally hostile to religion per se.... They worked to undermine religion more subtly, feigning respect through the occasional use of religious language...all the while working intentionally to disabuse believers of their religious faith and divest religious organizations of public authority. These were not men who accidentally slighted religion. These were skeptical Enlightenment atheologians, personally devoted apostles of secularization.[13]

Dynamic Sociology

We might think that Smith is writing about sociologists teaching in our American universities in the 1960s, but as we've seen, that's off by about a hundred years. He's actually speaking of sociologists such as Lester Ward, whose *Dynamic Sociology* was one of the most popular sociology textbooks in American from its publication in 1883. Ward's biography beautifully illustrates the sociological revolution and its connection to liberal progressivism in politics.

Lester Ward did not have to cross the ocean to Germany to get his radicalism—a fact that illustrates how early the radical wave hit our shores. He was born in 1841, raised in an evangelical Protestant household, and encouraged by his mother to enter the ministry. Ward attended the Presbyterian Susquehanna Collegiate Institute in the early 1860s, but he had already come to have doubts about Christianity by then, shifting to something like Unitarianism.[14] The Civil War broke out, and in 1862 Ward joined the Union forces; he was a staunch abolitionist.

After the war, he went to work in Washington as a clerk for the U.S. Government, first at Treasury, next in the Bureau of Statistics, and then, in the early 1880s, as a geologist in the Geological Survey. Ward saw Lincoln's massing of the power of the federal government to eradicate the great social evil of slavery as an example of what a strongly interventionist government could do for social progress. As historian Gillis Harp points out, "Ward's government service bolstered his confidence in the ability of the bureaucratic state to manage society and solve problems."[15]

At the same time Ward was working for the government, he was reading ever more radical Enlightenment material (including Paine's *Age of Reason*), while working on his B.A. at Columbian College (now George Washington University), then a Bachelor of Law, and finally a Master's. He was active in an intellectual circle of Washington bureaucrats who believed that future progress lay in liberal progressivism established through a strong central government led by scientific experts—what can very accurately be called "dynamic sociology," to quote the title of Ward's book.[16] Ward's progressive intellectual community in Washington had great plans. As Harp explains,

> Such men viewed science as more than just an empirical method; science was a progressive and integrating worldview

that implied social improvement and reform. Scientific enquiry also represented the way in which Washington's scientific bureaucracy would become an indispensable part of the policymaking process. The administrators of the new, empirically oriented bureaus would now advise Congress and the Executive Branch in their new role as scientific experts. Many in the community looked forward to forging such a close relationship with legislators and administrators.

"Dynamic sociology" expressed Ward's belief that "social physics" had to be "applied physics." In both social evolution and physics, claimed Ward, "all results are accomplished by force." Force must be applied for progress to be made. If it were properly applied by an elite under a popular, majoritarian form of government—think of Rousseau's General Will, and his claim that citizens who deviate from it must be forced to be free—the "coercion which is now so fruitless" would produce "a positive and increasing future benefit."[17]

In order to apply truly effective and beneficial coercion in a democratic society, Ward believed that sociologists must guide Congress through its deliberations, with the social scientists doing the actual investigating, defining the issues, and recommending policies. Ward also advocated a significantly strengthened executive to enable "dynamic sociology" to achieve real progress.[18]

The fact that that "dynamic sociology" was to be secular—in other words, radically anti-Christian—is clear from Ward's other activities in Washington during this period. He and his wife soon found even the Unitarian church to be too dogmatic, and Ward began his explicit attacks on Christianity and the church. With a few fellow bureaucrats, Ward formed the National Liberal Reform League, a secret society aimed at the complete refutation of all Catholic and Evangelical doctrines. As Harp notes, "the league's aim was to encourage affiliated groups in other cities, and Ward appealed to all 'Liberals, Skeptics, Infidels, Secularists, Utilitarians, Pantheists, Atheists, Freethinkers'" to join forces.[19] Ward and his wife did their part, publishing a newsletter, the *Iconoclast*, which made clear (in perfect Comtean terms, reinforced by John Stuart Mill) that Christianity and science were at war in history and that for social progress to occur, Christianity had to be eliminated.[20] There is no doubt that Ward conceived of his dynamic sociology as both secular and secularizing; that was the very meaning of "progress." And there is no doubt about Ward's influence on Theodore Roosevelt, Woodrow Wilson, and Franklin Roosevelt—that is, on the first great progressive presidents.

One last illuminating note on Lester Ward. Ward is also famous for his internecine battle with the "right wing" of America's secular sociologists, those beholden to the British Darwinist Herbert Spencer, such as William Graham Sumner (1840–1910). Spencer and Sumner were, on the basis of Darwinism, hearty advocates of a classical liberal *laissez-faire* approach. They wanted government to be non-interventionist, letting the market work, like the laws of evolution, for the ultimate benefit or at least the ultimate efficiency in the production of wealth—a very Lockean approach, as modified by Adam Smith and Darwin.

Ward opposed this classical liberal approach with his radical liberal approach. He argued that the intervention of the state was necessary to overcome the evils of capitalism, for the sake of the greatest benefit of the greatest number—a Rousseauian egalitarian approach, modified by the utilitarianism of J. S. Mill and the Darwinian notion that future evolution could be directed intelligently. In this dispute among the early sociologists we have a clash between the first wave of liberalism and the second, but it is still a debate internal to liberalism; each side assumes an entirely secular view. Spencer's side is taken today by "conservatives," still hailing Locke and Smith, and Ward's side is taken by most of academia and the Left in politics, who regard FDR and LBJ (and now BHO) with reverence.

Social Physics in the Ivory Tower

Although Ward's books had already become standards in the new academic discipline of sociology earlier, he himself only went into academia full time in 1905, taking a position at Brown University, moving from bureaucrat to professor.

Ward was by no means the only academic revolutionary in sociology. Other leading lights in the establishment of sociology at the end of the 1800s and beginning of the 1900s—Albion Small, Edward Ross, George Vincent, Franklin Giddings, and James Dealey, among others—had experienced the same "revelation" at Germanized universities in America or in Germany itself. They, too, were "personally committed apostles of secularization."[21] They would achieve the reform from within education, spreading the secular Good News ever more broadly by way of the influence of fresh waves of students.

In their sociology textbooks, students learned that primitive people believe in spiritual realities out of ignorance but that the advance of science demonstrates that everything can be explained according to material realities. "Eternal matter with its eternal activities suffices to account for all the phenomena of the universe," explained Ward. Thus, "Among people acquainted with science, all...supernatural beings have been dispensed with, and the belief in them is declared to be wholly false and to have always been false." Therefore, "society should first specially aim to convert all pseudo-ideas into true ideas," that is, all religious ideas into purely secular, materialistic ideas.[22] So declared the experts.

But Ward the professor aimed at more than merely disabusing the masses of religious pseudo-ideas. Our ability to control matter must be extended to our ability to control human matter, for "the laws of nature have always proved capable of being turned to man's advantage...and there is no reason to suppose that those of human nature and of society will form an exception."[23] If knowing the laws of physics has proven so miraculously beneficial in controlling nature, then knowing the laws of social physics will perform greater miracles still in our future society. As similarly inspired sociologists Albion Small and George Vincent declared, "the factors of human welfare are intelligible; and...the forces by which the conditions of human welfare are to be secured and maintained are within human control."

"Why," asked another sociologist, Edward Ross, isn't it legitimate to investigate "social phenomena in hopes of discovering how they may be controlled to suit our wishes?"[24]

The result of such applied sociology would be real progress in creating this-worldly perfection, a society cured of evil and unhappiness. This utopian vision of what the new social physics would do—if only it were given the power—was essentially religious. Sociology would displace Christianity; it offered a new secular salvific vision. As James Dealey enthused,

> [Humanity] looks forward to the time when man will come into his kingdom; when misery, vice, and human discord shall have been outgrown, and peace, good will, and joyous emulation in achievement will prevail among men. In anticipation he feels himself to be part of this glorified humanity, since he also does his share in the world's work, and builds up, be it ever so little, the achievements and happiness of mankind.[25]

As if to recall the warnings of Machiavelli, Edward Ross informed his fellow elites that, in order to keep from ruffling feathers of the unenlightened masses, "The wise sociologist will show religion a consideration," and "He will not tell…[the ordinary man] how he is managed." Rather, he will speak the truth only to the other liberal intellectual elites—"teachers, clergymen, editors, law-makers, and judges," as well as "poets, artists, thinkers, and educators"—all those "who wield the instruments of control" and "guide the human caravan across the waste."[26]

Liberal Christianity

The inclusion of "clergymen" on this list is worth noting. Along with Machiavelli, Hobbes, and Spinoza, the sociologists generally believed that religion of some kind was necessary, or at least useful at the current stage for controlling the ordinary men and women at the bottom of the pyramid. But as Spinoza had proposed, a new religion could be designed by liberalism for its own purposes. There could be a church as long as it was not doctrinal, accepted the dictates of secularizing modern scriptural scholarship, and adhered to the liberal notion of salvation in this world—in short, as long as it toed the line drawn by the "experts," the liberal elite.

As we have seen, this meant the church would be confined to preaching a kind of moral gospel. As George Marsden has shown in detail in his *The Soul of the American University*, the acceptance of the structure and substance of German learning in American graduate education in the 1800s was considerably lubricated by the liberal strategy of de-emphasizing doctrine (about which people tended to disagree) and emphasizing morality (about which people tended to agree). The revolutionaries assured their audiences and skeptical critics that there was no danger from the new learning because it affirmed the same moral core that all Christians affirm.

Duplicating Spinoza's strategy, the sociologists dictated what Christians could legitimately believe (a very general moral message, aimed at well-being in this world), and what they couldn't (miracles, resurrection, heaven or hell, any absolute claims of doctrinal truth). Thus was born among American sociologists yet another version of "liberal Christianity"—a form of the Christian religion that could be established by the secular state they were envisioning.

Liberal Christianity was what sociologist Edward Ross called "social religion," which, as Christian Smith notes, "involved nothing supernatural, but was an entirely human affair." It had its own doctrine—but in Ross's words, "Not the doctrine about the gods, but the doctrine about men." And the church? "The church of necessity must become either an anachronism, or else must work toward a higher stage of usefulness...endeavoring to serve...as a prophetic guide for man's idealistic longings." Christian Smith sums up Ross's position, shared by his fellow sociologists: "In sum, religion must reinvent itself to be not about God, but about Man. This was the modern gospel that these allegedly objective, positivist sociologists proclaimed about the purpose and future of religion in a progressive social order."[27]

To make the complexity of the situation in the nineteenth and the beginning of the twentieth century a bit clearer, we must remember that even very orthodox Christians seemed to have some common ground with secular liberals. Both were rightly concerned about the ill effects of industrialization: the horrible conditions in the city's slums, the unconscionable treatment of children in mines and factories, the misery of many adult workers, governmental corruption, and the economic despotism of monopolies.

Thus some kind of commonality seemed to exist between Christianity and secular liberalism, precisely because of Christ's charge to feed the hungry; clothe the naked; care for widows and orphans, for the poor, and for the oppressed. Christianity was directed by Christ toward the next world, but one's fate in the next world was bound to how one cared for others' physical needs, as well as their spiritual needs, in this world. The Christian church could not abandon its care for the world without ceasing to be Christian. And so secular liberal progressives and Christians—even Christians who had *not* jettisoned their belief in the supernatural—seemed like natural allies in the crusade to alleviate the suffering of the poor, the oppressed, and those suffering from the ills of industrialized, capitalist society. They seemed to have common moral ground.

The Common Moral Ground Proves to Be Sand

But that common ground was an illusion. The materialism at the heart of secular liberalism from Machiavelli and Hobbes onward was utterly incompatible with the orthodox Christian belief in the reality of the soul and the world to come—though perhaps not with the new this-worldly liberal version of Christianity. Materialism cannot accept the virtue-based morality that follows from the existence of God and the soul, but only a hedonist morality. If nothing exists but bodies, then good and evil are ultimately defined by physical pleasure and physical pain.

Thus, as we have seen, in liberalism morality is reduced to claims of rights, which in themselves are merely proclamations of individual desires.

"This feels good" and "I want" become "I have a right to." "This feels bad" and "I don't want" become "I have a right to be protected from." Since each individual has different desires, morality is entirely relative, that is, reducible to individual, subjective desires and the consequent discordant claims of rights to satisfy them.

But the utter incompatibility between orthodox Christian and secular liberal morality was made manifest at the point in history at which liberalism moved on from eliminating pains to maximizing pleasures. As we have seen, in the late nineteenth and early twentieth centuries liberals were full of zeal for projects orthodox Christians could cooperate with enthusiastically—feed the hungry, clothe the naked, relieve the oppressed. (One suspects that liberals' zeal for these projects may have arisen at least in part from a regret at losing their Christian faith and a desire to make up for having to give up all otherworldly hopes by zealously attacking real this-worldly social evils. Ameliorating evils that had so stubbornly resisted the centuries-long efforts of orthodox Christianity would also prove that giving up Christianity was a net gain, not a loss.)

But in the twentieth century, progressive liberalism moved on from the program of addressing and eliminating the pains of poverty, oppression, and hideous work conditions. Liberals now embraced a positive program of expressive hedonism—liberating sexual pleasure from the confines of morality and from marriage. At that point, it became increasingly and painfully obvious that orthodox Christianity and liberal progressivism were irreconcilable worldviews.

Much of the twentieth century after World War II was taken up with the clash between orthodox Christians and liberals, as liberalism moved from reducing pain to promoting pleasure. Liberalism slowly won out. The specific moral positions by which Christianity had so clearly distinguished itself from pagan Rome and that had formed the moral framework of Western culture for over a thousand years, began to fall one after the other. Contraception, abortion, homosexuality, euthanasia—one by one, practices that had been held to be sinful were normalized. (Homosexual marriage and infanticide are currently on the agenda.) This revolution occurred first in the universities, from which it spread to the other areas of our culture, using every available means from the media to literature, but especially public education and the federal courts to impose the new liberal morality. This moral revolution could not have succeeded without excluding the churches—or should we say "separating" them?—from the public square and ushering them into the realm of harmless private institutions.

But there was one brand of Christianity that was a friend of the revolution, an ally. Liberal Christians accepted the entire hedonist revolution, from sexual liberation to abortion to homosexual marriage. Liberal Christians had long since shed the theological doctrines that conflicted with the secular revolution. Now they found it easy to shed the moral doctrines as well. Thus liberal Christianity assured itself favored status. Secular revolutionaries found its adherents both useful and harmless.

But to orthodox Christians, it looks like we are rapidly approaching the situation that prevailed two millennia ago. Once again, we face a hostile pagan state with its own established religion and the morality to go with it.

An Evitable Revolution

That is what has happened. But did it have to happen?

According to liberalism, yes. The inevitable progress of humanity in this world means liberation from Christianity and the next world. As Comte declared, this advance *has to happen* according to the "laws of history." The triumph of secularism is inevitable, and so also is Christianity's demise.

But "laws of history" are figments of the fevered liberal imagination. They're not rooted in necessary laws of the mind, as Comte believed. They are only something in liberals' minds—born of the fervent desire that history would leave Christianity behind and embrace materialist science (and Comte's Religion of Humanity) as the new faith.

The secular revolution was not the inevitable march of progress in history. It was an intentional revolution, both in Europe and in America. As Christian Smith explains, "the secularization of American public life" was "the successful outcome of an intentional political struggle by secularizing activists" whose aim was "to overthrow a religious establishment's control over socially legitimate knowledge," that is, over the truth and who gets to proclaim it:

> The rebel insurgency consisted of waves of networks of activists who were largely skeptical, freethinking, agnostic, atheist, or theologically liberal; who were well educated and socially located mainly in knowledge-production occupations; and who generally espoused materialism, naturalism, positivism, and the privatization or extinction of religion.[28]

As we've seen the radical Enlightenment was carried to our shores by American students with Ph.D.s from German universities, where they had imbibed "some version of the skeptical or revolutionary Enlightenment traditions received from eighteenth-century Europe."[29] These revolutionaries imposed radicalism on American society not out of necessity but to spread their own faith.

"What these secularizers were actually pursuing," Smith maintains, "was not primarily a neutral public sphere, but a reconstructed moral order which would increase their own group status, autonomy, authority, and eventually income."[30] The Christian church had to be separated from the state to make room for a rival secular church defined by the radical liberal moral order, moral relativism, "rights" instead of natural law, and utilitarian hedonism. The de-Christianized secular public square is by no means morally or theologically neutral.

Secular liberalism has no problem with welcoming a weak and obedient liberal Christianity into the public square—or Deism, or atheism, or some harmless liberalized form of an Eastern religion. It is orthodox Christianity that liberals can't stomach because it has very definite theological and moral doctrines directly opposed to the secular worldview and the state that supports it.

Liberalism has its own vision of human redemption. The revolutionary "secularizers sought to increase their own power in part because they genuinely saw themselves as bearing the vision and means for a better world" as Christian Smith explains.[31] That vision, the liberal vision we have outlined over the last few chapters, is a counter-faith to Christianity, one with a rival view of history's consummation: the establishment of a secular utopia. Liberalism is a fundamentally religious faith, one formed in reaction against Christianity and taking on the form and functions of the Christian church it seeks to displace. Secular liberalism aspired to fulfill all that Christianity had promised—and more. In attempting to fill the entire "space" left by the exclusion of Christianity, and to satisfy in this world all the longings that Christianity offered to satisfy in the next, secular liberalism made of itself a kind of utopian this-worldly faith, an anti-church with its own evangelical mission:

> Religion's historical marginalization in science, the universities, mass education, reform politics, and the media was a historical accomplishment, an achievement of specific groups of people, many of whom intended to marginalize religion. The people at the core of these secularizing movements, at least, knew what they were doing, and wanted to do it. They were activists, secularizing activists....[32]

They knew what they were about.

The secular revolution in our culture did not have to happen. The initial success of radical secularism was not inevitable in the nineteenth century and its ultimate triumph is not inevitable now. What has been done can be undone.

CHAPTER 15

SECULARIZATION, AMERICAN STYLE

C learly, radical ideas from the European Enlightenment made their way across the ocean in the nineteenth century. But can we really blame them for the "separation of church and state" that prevails in twenty-first-century America? And—this is the really crucial point—if the regime of "separation" is not rolled back, do we really have to look forward to the fulfillment of the schemes of Machiavelli, Hobbes, Spinoza, and Rousseau? Is a complete revival of the paganism, materialism, and state-worship that held sway in the Roman Empire in our future? Might we even live to see actual persecution of Christians in the United States?

The reader may be tempted to think that we've been overestimating the power of secularizing Enlightenment ideas on American society: "But surely it's the First Amendment that's responsible for separation of church and state?" We've all heard that the Establishment Clause requires that separation. That has been the conventional wisdom since the watershed *Everson v. Board of Education* case was decided by the Supreme Court in 1947.

But if that's true, then just why did it not become clear that the separation of Christianity from the state was constitutionally mandated until more than 150 years after the Bill of Rights took effect? That's a question well worth investigating in some detail.

A Closer Look at *Everson*

At issue in *Everson v. Board of Education* was whether a school district could reimburse the parents of private religious school (particularly Catholic parochial school) children for transportation to school. The New Jersey taxpayer who brought the case believed that using public tax money in this seemingly innocuous way somehow meant that the government was violating the First Amendment.

As with so many other Supreme Court cases, the justices in *Everson* used a small defeat for the liberal side in the case to cover for an even greater victory; that is, the majority ruled that *in this particular case* there was no violation of the Establishment Clause, but their decision awarded new and hitherto unsuspected meaning and force to that clause—which, as we shall see, is really just one part of a sentence ripped out of its proper context in the First Amendment.

We've noted that the Supreme Court made two key declarations in *Everson*: (1) that the First Amendment's Establishment Clause demanded the erection of "a wall of separation between church and state," and (2) that the Establishment Clause could be applied to the states—rather than only the federal government—through the Fourteenth Amendment.

Once *Everson* established those two principles, the separation of religion from public life proceeded apace. As I laid out in the first chapter of this book, after *Everson* there was an avalanche of Supreme Court cases applying the power of the federal government to drive religion from public institutions. Prayer, Bible reading, and even a "moment of silence" were banished from schools. The Ten Commandments were taken down or, in an exceptional case, allowed on public land only if their display served a "secular purpose" (whatever that means).

The effect of *Everson* has been to remove Christianity bit by bit, chunk by chunk from public influence and even public view. It turned the First Amendment, or at least the Establishment Clause, into a kind of engine of secularization, or we might say, of de-Christianization, used by the state. The secularized state is the result of de-Christianization through *Everson*.

All the secularizing Establishment cases that followed in the wake of *Everson* assumed that the First Amendment must be interpreted in terms of what Justice Black, following Thomas Jefferson, believed it implied, rather than in terms of what the First Amendment actually *says*. The cases that followed in the wake of *Everson* enshrined in American life Justice Black's momentous assertion, borrowing from Jefferson's letter to the Danbury Baptists, that "the clause against establishment of religion by law was intended to erect 'a wall of separation between church and state.'"[1]

But that's not what the First Amendment says. There's nothing in it about a wall of separation. Let's look at the significant differences between the actual words of the Constitution and the interpretation of Jefferson and Black, so that we understand the full import of exchanging the words of the Amendment for theirs. The actual relevant text of the First Amendment simply declares that "Congress shall make no law respecting an establishment of religion, or prohibiting the free exercise thereof...." (That's literally all the First Amendment says about religion before moving on to freedom of speech, of the press, to assemble, and to petition the government.)

Let's be careful readers. Note, first of all, this key difference: the First Amendment refers to "Congress" while Justice Black's formulation is focused on "the state." That change represents a shift from the First Amendment's original meaning—protecting the states (plural) *from* the national Congress—to the "state" (singular) as the sole political entity of any consequence, now empowered to impose separation of church and state *on* the states. The "state" has replaced the states as the focus. Justice Black's assertion that the Establishment Clause must be applied by the federal government to the states through the Fourteenth Amendment was a radical departure from the original intentions of those who framed and ratified the Bill of Rights.

This becomes even clearer when we note another major change from the language of the First Amendment to the language of *Everson*, from "make no law" to "separation." This represents a shift from the original negative limitation on federal power to a notion that the federal government is now positively charged with the task of removing religion from the (ever-increasing) domain overseen by the state—constructing a great wall to ensure that believers are kept out of that domain. A negative restraint on federal power has become a positive mandate for federal power.

And then there's the question of the "Establishment Clause" itself. The Court created a kind of mandate for secularization by cutting the guarantee of religious liberty in the First Amendment in half. The Supreme Court has played divide and conquer with this guarantee, splitting it into two clauses, the so-called Establishment Clause—"Congress shall make no law respecting an establishment of religion"—and the so-called Free Exercise Clause—"or prohibiting the free exercise thereof." It then uses the Establishment Clause against the Free Exercise clause, as a tool to de-Christianize the culture.

But of course both "clauses" are very obviously meant to be read together. They are *one* clause, meant in its entirety to limit federal power. Unless the first, "establishment," part of the sentence is ripped out of context, the second, "free exercise," part prohibits government from eliminating Christianity—thereby keeping intact the original intention of the First Amendment as a restraint on federal power.

Thus the Supreme Court's attempt to split "no...establishment" off from "free exercise" has led to enormous confusion in First Amendment jurisprudence. The effort to eliminate Christianity via the Establishment Clause is now running smack into the protection of Christianity via the Free Exercise Clause. So, for example, in *Widmar v. Vincent* (1981), the public University of Missouri, following the line laid down by the Supreme Court's decision in *Everson*, decided the university could not allow its facilities to be used by religious student groups for purposes of prayer, Bible reading, and religious discussion because that would violate the Establishment Clause, but the Supreme Court itself decided in favor of the students because they were protected by the Free Exercise Clause.

But there is no contradiction between the two "clauses" if we simply admit that they go together, and that the entire guarantee of religious liberty in the First Amendment was meant as a protection against incursions by federal power, not a writ for the government to wall religion off and away, out of mainstream American life.

The real source of the reasoning in *Everson* and the cases that follow it is not the Constitution in general or the Establishment Clause in particular, but the notion of secular progress that was shared by both Jefferson and Black, and that, as we've seen, was firmly entrenched in the upper echelons of American intellectual life by the mid-twentieth century. According to that view, the irrationalities of Christianity must be left behind (separated off) so that humanity may march forward to a brighter secular future. In *Everson* Justice Black was reaching back and picking up from Jefferson, our nation's most liberal and secularizing founder, the particular view that happened to fit his own—one in accord with the secular Enlightenment view of progress. That view was at the extreme left of American politics at the beginning of the nineteenth century, but by the middle of the twentieth century it was widespread among our elites, including our judicial elites.

It's evidence that Justice Black was reasoning from the dominant secular liberal worldview rather than from the actual words of the First Amendment that he was very selective in his use of history to back up the Court's decision in *Everson*. His account of the historical pedigree of the Court's decision[2] displayed, in the words of legal scholars John Jeffries Jr. and James Ryan, "little research and zero interest in conflicting evidence, competing inferences, or alternative interpretations."[3] Black ignored the evidence of the original meaning of the Bill of Rights, such as the debates at the time of its ratification, and latched onto Jefferson's words as if they were the definitive explication of the First Amendment. But the result in *Everson* is far from what the founders intended and even further from the actual words ratified by the states.

Interestingly, what Black achieved in *Everson* differs in some important ways even from what Jefferson intended. Jefferson wanted America to leave behind doctrinal Christianity based upon the Bible. But he would have been quite happy with a Deist foundation for America's civil religion—something in accord with Locke. But by the mid-twentieth century, the more radical liberalism spawned by Spinoza and Rousseau held sway, so that the scene was set for full-bore secularization.

It was the secular liberal revolution, not the First Amendment, that required the "separation" of the Christian church off from public life and public influence in the United States. The Supreme Court's *Everson* decision in 1947 was simply the way in which Spinoza, Rousseau, and radical Enlightenment liberalism were imposed on America, using the power of the Court and the weight of Jefferson's words.

Christians Divide and Secularists Conquer

But there is also another trend in American culture that bears an important share of the responsibility for the *Everson* decision and the increasingly radical "separation of church and state" that has followed in its wake.

What was at issue in *Everson* was not the use of public tax dollars to fund religion in general, but the use of public funds to transport *Catholic* children to *parochial* schools. The significance of this fact can be seen if we take a big step back in history.[4]

As Jeffries and Ryan point out, there were actually two sources of the push to have the federal government deny aid to religious schools. "Most visible was the pervasive secularism that came to dominate American public life [by the mid-twentieth century], especially among educated elites, a secularism that does not so much deny religious belief as seek to confine it to the private sphere. This public secularism appears on the face of Supreme Court opinions and is deeply embedded in Establishment Clause doctrine."[5]

But there was also a second source for the campaign to deny public funding to private schools: Protestant antipathy to Catholicism. America was a predominantly Protestant nation, and in the mid-nineteenth century Protestant America had established a kind of religious-moral backdrop in public schools that was intended to define American culture through common public education. The presence of separate Catholic schools challenged that establishment. According to Jeffries and Ryan, even up into the first half of the twentieth century,

> the ban against aid to religious schools was supported by the great bulk of the Protestant faithful. With few exceptions, Protestant denominations, churches, and believers vigorously opposed aid to religious schools. For many Protestant denominations, this position followed naturally from the circumstances of their founding. It was strongly reinforced, however, by hostility to Roman Catholics and the challenge they posed to Protestant hegemony, which prevailed throughout the nineteenth and early twentieth centuries. In its political origins and constituencies, the ban against aid to religious schools aimed not only to prevent an establishment of religion but also to maintain one.[6]

Protestantism had worked hard in the nineteenth century to establish itself, especially through public education, as the country's civic religion. The large numbers of Catholics immigrating from Europe threatened that establishment, and no aspect of the situation seemed more threatening than the presence of the Catholic school system running parallel to the public school system, which was effectively Protestant (though, as we shall see, its Protestantism was of an attenuated variety, a sort of least-common-denominator faith). Thus Protestants cheered *Everson* in 1947, still holding to the Protestant antipathy to any public funding for Catholic schools that went back an entire century.[7]

Naturally secular liberals were (and are) happy to use Protestant-Catholic antipathy for their own purposes. But secularists are no real allies of any Christian church. They have eagerly turned the weapons forged in *Everson* against the Protestant establishment that welcomed the decision at first.

We find this same pattern again and again: divisions among Christians are used by secular activists (and the Supreme Court) to advance the secular cause. Consider an earlier example: Who first pushed for the prohibition of Bible reading in public school? Who first asked for their children to be excused from having to listen to the daily Bible readings in school? Rabid secularists? The ACLU?

No. It was Catholics. In this case, it was anti-Protestant Catholics who objected to religion in the public square—and provided an opening for the radical secularists interested in the complete disestablishment of religion from American public life. Daily Bible reading had been mandated in America as part of the common school movement beginning in the 1830s, and the version of the Bible to be used was chosen by Protestants. As Catholic immigrants began to flow into America in the second half of the nineteenth century, they bristled at having to read the Protestant King James Bible instead of the Catholic Douay-Rheims. Catholics were expelled from public school for refusing to read from the KJV, and in a Massachusetts state court case in 1859 it was declared legal to beat Catholic students who wouldn't read it.[8] Catholics did not want to be forced to read the Protestant Bible, and they would rather have the Bible not read at all than be compelled to read the Protestant version. Or, failing that, they would start their own schools.

The extensive Catholic school system we now take for granted in America was the result of Catholics deciding that the public school system was too Protestant for them. And then once Catholic schools came into existence, Protestants did not want public money to go to supporting them. Hence their support for *Everson*.

If that weren't irony enough, the fact that the Bible was read in public schools in the first place was in its origin a result of religious conflict among Protestants themselves. The problem facing the incipient movement for "common schools" (the forerunners of our modern public school system) was that, while all the various Protestant denominations were in favor of the schools' having a common Protestant religious-moral foundation, the theological conflicts between the various denominations were so intense that no headway could be made as to the content of the common religious education.

The solution was offered by none other than Horace Mann (1796–1859), a very liberal Unitarian. As an ingenious compromise, Mann advocated reading the King James Version of the Bible (which all Protestants accepted) *without comment* (so that no particular denomination could interpret the Bible according to its own doctrines).[9] In other words, both teachers and children were to keep silent about doctrinal differences that they held *privately*, while the Bible would provide the common moral foundation for common *public* life.

Mann's assumption—an assumption at the very heart of his Unitarianism, which denies the divinity of Christ, just as Jefferson did—was that what is of real value in Christianity is the moral core. For Mann, as for all Unitarians, Jesus Christ was not divine (thus Trinitarianism should be reduced to Unitarianism). But Jesus the man was a great moral teacher, and the Bible contains his great moral teachings. Since Christ was not divine, the particular theological doctrines about which the various Christian denominations disagree and fight are of no consequence. Horace Mann's limiting the religious instruction in the "common schools" strictly to Bible reading alone was originally a way to exclude doctrinal disagreements by eliminating doctrine, leaving behind only the moral core of Christianity. It was less drastic than Jefferson's cutting all the miraculous and dogmatic passages out of the Bible. But the Enlightenment Deist and the nineteenth-century Unitarian were essentially on the same page.

So that's how regular Bible reading became part of the public school day. To complete the irony, in the post-*Everson* Supreme Court case that declared Bible reading to be unconstitutional, *Abington Township School District v. Schempp* (1963), Edward Schempp, who brought the suit against the school district, was a Unitarian Universalist, a theologically even more liberal heir to Horace Mann. The case was a sign of how much farther toward a fully secularist outlook America had moved between the nineteenth and the twentieth centuries. Edward Schempp's son Ellery purposely lit the spark that led to the famous court case by refusing to stand during Bible devotions and defiantly reading a copy of the Koran instead!

I cannot mention *Schempp* without quoting the extraordinarily prescient dissent by Justice Potter Stewart: "a refusal to permit religious exercises [in public schools] thus is…not…the realization of state neutrality, but rather….*the establishment of a religion of secularism*, or, at the least … government support of the beliefs of those who think that religious exercises should be conducted only in private" [emphasis added].[10]

Liberals are always happy to make use of Protestant-Catholic antipathy—or Protestant-Protestant antipathy—to forward their own secularizing aims. In a very real sense, a very painful sense, the current success of the Supreme Court in disestablishing Christianity from public life (and not just from public schools) is the result of centuries-old religious disagreements among Christians.

It's a painful truth. Secular liberalism's success in supplanting Christianity can be laid, in part, at the door of Christians—all Christians, Catholic and Protestant. But only in part. Secular liberalism isn't merely a reaction to religious conflict. As we've seen in great detail, it is a substantive revolution in its own right, a revolution with its own view of human nature, good and evil, happiness, the goal of political life, and so on. Secularism is not what you get left over after you subtract religion. It's the other way around. The subtraction of religion is what you get when you have secular liberals bent on erasing Christianity from public life to make way for something else—an entirely secular world. The disestablishment of Christianity from culture prepares the way for the establishment of a culture built upon the rejection of Christianity. The wall of separation that keeps Christianity out also doubles as a wall propping up the construction of a new secular society defined against Christianity.

Not Made in America

The "separation of church and state" Supreme Court cases that stripped Christianity from our public square in the twentieth century looked "made in America," but really they are understandable only in light of the larger historical sweep of secular liberalism we've covered in previous chapters.

For a century and a half before *Everson*, the notion of a declared *separation* (as opposed to distinction) between church and state was directly associated with active *secularization*—that is, the removal and exclusion of Christianity from public and legal influence, the demand that all marriages be civil marriages, the driving out of clerics and pastors from education, the closing of religious schools, the taking down of crucifixes and crosses, the renaming of streets and towns that referred to saints or Christian luminaries, the closing of convents and churches, the secular co-option of sacred holidays, the public mockery of Christianity, and the persecution and even slaughter of priests, nuns, pastors, ministers, and faithful lay Christians. It had been so in the French Revolution with formal separation in 1795, in the secular government of Colombia in Latin America in the mid-1800s, in the secular French Third Republic beginning in 1870 and culminating in the 1905 law on the Separation of Church and State, in militantly secularist Mexico with the Queretaro Constitution of 1917 explicitly modeled on the French law of Separation of Church and State, in 1920s Russia when Bolsheviks crushed the opposition of the Russian Orthodox Church, and in radically secularist Spain in the 1930s.[11]

What has occurred (and continues to accelerate) in the United States following the Supreme Court's ruling in *Everson* in 1947—the exclusion of Bible reading from schools, the forbidding of public prayer, the taking down of Ten Commandment plaques, the forced removal of crucifixes, crosses, and crèches, and the whole "war on Christmas"—*must be understood as part of the larger historical sweep of enforced secularization that had already been occurring in Europe and Latin America in the previous two centuries.*

I really am saying what you think I am saying: neither the Constitution nor the First Amendment is the source of the notion that we must erect a wall of separation between church and state. Nor does it come from Christianity itself—although, as I shall not tire of repeating, the understanding that the church and political power must be *distinct* in form, function, governance, and ultimate aim is a great gift from the church. The notion of a *separation* that demands secularization comes from secularists, that is, from those demanding the liberation of this world from all considerations of the next. That is the liberation at the origin and heart of liberalism.

Moreover, as that same period of history running from the French Revolution to the present makes profoundly clear, the forced exclusion of the church through secularization has nowhere resulted in the establishing of a neutral, non-religious political state, but rather always in a state with a quite different, hostile political religion—the Religion of Reason, the Religion of Humanity, the worship of the nation as incarnate Spirit, the worship of nature, the worship of race, the worship of human self-deification through human technical progress, the worship of sexuality, the worship of liberty, the worship of equality, the revival of neo-pagan cults, and who knows what shall be next. Since all of these new worships funnel their aspirations through the state, the state itself becomes the object of worship, a great mirror in whose reflective and magnifying power we can worship ourselves, and concentrate the beams of our own energy to a burning point that scorches all that stands in the way of progress toward earthly utopia.

Secular liberalism is not a neutral view, as it pretends to be so that it may serenely govern our culture from above. It is one particular philosophical and religious worldview—a worldview defined by antagonism to Christianity. And that secularism is now our established religion. The only cure for the threat it poses to our religious liberty is disestablishment. To that hope, and challenge, we turn in the next chapter.

PART VI

DISESTABLISHMENT

CHAPTER 16

DISESTABLISHING SECULAR LIBERALISM

The first step in disestablishing secular liberalism as our *de facto* state religion is to unmask its pretensions to neutrality. Secularism has prevailed throughout our society by means of the fiction that it is a kind of neutral least common denominator—the pretense that, while conflicting religions are in competition with one another, secularism is simply what is left over after all competing religious claims are ruled out of bounds (that is, separated behind a wall). But in reality, secular liberalism is itself a religion, or an anti-religion—a complete worldview and an agenda in direct and fierce competition with Christianity.

The domain covered by secular liberalism is as extensive as that of any religion and in particular of Christianity, the religion that it has displaced. Liberalism is not agnostic about the meaning of life. It makes very specific claims about the universe and our place in it. According to secular liberalism, we live in a godless cosmos, one in which all causes and effects are material. Spiritual realities—souls, angels, demons, gods, and God—do not exist. There is no source of rational order in the universe but human thought. Thus the secular liberal view of rationality is not neutral either: to be rational, according to the liberals, means to think that we live in a godless cosmos in which all phenomena can be reduced to physical cause and effect. Determinist scientific materialism is the only respectable way of understanding the universe.

Besides its own cosmology, secularism has its own moral philosophy, as we have seen. Materialism requires that all morality be reduced to hedonism—because good and evil are nothing more than bodily pleasure and pain. Thus for secular liberals there are as many notions of good and evil as there are particular material desires of individual bodies, so that good and evil are relative to individual choice.

Since according to the secular worldview there is no objective morality, no universal good and evil, the two-fold purpose of government is to protect and enhance the "rights" of individuals to pursue their own private desires, and to guide society toward ever-greater this-worldly pleasures while reducing pain, toil, and discontent.

This is what secular liberals passionately believe. This is the notion of historical progress that animates their efforts. This is the mission they wish to impose on the rest of the world through evangelization and political force. (In this effort the United Nations would seem to be the functional equivalent of the universal Catholic Church.)

Secular Liberalism Is a Religion

But secular liberalism doesn't just take up the space that Christianity used to occupy. As we have seen, liberals have historically envisioned their movement in fundamentally religious terms, from the French Revolution's Religion of Reason through Auguste Comte's Religion of Humanity to the all-encompassing aims of nationalism and then of socialism and sociology as they permeated the West's liberal democracies in the early twentieth century and to the political religions of Nazism and Fascism. In each case—in some with more shockingly horrific results than in others—the natural religious devotion that should be directed to God was bent on the worship of ourselves, our nation, our ideas, our race, our technological or economic progress, our emancipation from all natural and moral restrictions.

The liberalism that dominates the public square in America today is part of that same history, in which Christianity is replaced by some form of a secular religion. It is just as adamant and extensive in its dogmatic claims as any religion. But those claims are mostly negative. Secular liberalism defines itself against Christianity, self-consciously and dogmatically denying what Christianity affirms. Let's summarize how the two line up, creed versus anti-creed.

Christians affirm that there is only one God, and he created heaven and earth. Secular liberals assert that there is no God, and that nature is the result of blind laws and chance interactions.

Christians believe that the world is full of meaning because it was created by a wise and loving God. Liberals believe that the universe and life itself are ultimately meaningless. Meaning itself is an entirely human and artificial construct.

Christians believe that human beings are made in the image of God and are the very pinnacle of creation. (Guided evolution, understood as creation over time, is compatible with Christianity.) Liberals believe that a human being is just one more animal, an accidental artifact of blind evolution. (They will not allow any theistic alternative account a hearing.)

Christians believe that the world is fallen, and that sin infects and distorts every human endeavor. Liberals believe that human beings are naturally good, and that "evil" is only the result of a bad environment (that is, an unfortunate set of proximate material causes).

Christians believe that the grace of God is necessary to heal human wickedness. Liberals believe that human beings may manipulate their material surroundings, and even human nature itself, to effect their own salvation by their own works.

Christians believe that God became incarnate in Jesus Christ, who is fully divine and fully human, the only God-man in history. Liberals deny the divinity of Christ, proclaiming that he was only human and that there is no God; they believe that human beings can become their own gods.

Christians believe that political life in this world is tainted and hindered by the presence of sin, so that we cannot place our ultimate hopes in a kingdom of this world. Liberals believe that this world is all we have, and that we can bring about an earthly paradise if we unite political and technical power.

For Christians the fundamental institution is the church, the Body of Christ, with Christ as its head. The kingdoms of this world—the nations, the states aimed at sustaining bodily existence and social order in this life—are secondary. Church and state are complementary, but truly distinct in institutional form and function. Liberals, denying the reality of the next world, make this-worldly kingdoms, nations, and states the primary and exclusive powers. If they allow the church to exist, they make it subordinate to the political power or render it an impotent private glee club.

A sign that the secular state is now elevated to the dominant institution is that it has displaced the Gospel of the church with its own gospel, taking over the task of defining human nature, fundamental human institutions, and the human good.

To cite an obvious example, Christianity historically defined marriage as the exclusive and permanent union between one male and one female. One of the first actions of modern secular states from the French Revolution onward has been to institute civil marriage and easy divorce and to deny the validity of ecclesiastical marriage. This continues today, with the state imposing gay marriage and civil unions.

Christian sexual morality is defined by the goal of exclusive heterosexual marriage; thus premarital sex, pedophilia, homosexuality, and adultery are grave moral violations. Liberalism, in rejecting Christianity and redefining marriage, has redefined all of human sexuality, declaring liberation from Christian morality (and the attendant guilt and shame) to be the sexual good.

Christianity affirms that human life is made in the image of God. Christians hold that human beings have an immortal soul from the moment of conception, a soul that is essentially united to the body until natural death. Liberalism denies the soul, and therefore takes upon itself the authority to define what kind of human life is (and is not) worthy of the protection of the law. In reducing human beings to a growing mass of cells, liberals deny the humanity of the unborn, the partially born, and now those who are born with disabilities. Liberals also seem to revel in any and all manipulation of the human genome and of living human embryos. Finally, liberalism takes upon itself the authority to proclaim when life at the other end is not worth living, and so liberals champion the right to euthanasia.

We could go on, but the point should be clear. In defining itself from top to bottom directly against Christianity, secular liberalism is a kind inverse image, like a photo negative, of the religion it has so energetically worked to displace for the past several centuries. It is a kind of anti-Christian religion as extensive in its claims as the Christianity it denies, with its own set of passionately held beliefs and dogmas. It doesn't just look like a religion. It doesn't just function like a religion. It *is* a religion.

I emphasize that liberalism both *acts like* a religion and *is* a religion to make clear that it satisfies both definitions of religion offered by scholars, the functionalist and the substantivist definition.[1] Thus we should be able to proceed, through the courts, to disestablish it. Liberalism is the worldview that has been enshrined in American law as the default position wherever Christianity has been ruled out of bounds and "separated" from our public life. But that is unconstitutional—as the establishment of any religion would be unconstitutional. The establishment of secular liberalism should be litigated against as a violation of the First Amendment. Secular liberalism can and must be disestablished.

That doesn't mean that secular liberalism should be outlawed. But it must be placed on the same level as any other religion. It must be disestablished, and secular liberals must be forced to make their case in the public square by moral persuasion, like the adherents of any other religion, rather than relying on the state to impose liberalism by force.

In the half century since *Everson*, Christians have been hounded out of the public square. But the secular liberalism that has displaced Christianity is—as we have demonstrated—a particular worldview, no more rational than its rivals. More has been, and more can be, done. For example, the philosopher Alasdair MacIntyre, with whom I had the privilege to study, has made a key contribution to this important project of unmasking liberalism's pretense of neutrality by showing it to be a quite particular tradition with its own questionable assumptions.[2] The more these assumptions are understood, the clearer it will become that secular liberalism satisfies the definition of a religion. And the more the history of secular liberals is known, the more obvious it will be that they have seen liberal secularism explicitly as a religion. All of which should bolster the efforts for disestablishment. But if these efforts are to be effective, we will need to be careful to avoid the traps that secularists have set for believers in the past.

Don't Default to Unbelief

Liberals would have us believe that our public political space must be defined by *unbelief*. It's easy to see why—after all, unbelief is liberalism's foundational belief. Secularizing the public square means secularism wins. But why have Christians so often gone along with this stripping of belief from the public square, even aiding and abetting it?

Because again and again they've fallen for one of the secularists' classic traps. This particular trap has a couple of basic forms (with variations). In the first, the secularists say to the Baptists in a friendly way, "You don't want to be ruled by Anglicans! It's so much better for public space to be secular than for the government to bully you into accepting someone else's notion of the sacred." And then to Anglicans, "You wouldn't want Catholics using public power to set the rules, would you? Better *no* beliefs, than *their* beliefs." And then to Catholics, "You certainly don't want Baptists defining the law of the land! Better let *no one's* religious beliefs define the public square, decide what the laws will be, control education, and so forth, than to let Baptist beliefs rule."

But secularism isn't "no one's beliefs"; it's the religion of the secularists. When unbelief becomes the established belief, secular liberalism is in control. Secularists have been trying this trick at least since Jefferson played one Christian denomination off another so that, once he had subtracted all the rival doctrines about Christ's divinity, Jefferson's own Deism would be the default established position. Today liberals more radical than Jefferson use the same trap to establish atheism as the *de facto* state religion.

Don't Accept Secular Liberal Morality as Neutral

There's another form of this trap that we might call Spinozan because it's a strategy cleverly designed by Spinoza and his followers. Here the liberal secularists say, "Look at Spinoza. He's an atheist, but he's a man of impeccable morals. He's so peaceable and law-abiding—unlike many Christians! What harm can private unbelief be? Religious freedom must include the freedom *not* to believe."

The trap here is the proposition that law-abiding "unbelief" actually shares a common moral foundation with Christianity. This common morality, so the argument goes, can form the foundation of society. Thus religious belief can be separated off privately, and unbelief may define our public square. But what that actually means, as we've discovered, is that the radical atheism of a tiny minority ends up defining what beliefs are acceptable in the public square. Once this occurs, the particular morality of "unbelief," the morality of secular liberalism, becomes the view imposed on everyone else. Unbelief wasn't morally neutral after all!

The Spinozan strategy has been an effective one for secular liberalism. But today it has been exposed as the "bait and switch" tactic that it really is. It is now crystal clear that secular liberalism has definite moral beliefs, quite different from Christian morality, which liberals are trying to impose by governmental force: contraception, abortion, infanticide, sexual libertinism, easy divorce, the continual redefinition of marriage, euthanasia, and so on.

While secular liberals may have shared the same moral views as Christianity in the seventeenth century, when Spinoza lived, that surface agreement didn't last very long. It soon became apparent that a this-worldly secularism grounded in materialism dictated a new morality, based entirely upon the pleasures and pains of bodily existence—hedonistic utilitarianism. By the nineteenth century the moral differences between Christianity and secular liberalism were becoming ever more apparent. And secularism aggressively asserted its own moral agenda in the twentieth century.

Today, as the fundamental moral conflicts between Christianity and secular liberalism become ever more intense, it is clear that we're dealing with fundamentally different and conflicting moral views—that the affirmation of liberal moral positions is the denial of the Christian moral view. The two rival moralities arise from conflicting beliefs about the way the world is, what human beings are, and how we should define the human good.

The non-neutrality of liberal morality is obvious in an ever more stunning way as we see liberalism reversing the course of history. Liberal secularism has in fact moved the West back toward an affirmation of the moral worldview of pagan Rome. Liberal morality is a kind of utilitarian hedonism, rooted in materialism, that is taking us right back to paganism.

Don't Fall for Moral Relativism

Christians must also avoid falling into the moral relativist version of the don't-let-the-Anglicans-persecute-you trap described above. It goes something like this: "You see that there are any number of different moral views, and no way to reconcile them. We each have the right to define our own beliefs about morality, and the state has no right to interfere. Thus the state must allow for, and protect, those who want abortion, infanticide, casual non-marital sex, homosexuality, lesbianism, pedophilia, easy divorce, cohabitation, a new and different definition of marriage, euthanasia, the endless manipulation of human genes, experimentation on living embryos, genetic screening to eliminate babies for any reason including sex selection, and so forth."

This is simply a victory for liberalism over Christianity. Affirming any and every view as equally legitimate means that the default position becomes moral relativism, which is the fundamental assumption of liberalism going all the way back to Machiavelli, and which underlies Hobbes's notion of amoral "rights." There is no good and evil. There is just the human will, the heart that "wants what it wants," as Woody Allen explained (in justification of his creepy affair with Mia Farrow's daughter). The ultimate result, of course, is not real moral freedom for everyone but the imposition of liberal morality by the state, and the fiction that one's particular desires, whatever they may be, define one's legal rights. Liberalism is not even actually interested, as it claims, in allowing for a real tolerance of differing moral views. Rather, liberals use the state to impose their own moral view on everybody else.

From Tolerance to Persecution

That was precisely what was going on in Obama's first term, when Obamacare was used to push a mandate through Health and Human Services demanding that all employers, regardless of their religious or moral beliefs, must provide insurance coverage for contraception, abortifacients, and sterilization. The HHS mandate was especially aimed at Catholic hospitals and universities—as a way for secular liberalism to show its muscle against its greatest, most unified rival. Another obvious example is the use of federal power over public education to push sexual education that is aimed at sexual liberation, that is, freedom from the moral restrictions on sexuality historically rooted in Christianity. Or consider the imposition of a liberal abortion regime by the Supreme Court in *Roe v. Wade*. Or the use of state power to impose homosexual marriage, and the re-definition of opposition to homosexuality as "discrimination"—as in the case of the New Mexico photographer who was fined $6,600 for declining to photograph a lesbian "commitment ceremony."[3] When the state threatens to drive Christian businesses and charities out of business for witnessing to Christian moral principles, it is time to start using the word "persecution."

The examples are endless. Liberals have moved from agitating for tolerance of a variety of moral views—only the first step in their strategy—to imposing their own particular moral views with the full force of the state. Liberalism once appeared to be about freeing everyone, believers and nonbelievers alike, from government-imposed religion and morality, but it has shown that that was just a ruse for establishing its own particular worldview, one that is fundamentally antagonistic to Christianity.

Putting the First Amendment Back Together Again

We must remove liberalism from its privileged established position. But that doesn't mean going to the other extreme, and—as liberalism has done to Christianity—driving it out of the public square. It simply means demoting liberalism from the federally established worldview it is today and placing it back on an equal footing with every other view, so that it has to make its case by argument rather than by state coercion.

A start can be made by using the Free Exercise Clause against the Establishment Clause, so that any attempt by the federal government to impose secular liberalism via Justice Black's Jefferson-inspired reading of the Establishment Clause is rebuffed as an encroachment on the First Amendment's guarantee of the free exercise of religion. As we saw above, this strategy has already been used successfully in *Widmar v. Vincent*. And it has been repeated successfully in later court cases: *Rosenberger v. University of Virginia* (1995), *Mitchell v. Helms* (2000), and *Zelman v. Simmons-Harris* (2002).

In pursuing this strategy, even though we will be using one part of the First Amendment (the Free Exercise Clause) against the Court's interpretation of another (the Establishment Clause), we should be clear that the goal is not to follow the Supreme Court in cutting up the Constitution and Bill of Rights, but to reunite the pieces so that the First Amendment's guarantee of religious liberty can function once again as a unity: "Congress shall make no law respecting an establishment of religion, or prohibiting the free exercise thereof. . . ."

When the day finally comes that the Free Exercise Clause is reunited with the Establishment Clause (through a series of judicial precedents making it clear that any attempt to use the latter to impose secularism is a violation of the former), then we will have arrived again at the Amendment's original purpose—to prevent the federal government from either interfering with citizens' religion or establishing a religion of its own choosing (including an anti-religious religion like secular liberalism).

Reclaiming Education

But even straightening out the judicial system, while it would be a very good start, will not be enough to disestablish secular liberalism. As we recall from previous chapters, radical liberalism entered America through the university system in the 1800s, and the liberal revolution was first of all a revolution achieved in and through education. In fact, the liberal intellectual revolution had a profound effect on legal studies and bears a great deal of responsibility for the judicial imposition of "separation of church and state" on our society. The triumph of secular liberalism in academia was largely responsible for the pervasive secularism that came to dominate American public life among educated elites by the mid-twentieth century, including elite lawyers.

The education of our judicial elites followed the same pattern as we've seen in regard to the other disciplines. In the 1870s began the move for academic professionalization of the law. A "science" of law was set up against the earlier notion that judges and lawyers should be trained in the practice of the common law, which had been informed by Christianity. This "science" was not yet opposed to Christianity, but it rested on a kind of quasi-Enlightenment notion of a merely moral shared Christianity. Then, beginning with Oliver Wendell Holmes (nominated for the Supreme Court by Teddy Roosevelt), we have an entirely secular rights-based approach to law. (Holmes was, at best, agnostic, and a great admirer of Comte, J. S. Mill, and progressivism.) Other liberal judges followed, such as Louis Brandeis, Benjamin Cardozo, and of course, Justice Hugo Black, who in *Everson* was able to orchestrate the complete separation of religion from the secular state. This secular liberal approach continues to define legal education and the legal profession today, and hence largely determines the courts.[4]

But obviously secularism has not been confined only to lawyers and the legal profession. Academic liberalism has been a powerful force for reshaping all of American society. Realizing how important it is to capture minds while very young, liberals begin imposing their views on children long before college. Given that the secular takeover of education was the mode by which liberalism gained cultural hegemony, it should be no surprise that the majority of the "separation of church and state" cases beginning with *Everson* dealt with public education.[5] Liberals understood that secularizing public schools was essential, because it is in these schools that they can exercise the most pervasive top-down control, and do the most to direct the intellectual and moral formation of future generations.

So the secular liberal takeover that occurred in America's colleges and universities in the latter half of the 1800s had its parallel in the American public school system. Consider the history of the National Education Association, the nation's largest teachers' union and advocacy group for public education. It was founded in 1857, under its original name, the National Teachers' Association, and renamed the National Education Association in 1870. From the time of its founding the NEA was explicitly Christian, and as part of the common school movement among Protestants it remained so for some time, advocating Bible reading and Christian moral instruction as essential to the public school curriculum. Generally, those in charge of the NEA were liberal but committed Protestants.

But then in the 1880s the NEA experienced an influx of liberal educational elites that had received instruction at America's by-then secularized colleges and universities. As Kraig Beyerlien details, these elites moved immediately to secularize the NEA. "By the turn of the century, the educational secularizers in the association had won."[6] Thenceforth the secularized NEA had enormous impact on the formation of America's public schools and on the training of public school teachers—at the very time when public schooling was becoming mandatory, and less than a generation before Progressives made an enormous push for expansion and federal control of American public schooling.

And so the entire educational system, top to bottom, from the Ph.D. to first grade, was controlled and defined by a liberal elite. The takeover was largely completed before the beginning of the twentieth century. If there is to be an effective counterrevolution, it must occur first of all in education.

Teaching What Really Happened: the Invention of the University

No doubt what I'm going to suggest will appear, at first glance, less than revolutionary. The radical revolution against Christianity in America occurred first of all in its universities, and that is where the counterrevolution must be launched. All that counterrevolutionaries need to achieve in education in order to undermine the establishment of liberal secularism is—brace yourself!—to ensure that *what really happened* in the past be taught in our history classes.

Teaching the truth about the past seems too simple—it seems so obviously the right thing to do that everyone, even liberals, ought to be able to agree on it—but it is not what has been going on in our educational system for some time. History in our schools, and especially the history of ideas and of institutions, has been truncated and skewed to serve the secular liberal revolution. Teaching what really happened in history class is revolutionary precisely because it undermines the Comtean script for human progress, wherein humanity moves historically from religion to secularism. It's a compelling story—mankind's valiant struggle to cast off the shackles of religious prejudice and stride boldly into the wonderful world of freedom, tolerance, scientific truth, and technological progress. *But it's not what actually happened.*

Let's look at a few examples of historical truths that challenge the accepted account that's now taught in our history classes. Consider, first of all, the invention of the university itself. Where did the university come from? Did it arise as poor benighted human beings shook off the chains of religion in the eighteenth-century Enlightenment? No. The university is an invention of the Christian Middle Ages. Yes, that quintessential era of religious backwardness—or so we're told! Universities did not exist in any other time or place prior to that. If Christians had not invented them, there would be no universities today. Universities were originally an explicitly Catholic educational project. Institutions of higher education began in cathedral schools and spread all over Europe during the period between 1200 and 1500.

And from the beginning they provided more than just a theological education. Medieval university students who were going to study law, theology, and medicine had first to study mathematics, geometry, astronomy, and music, and also grammar, logic, and rhetoric—that is, they spent the beginning years of their education studying the natural sciences, mastering a strong mathematical curriculum, and undergoing a very rigorous education in language and logic. This curriculum was the ultimate foundation of all university education as it continued to develop after 1500.

Universities educated hundreds of thousands of people from all stations in life in the Middle Ages. Until that time, only a handful of people in all previous civilizations had ever been educated in the most advanced subjects. But thanks to the church's invention of the university, an unprecedentedly large number—again, hundreds of thousands in the Middle Ages alone—got top-class educations.[7]

That is what happened. The question is, can what really happened be taught in today's public universities and secondary schools?

The problem for secularists is that the church itself, in the supposedly benighted Middle Ages no less, was the great guardian and nurturer of reason and science, responsible for the largest, most expansive push for universal education that the world had ever known. Our educational system owes its origin to Christianity—though that system has now been largely taken over by a worldview hostile to the Christian religion.

But precisely *because* that is what happened, to truly understand *why* it happened one needs to study the Middle Ages more carefully and respectfully, and in fact to dig deeply into the fundamental theological doctrines of Christianity and find out why it was here, in Christendom alone, that we find the birth of the university, and with it the historically unprecedented spread of education on all levels. In other words, if we are even to understand our own educational institutions, Christianity would have to receive a sympathetic study, rather than hostile rejection.

If the inconvenient facts that the invention of the university and the unprecedented spread of education beyond a tiny elite occurred in Christendom alone were widely known, students might begin to question the liberal version of salvation history, wherein the human race is always being rescued from backwardness and ignorance by benevolent secular liberalism.

Teaching What Really Happened: the Origins of Modern Science

As we've seen, secular liberalism's view of human history is that human progress is defined by salutary secularization, leaving behind the superstitions and irrationalities of Christianity and embracing scientific materialism. On this view, modern science is something that developed in rebellion against Christianity. That was the view enshrined in Andrew Dickson White's *A History of the Warfare of Science with Theology in Christendom* (1898) and William Draper's equally famous *History of the Conflict between Religion and Science* (1874).

The problem with the "war between science and religion" thesis is that it is not supported by the actual facts of history. Over the last quarter of a century, historians of science have completely disproven the secularist notion, championed by Draper and White and a host of other peddlers of liberal secularist salvation history *à la* Comte, that the history of science is a history of conflict between the church and scientific truth. What they have found is quite the reverse: when you try to uncover the actual origins of modern science, you actually find yourself going all the way back to the early Middle Ages, to the universities and monasteries of Christendom.

The truth is that the first great modern scientists were medieval monks, priests, and bishops; the achievements of modern science rest on their accomplishments.[8] The origins of modern science are inextricably tied to the medieval university. As historian of science Michael Shank makes clear, "the medieval period gave birth to the university, which developed with the active support of the papacy," and that development had momentous consequences:

> This unusual institution sprang up rather spontaneously around famous masters in towns like Bologna, Paris, and Oxford before 1200. By 1500, about sixty universities were scattered throughout Europe. . . . About 30 percent of the medieval university curriculum covered subjects and texts concerned with the natural world. This was not a trivial development [for the history of science]. . . .
>
> If the medieval church had intended to discourage or suppress science, it certainly made a colossal mistake in tolerating—to say nothing of supporting—the university.[9]

Of course, Shank is being ironic here. As he makes clear, the church didn't discourage or suppress science but instead instituted a standard curriculum that deeply nourished it. All students had to take the seven liberal arts, divided into the quadrivium (arithmetic, geometry, music, and astronomy) and trivium (grammar, rhetoric, and logic). It was this heavy emphasis on mathematics in the quadrivium (both music and astronomy were mathematically based) along with the focus on natural science that laid the groundwork for future advances. The mathematical underpinnings of modern science would have been impossible without the extraordinary spread of mathematical knowledge in the universities of Europe. As Shank reveals, "Between 1150 and 1500 more literate Europeans had had access to scientific materials than any of their predecessors in earlier cultures, thanks largely to the emergence, rapid growth, and naturalistic arts curricula of the medieval universities."[10]

You see the secularists' problem with teaching what really happened? The whole Comtean Enlightenment scheme of progress is demonstrably false. Christianity isn't at war with science. It gave birth to and nurtured science. The development of science is not understandable without a thorough study of its beginnings in Christendom, among Christians, and even worse, among monks, priests, and bishops. Moreover, in order to understand why modern science developed in Christendom and nowhere else, one would have to investigate the particular Christian doctrines and policies of the church that led to this result. So, to really understand the origins of science—to teach it to students in universities—you'd have to teach Christian theology and church history.

And if those students were really going to understand the history of science, they'd also have to learn about the materialist takeover of science, looking at when and how science came to be defined as hostile to Christianity. They'd have to study the quite patently non-scientific origins of scientific materialism and hostility to religion. They'd read Machiavelli and Hobbes, Bacon and Descartes.

Teaching What Really Happened: the History of Warfare, Religious and Otherwise

So real history debunks the "war between science and religion" thesis. And there's yet another warfare-related thesis that would be completely exploded if students in our schools knew what really happened: the liberal notion that religion, especially Christianity, is the source of history's continual wars. Whatever else Christianity has given us, secular liberals never tire of reiterating, the perpetual divisions and conflicts among different sects of Christians have been the source of history's most bloody and destructive wars. This point has been drilled home in recent years by atheists such as Richard Dawkins, the late Christopher Hitchens, and Sam Harris. When we look back over history, according to this view, we see that religious passion and especially irrational religious controversies are *the* cause of war. Thus the world will never have peace until religious passions and religious differences are rendered harmless by separating the church from the state. To avoid perpetual violence, we must exile religion from the public square.

The problem with this argument is that it depends on another historical falsehood.

The dreadful Thirty Years War that occurred in the first half of the 1600s is the paradigmatic event that secularists always point to as *the* illustration of the essentially destructive nature of irrational religious belief and its passions. In their telling, the Thirty Years War is the key to understanding history—it proves the truth that religion leads to conflict (while human reason, materialist science, and a secular liberal worldview will lead to universal peace).

The problem, once again, is that that's not what actually happened. Let's take a quick tour through wars and related violence in world history, measuring their severity by the numbers of dead.[11]

The death toll of the Persian Wars between the Persian Empire and the Greek city-states struggling not to be absorbed by that empire in the fifth century BC was about 300,000. Soon afterward, when the Greeks themselves were engaged in acquiring an empire under Alexander the Great, about a half a million people were killed.

When the expanding Roman Republic clashed with Carthage in the Punic Wars, the butcher's bill was about 1.1 million dead. Another million died in the Roman slave wars during the growth of the republic, another 300,000 in the Roman Social war of the first century BC, and another 700,000 as Rome conquered the German barbarians. Rome itself became an empire, and its imperial prestige was displayed in its famous gladiatorial games, the huge spectacles of carnage that took place not just in Rome but throughout the empire. A reasonable estimate of the total number of prisoners of war, criminals, and professional fighters killed is about 3.5 million. Before Rome fell, somewhere around 7 million more died in ongoing efforts to expand and defend its imperial borders or fell in the barbarian invasions that finally resulted in the fall of the empire.

Note well—all of this carnage occurred for reasons other than religion. The cause of most of it was the desire for empire, along with the riches and luxuries that go with it. Such were the motives that killed millions of people before Christianity existed, and millions more before it became culturally powerful.

And what about wars beyond the borders of Western civilization? The history of China is exceedingly bloody, with millions upon millions slaughtered because of dynastic political ambition, the ambitions of local warlords, and the revolts of the unfortunate beneath them—*not* because of religious beliefs. Tens of millions were killed in the Chinese dynastic wars of the second and third century AD alone. Further dynastic wars in early seventh century AD took another 600,000 lives. More tens of millions died in wars of rebellion against the ruling dynastic power in the eighth century AD.

If we turn to America before it was touched by Christianity, we find battles of political ambition among the Mayans of Mexico and Central America costing a couple million lives in the ninth century AD.

And then back in Asia we mustn't forget the invasions of the Mongol leader Genghis Khan, which resulted in tens of millions of deaths, with another 800,000 under later Mongol leaders. When the Mongols warred with the Chinese in the mid-fourteenth century BC, perhaps 30 million were killed. In the last quarter of the fourteenth century, the notoriously ruthless Turk Timur (or Tamerlane) was responsible for the slaughter of some 17 million in central Asia. When the Chinese conquered Vietnam in the fifteenth century AD, about 7 million were killed. The chaos involved in the collapse of the Ming dynasty in China in the seventeenth century resulted in some 25 million dead. The Chinese wiped out about 600,000

Mongols in the eighteenth century AD, and in the last part of the nineteenth century and the middle of the twentieth Sino-Japanese wars took about 10 million.

But even in Christian Europe the vast majority of the violence was political rather than religious. There were many purely political wars in Europe over dynastic rivalries. William the Conqueror's invasion of England killed about 100,000, and the Hundred Years War (1337–1453) between France and England cost perhaps 3 million lives. As nation-states in Europe began to develop and assert their ambitions and claims to land, trade, and empire, we see a tiresome series of wars, both wars that had nothing to do with religion, and wars in which political figures sought to use differences in religion for dynastic or national advantage. The War of Spanish Succession (1701–1713) cost 700,000 lives, the War of Austrian Succession (1740–1748) another half million, the Seven Years War (1756–1763) 1.5 million.

And let's not leave out Africa, where one and a half million were killed in Zulu wars in the early 1800s, one million were killed in the war between Nigeria and Biafra in 1966–1970, and Idi Amin in Uganda took out about 300,000. Another 2 million were killed in wars spurred by communism (and ethnic tensions) in Ethiopia between 1974 and 1991, 800,000 in civil wars in Mozambique, a half-million in civil wars in Angola, and another half-million in Ugandan civil war during the same time period. And then we have the horrible Hutu-Tutsi conflict in Rwanda in 1994 taking about a million lives, soon to be outdone by the Second Congo war between the same two tribes in 1998–2002, which claimed almost 4 million lives. While religion may have played a part in these conflicts, the overriding causes were tribal, political, or ideological.

But what about the famous European Wars of Religion—the Thirty Years War in Germany and the violence between the Catholics and the Protestant Huguenots in France? These are the wars almost invariably held up by the secularists to prove that religion is *the* source of war. But even if we were to accept for the sake of argument that these two wars—with 7.5

million dead and 3 million dead respectively—were solely religious-based wars, their death toll is dwarfed by comparison to the carnage in all the other non-religious wars that have occurred throughout world history.

But the death toll in those wars *cannot* be ascribed to religion, either alone or even primarily. As a number of scholars have now established in great detail, the so-called "Wars of Religion" in sixteenth- and seventeenth-century Europe were primarily national and dynastic wars in which political figures *used* religious differences to achieve their ambitions (think the Catholic Cardinal Richelieu, who secretly supported the Protestant side in the Thirty Years War to weaken the Hapsburg dynasty because they were a threat to France).[12] It is not that differences of religion didn't play a part in the violence—for that Christians must take their share of the blame—but that religious differences weren't the exclusive or even the primary motivating factors for these wars.

And if religion has sometimes fuelled violence, secularism has been responsible for much, much more. The horrors of the French Revolution—as we've seen, a quarter of a million slaughtered in the Vendée alone—came with the attempt to extinguish Christianity and establish a Religion of Reason. The flowering of nationalism in the nineteenth century was the cause of far more bloody and destructive wars than Christians ever waged on behalf of their faith—the Franco-Prussian war alone tallied about a half million lives lost. The violence only became more destructive in the twentieth century, as idolatrous nationalism united with various political religions in World War I (15 million dead) and even more obviously and horrifically in World War II (between 50 and 70 million killed). Finally, we cannot fail to mention the epic destruction caused by Marxism, the ultimate secularist ideology bent on creating a heaven on earth, which can boast 100 million slaughtered in the Soviet Union, China, and elsewhere. The truth is that, in one form or another, the religion of secular liberalism has caused far more slaughter than any religion that acknowledges God's existence.

The notion that religion is *the* cause of war is patently ridiculous.

And so we may dispose of another argument liberals use to assert that the church must be driven from the public square and kept behind a wall of separation.

If you really wanted to separate what has caused the most wars from the state, it wouldn't be the church. You'd have to separate dynastic ambition, ethnic rivalry, economic ambition, national and tribal identity, the desire for glory, the desire for luxury and a life of ease, technological power, and the power of propaganda from the state—for these have been the overwhelming motives for war and the actual causes of its destructive toll in human history. Doesn't sound very practical, does it?

But here's a modest proposal that might just work: if you wanted to (at least) prevent the horrors of the very bloodiest wars in world history from ever being repeated, you'd separate *secularism* from the state. If you could somehow guarantee that anti-Christian state-worshippers would never again come to power in any government, you'd foreclose the possibility of any repeat of the horrors perpetrated in the twentieth century by revolutionary communists and Nazis.

Teaching What Really Happened: the Bible and the Distinction between Sacred and Secular Power

Beleaguered Christians have resorted to sneaking the Bible back into university curricula by teaching it "as literature." After all, given the Bible's immense influence on the great works of the Western canon, any educated person should at least be familiar with its contents. Dressing up the Bible as literature is a way to obscure its religious significance, so that it doesn't fall prey to the attacks of the ACLU armed with the Establishment Clause.

But there is a much better reason to teach the Bible in our universities. The history of the "separation of church and state" so precious to the ACLU is impossible to understand without the Bible. Can you see the ACLU bringing an Establishment Clause case to prevent a public university from assigning the Bible in a course exploring the history of church-state separation?

So can I. All the more reason to go ahead—to draw attention to the absurdity of the secularists' position.

We have seen that the very distinction between church and state can ultimately be traced back to the Bible. The truth is that the deep distinction between religious and political power arose *in Christianity alone*. Aside from Christianity, politics and religion are fused. Both kinds of power were in the same hands in ancient Greece and Rome, to a large extent in Judaism, and quite obviously in Islam. And when secularism rejects Christianity, as we have seen, soon enough religion and politics merge once again. That's why we've seen so many political religions arise in modernity. When the sacred is denied its own domain outside politics, then the secular inevitably becomes sacralized. Divinized modern political leaders exercising totalitarian rule resemble nothing so much as divine pharaohs or Caesars.

But the fusion of pagan religion and politics actually goes beyond anything in ancient Egypt or Rome. Modern secularism is directed explicitly against Christianity. And its proponents push it with the evangelical zeal that has always animated Christians to win souls for heaven. In secular liberalism Caesar becomes Christ and attempts to force heaven down to earth.

The immensely destructive modern fusion of religion and politics was made possible, in great part, because of the attack on Biblical authority carried out by Spinoza and the many liberalizing historical-critical Biblical scholars that followed his lead. Once the Bible was no longer authoritative, the lessons that had been learned from it—that priests are distinct from kings, that no man is a god, that even kings sin, that God's law is above all human law, that every human being has an immortal soul and an eternal destiny so that salvation is open to all regardless of race or nation or gender, that salvation cannot be achieved here on earth even by the most powerful kings—were lost. The result was that men became gods in their own minds, priests of their own secular salvation. The laws of the state became the highest laws; there was no appeal against them. Within living memory, the Darwinian notion that only some human beings of some races are fit for salvation, fused with the liberal notion that we can indeed make a heaven on earth (and should do so no matter what the cost) led to the most widespread and horrific violence the world has ever seen. That doesn't mean that Christians are without sin—too many used the Bible to support racist ideas. But Darwinism, which provided a "scientific" foundation for racial eugenics, was the real source of the Nazis' racial creed.

But again, I'm not calling liberals here in America "Nazis." Barack Obama is not Hitler, or Stalin, for that matter. Thank God for that! But America doesn't have to turn into Nazi Germany or Soviet Russia to become a very uncomfortable place for Christians to live—or, we should add, for anyone who for *any* reason declines to get on board with worshipping the state and embracing the wonderful programs with which it proposes to usher in a hedonist's paradise by alleviating all suffering (right down to the unbearable inconvenience of paying for one's own birth control).

I believe it was James Burnham who first pointed out, "The difference between the Communists and the liberals is that the Communists know what they're doing."[13] I think it is fair to say that the men and women responsible for unleashing the secularizing forces in our society may not always understand exactly where their project is taking us. But the inexorable logic of liberal secularism is for the state to expand to fill all public space, entirely squeezing out the church and, ultimately, the individual conscience. Already our political leaders are proceeding full steam ahead to require that Christians violate their consciences and pay for abortion-inducing drugs as the price of participation in "the marketplace of commerce."[14] Unless the courts overturn the HHS mandate, it will be impossible for a practicing pro-life Christian to own a mid-sized business in the United States. The point has now arrived at which Machiavelli's five-hundred-year-old dream of re-founding Western politics on a pagan basis is on the very cusp of fulfillment. Hobbes's Leviathan—the completely powerful state as guarantor of the "rights" of its subjects to fulfill their bodily appetites—is finally within reach. Sooner or later, that absolutely powerful state will leave no room, no more space than the Roman Empire allowed, for the worship of anything but itself.

And so we are brought back to that most prophetic statement by G. K. Chesterton, which provided the defining epigraph for this entire book:

> It is only by believing in God that we can ever criticise the Government. Once abolish...God, and the Government becomes the God. That fact is written all across human history....The truth is that Irreligion is the opium of the people. Wherever the people do not believe in something beyond the world, they will worship the world. But, above all, they will worship the strongest thing in the world.

The Counterrevolution We Must Launch

The book you have in your hands is meant to serve as the template for a revolution against the triumph of liberal secularism—while there is still time, in the remaining window when that triumph is not yet quite complete. But I am certainly not calling for a bloody revolution. Christianity is not Jacobinism, or radical Islam. The revolution we need is a revolution of mind and heart. The courts and the universities are two places where, as sketched out above, we must begin to loosen the grip that liberal secularism has on our country. Neither the real meaning of the U.S. Constitution nor the actual historical truths about Christianity and liberal secularism support the liberal myth about history or the project to secularize our society. On the contrary, true history and honest constitutional interpretation cut against secular liberalism every time.

There is some solid hope in developments in First Amendment law over the past thirty years. As we have seen, Supreme Court cases beginning with *Widmar v. Vincent* in 1981 have revived the First Amendment's Free Exercise clause as a counterweight to the Establishment Clause—or rather, to the secularizing interpretation that has wrenched "no . . . establishment" from its original context in the First Amendment and made it a writ for the government to drive religion out of every public space. We must keep working for even better jurisprudence, which would read the First Amendment's language on religion in its entirety as it was originally meant to be read—as a guarantee of religious liberty against government interference.

But when we turn to the university things seem less hopeful. And that's of great concern because, as we've seen from the history of liberal secularism's success in America, what goes on in the educational system ultimately will determine what happens in the courts, and in society at large. (And as we've seen from what's happening in universities now, that means a kind of liberal totalitarianism.) The university was a Christian invention. Religious Americans should be on our home turf in the academy. But we all know that's not the case. The vast majority of universities across the United States have become entirely secularized—defined, inside and out, by the rejection of Christianity, and devoted to imposing the most radical notions of the secular Left, based on moral and philosophical relativism. As a result, they are becoming no longer universities but *multiversities*. The old university was an institution rooted in a common dedication to the belief that the truth can be known by the human mind because the world was made by a divine Mind. Reject belief in the divine Mind, and belief in truth soon goes too. The universe becomes a kind of chaotic free-for-all, and the university becomes a multiversity of incoherent disciplines whose methods of approaching their various subject matters are mutually unintelligible to one another. And, as we've seen, this relativism becomes the ground for establishing an increasingly more evangelical, more radical liberalism.

While a few religious colleges continue to swim against the tide, and some small progress has been made in reclaiming at least a tiny amount of territory at those venerable institutions that have been nearly completely secularized—the Witherspoon Institute at Princeton University comes to mind—the situation in education is dire. By and large, the next generation is being infused with secular liberalism throughout their formative years. Unless our educational system changes, the victory of the aggressively secular state may be irreversible. And there is no fixing the schools without first reforming the universities, from which the liberal secularist philosophy radiates.

It may be that we must actually re-found the university. The goal would be not reclusive retreat into a religious ghetto but evangelical outreach to the culture at large. New Christian universities should offer *more* than is offered at secular universities, not less—a better understanding of modern science, more thorough scholarship of the Bible, a mastery of every sort of philosophy, a deeper comprehension of history, and so forth.

And perhaps the re-founding of the university is itself a template for the larger task that faces us.

This is not the first time Christians have faced a pagan society bent on eradicating their faith from the public square. Christianity transformed the pagan Roman Empire, civilized the barbarians, and formed the culture that invented the university, modern science, and the freest political institutions that the world has ever known.

These achievements grew out of Christians' unflinching commitment to the Good News that the universe was created by a good and loving God who had sent his Son to redeem the fallen human race. Our freedom from political totalitarianism, as well as everything we have accomplished with our science, still ultimately depends on that central truth. All the realities that scholars and scientists study are ultimately meaningless without the recognition that the world has a rational Creator—and science and scholarship become increasingly incoherent and incomprehensible with our increasing distance from that recognition. Political freedom depends on the recognition that we are all created in the image of God, and all in need of redemption by him. Political oppression and disregard for the good of the individual in pursuit of impossible utopias inevitably increases with distance from those truths. It is only by proclaiming these truths again with evangelical zeal that we may achieve a successful revolution against the liberal secularism whose grip is tightening even as I write.

But we must emphasize that, above all, Christians as revolutionaries must also exceed everyone else in real charity—and not just toward other

Christians. When Christians were a small minority in the Roman Empire—yet large enough to be a thorn in the side of the empire—they won converts and grudging respect because of the way that they loved not only their own, but the pagans themselves. In real and active charity to the poor, the sick, and the outcast, the Christians in the empire did what the Roman pagans didn't do for themselves. In obedience to a direct command of Christ, they prayed for those who persecuted them and forgave those who hunted them down. To their unflinching adherence to the truths of the faith, Christians added an unearthly love that astounded their enemies, many of whom soon became their brothers and sisters in Christ. *That is how Christians conquered pagan Rome.* If we are to resist the final triumph of liberal secularism—if we are to remain free to worship God, rather than the state—there is no other way.

ACKNOWLEDGMENTS

I want to thank Bruce Schooley for greatly encouraging me in this project, Elizabeth Kantor for patiently wading through the manuscript and editing it with such finesse, and, as always, my dear wife, Teri, and all my children for the great privilege of being a husband and father.

NOTES

Epigraph

The epigraph to this is book is from G. K. Chesterton, *The Collected Works of G. K. Chesterton*, vol. 20, Christendom in Dublin, Irish Impressions, *The New Jerusalem, A Short History of England*, ed. George J. Marlin, et al. (San Francisco, CA: Ignatius, 2001), pp. 57–58.

Chapter 1: Reading the Signs of Our Times

1. "FFRF Places Its Natural Nativity Scene, Winter Solstice Sign in Wis. Capitol Rotunda," Freedom from Religion Foundation website, November 26, 2012, http://ffrf.org/news/news-releases/item/16165-ffrf-places-its-natural-nativity-scene-winter-solstice-sign-in-wis-capitol-rotunda.

2. Noel Sheppard, "Jamie Foxx: 'Our Lord and Savior Barack Obama,'" November 26, 2012, http://newsbusters.org/blogs/noel-sheppard/2012/11/26/jamie-foxx-calls-obama-our-lord-and-savior#ixzz2EfGyswuP.

3. "FFRF Places Its Natural Nativity Scene."

4. Collecting messianic utterances about Obama became an internet hobby of the less than devout. For these quotations and others, see "The Beginning of the Gospel of Barack Obama, the Son of God (According to Mark Shea)," 2008,

Mark-Shea.com, http://www.mark-shea.com/obama.html; "Obama '08 for Messiah," http://obamaformessiah.com/; and "Is Barack Obama the Messiah?" blog, http://obamamessiah.blogspot.com/.

5. "Farrakhan on Obama: 'The Messiah Is Absolutely Speaking,'" World Net Daily, October 9, 2008, http://www.wnd.com/2008/10/77539/#Dgzl1IG56yTeYKAF.99.

6. For the history of this display in Santa Monica see the website, "Santa Monica Nativity Scenes, since 1953," http://www.santamonicanativityscenes.org/History. html.

7. Troy Anderson, "Finding Room for the Inn," tothesource, December 6, 2012, http://www.tothesource.org/12_5_2012/12_5_2012.htm.

8. Billy Hallowell, "'Obey the Constitution!': Atheists Announce Lawsuit against Montana Jesus Statue," The Blaze, February 1, 2012, http://www.theblaze.com/stories/obey-the-constitution-atheists-announce-lawsuit-against-montana-jesus-statue/#.

9. Billy Hallowell, "Alabama Town Bows to Atheists and Removes Bible Verse from Welcome Signs," The Blaze, April 26, 2012, http://www.theblaze.com/stories/al-town-bows-to-atheists-infuriates-residents-after-removing-bible-verse-from-welcome-signs/.

10. Billy Hallowell, "Air Force Bows to Atheist Complaints: Will Remove Bible Requirement for On-Base Lodging," The Blaze, April 25, 2012, http://www.theblaze.com/stories/air-force-bows-to-atheist-complaints-will-remove-bible-requirement-for-on-base-lodging/.

11. Aaron Sankin, "Oakland Zoo Ten Commandments Removed after Outcry from Atheist Groups," *Huffington Post*, July 26, 2012, http://www.huffingtonpost.com/2012/07/26/oakland-zoo-ten-commandments-removed_n_1707718.html.

12. Todd Starnes, "Charlie Brown Embroiled in Christmas Controversy," Fox News Radio, November 19, 2012, http://radio.foxnews.com/toddstarnes/top-stories/critics-target-charlie-brown-christmas.html.

13. Bob Dunning, "Bah, Humbug! No Christmas Play Here," October 10, 2012, The Davis Enterprise, http://www.davisenterprise.com/local-news/dunning/bah-humbug-no-christmas-play-here/.

14. Marie Waxel, "School Asked to Nix 'Silent Night' from Christmas Program," December 14, 2011, News 48, http://www.waff.com/story/16325444/school-asked-to-nix-silent-night-from-christmas-program.

15. Tim Daly, "Holiday Decorations off Limits at Stockton School," December 2, 2011, News 10, http://www.news10.net/news/local/story.aspx?storyid=165912.

16. Warren Richey, "Nativity Scene Is Too Religious for New York City Schools," *Christian Science Monitor*, February 22, 2007, http://www.csmonitor.com/2007/0222/p04s01-ussc.html.

17. For the classic discussion of political religions see Eric Voegelin, *The Collected Works of Eric Voegelin, vol. 5: Modernity without Restraint, The Political Religions* (Columbia, MO: University of Missouri Press, 2000).

18. Leo Strauss, *Natural Right and History* (Chicago: University of Chicago Press, 1971), pp. 42–43.

19. Obviously I have benefitted from Pierre Manent, *An Intellectual History of Liberalism*, translated by Rebecca Balinski (Princeton, NJ: Princeton University Press, 1995), and Thomas Pangle, *The Spirit of Modern Republicanism: The Moral Vision of the American Founders and the Philosophy of Locke* (Chicago: University of Chicago Press, 1988), ch. 16–17.

20. See Richard John Neuhaus's classic *The Naked Public Square: Religion and Democracy in America* (Grand Rapids, MI: Eerdmans, 1986), 2nd ed.

21. See my *Ten Books Every Conservative Must Read, Plus Four Not to Miss and One Impostor* (Washington, DC: Regnery, 2010), all of part I, which is concerned with clarifying exactly what liberalism and conservatism really are, in their deepest, as opposed to their popular, meaning. See also Leo Strauss, *Liberalism Ancient and Modern* (Ithaca, NY: Cornell University Press, 1989), preface and chs. 1–3, which is immensely insightful, even while insufficient.

22. "LA Schools to Teach LGBT Curriculum in Anti-Bullying Effort," CBS Los Angeles, September 14, 2011, http://losangeles.cbslocal.com/2011/09/14/la-schools-to-teach-lgbt-curriculum-in-anti-bullying-effort/.

23. Greg Lukianoff, *Unlearning Liberty: Campus Censorship and the End of American Debate* (New York: Encounter Books, 2012), p. 97.

24. Ibid., pp. 100–1.

25. Ibid., p. 163.

26. Ibid., p. 110.

27. Ibid., p. 119.

28. Ibid., p. 192.

29. Ibid., pp. 163–80.

30. Ibid., pp. 57, 82, 90, 168–69.

Chapter 2: Back to the Beginning: the Church versus Pagan Imperial Rome

1. Here and throughout, except where otherwise noted, quotations of the Bible are from the Revised Standard Version (RSV).

2.   On Roman coinage in general see William E. Metcalf, "Roman Imperial Numismatics," in David S. Potter, ed., *A Companion to the Roman Empire* (Malden, MA: Blackwell Publishing, 2006), pp. 35–44.

3.   The Romans didn't much like the Jews either. The Roman historian Tacitus notes a discussion in the senate which "concerned the expulsion of Egyptian and Jewish rites" (the Egyptian rites in question involved the worship of Isis). The senate decreed that some four thousand adult ex-slaves "tainted with those superstitions" should be sent to Sardinia for enforced military service against bandits there: "If the unhealthy climate killed them, the loss would be small. The rest, unless they repudiated their unholy practices by a given date, must leave Italy." Tacitus, *Annals of Imperial Rome*, trans. Michael Grant (New York: Penguin, 1989, rev. ed.), II.85 (ch. 5, p. 118). See also a similar report in Suetonius, *The Twelve Caesars*, trans. Robert Graves (New York: Penguin, 1980), "Tiberius," III.36, (p. 132).

4.   Tacitus, *Annals*, VI.1 (ch. 8, p. 200). This was a dig at Tiberius. Sexual molestation of child slaves, male or female, was just part of the sexual liberties that the freeborn routinely took with their slaves, for whom serving the master included sexual service. (This was true even before greater sexual license had been imported to Rome from Greece.) But sex with a freeborn child (*pubem ingenuam*) was taken by the Romans to be crossing the line, something only a tyrant would do, and a sign of the evil of the times.

5.   Tacitus, *Annals*, XV.37 (ch. 14, p. 362). I have deviated from Grant's translation of Tacitus to better capture the meaning of *per licita atque inlicita foedatus nihil flagitii reliquerat*.

6.   As Tacitus relates, "Nero was already corrupted by every lust, natural and unnatural. But he now refuted any surmises that no further degradation was possible for him. For…he went through a formal wedding ceremony with one of the perverted gang called Pythagoras. The emperor, in the presence of witnesses, put on the bridal veil. Dowry, marriage bed, wedding torches, all were there. Indeed everything was public which even in a natural union is veiled by night." Tacitus, *Annals*, XV.37 (ch. 14, p. 362), and also Seutonius, *The Twelve Caesars*, "Nero," VI.28–29, p. 228.

7.   As Tacitus tells us. Yet even Tacitus notes that public sympathy was with the Christians, because it seemed that they were being so exquisitely slaughtered, "not for public utility" (*non utilitate publica*), but simply to satisfy Nero's insatiable lust for cruelty. Tacitus, *Annals*, XV.44 (ch. 14, pp. 366–67).

8. For an overview essay on sexuality in the Roman Empire with a large bibliography, see Amy Richelin, "Sexuality in the Roman Empire," in David S. Potter, ed., *A Companion to the Roman Empire*, pp. 327–53.

9. John Riddle, *Contraception and Abortion from the Ancient World to the Renaissance* (Cambridge: Harvard University Press, 1992), p. 3.

10. The ubiquity of pornography is evidenced at Pompeii and Herculaneum. See also the connection between imperial sexual perversion and pornography in Suetonius, *The Twelve Caesars*, "Tiberius," III.43–44 (pp. 135–36).

11. The *Fortuna Virilis*, the festivals associated with Venus, and the *Floralia*.

12. As attested by Augustus passing his famous law against adultery in 18 BC. For the complexities surrounding this law and the many and varied interpretations of scholars, see Catharine Edwards, *The Politics of Immorality in Ancient Rome* (Cambridge: Cambridge University Press, 2002), ch. 1. It is noteworthy that the prohibitions against adultery only dealt with sexual offenses against the freeborn, not with what the slaves and prostitutes did, or what the freeborn did with them. See Marilyn Skinner, *Sexuality in Greek and Roman Culture* (Malden, MA: Wiley-Blackwell, 2005), p. 207.

13. Given the desire to normalize homosexuality and lesbianism today, the literature in this area is vast, and also very often ideologically skewed. A good place to start is the article on "Homosexuality" in Simon Hornblower and Antony Spawforth, eds., *The Oxford Classical Dictionary* (Oxford: Oxford University Press, 1996), pp. 720–23.

14. See Tacitus, *Annals*, VI.1 (ch. 8, p. 200).

15. For a discussion of male-male marriages in ancient Rome see Karen Hersch, *The Roman Wedding: Ritual and Meaning in Antiquity* (Cambridge: Cambridge University Press, 2010), pp. 33–39. Tacitus is not our only source. Martial, the first-century-AD Roman poet, reports instances of male-male marriage as perversions, but not uncommon perversions. In one epigram he says mockingly, "You see that fellow there with the rough hair [i.e., beard], whose beetling brow frightens you.... Don't believe his looks. He took a husband yesterday." Martial, *Epigrams*, translated and edited by D. R. Shackleton Bailey, (Cambridge, MA: Harvard University Press, 1993), I.24. In another (12.42), "Bearded Callistratus gave himself in marriage to ... [a man named] Afer, in the manner in which a virgin usually gives herself in marriage to a male. The torches shone in front, the bridal veils covered his face, and wedding toasts were not absent, either. A dowry was also named. Does that not seem enough yet for you, Rome? Are you waiting for him to give birth?" In Juvenal's *Second Satire* (117), we hear of one Gracchus, "a former priest of Mars," who becomes a "blushing bride" with arms "hung

round 'her' husband's neck at a lavish wedding-breakfast," "decked out in bridal frills complete with train and veil.... Here's a wealthy, well-born man married off to a man...." Juvenal, *The Sixteen Satires*, trans. Peter Green, 3rd ed. (New York: Penguin, 1998), II.117–48. The notoriously debauched emperor Elagabalus (ruled 218–12 AD) married and divorced five women. But he considered his male chariot driver to be his "husband," and he also married one Zoticus, an athlete. Elagabalus loved to dress up as a queen, quite literally.

16.   The Roman Laws of the Twelve Tables (Table IV, Law I) mandated that a deformed child must be "quickly killed."

17.   See the article "Suicide" including classical references in Simon Hornblower and Antony Spawforth, eds., *The Oxford Classical Dictionary* (Oxford: Oxford University Press, 1996), p. 1453. For a more complex account, set within the larger context of the Roman views of death, see Catharine Edwards, *Death in Ancient Rome* (New Haven, CT: Yale University Press, 2007).

18.   Ian Dowbiggin, *A Concise History of Euthanasia: Life, Death, God, and Medicine* (Lanham, MI: Rowman & Littlefied, 2005), p. 7. Dowbiggin adds, significantly, "this doctrine about the equal value of all human lives would reign largely unchallenged until the eighteenth-century Enlightenment." At that time Voltaire, Montesquieu, d'Alembert, and Hume opened up the debate again, attempting to reintroduce the pagan affirmation of suicide. See Dowbiggin, pp. 30–34, and in more depth, Georges Minois, *History of Suicide: Voluntary Death in Western Culture*, trans. Lydia Cochrane (Baltimore, MD: Johns Hopkins University Press, 1999).

19.   See Richard Lipsey, et al., *Economic Transformations: General Purpose Technologies and Long-Term Economic Growth* (Oxford: Oxford University Press, 2006), pp. 335–37; Robert Jütte, *Contraception: A History* (Cambridge: Polity Press, 2008), ch. 1; John Riddle, *Contraception and Abortion from the Ancient World to the Renaissance* (Cambridge, MA: Harvard University Press, 1994) and *Eve's Herbs: A History of Contraception and Abortion in the West* (Cambridge, MA: Harvard University Press, 1999); and Jeffrey Reiman, *Abortion and the Ways We Value Human Life* (Lanham, MD: Rowman & Littlefield, 1998).

20.   *Didache* means, in Greek, "teaching" or "doctrine," the full title being, *The Teaching of the Twelve Apostles*. It begins with the ominous words, "There are two ways: one of life and one of death—and there is a great difference between the two ways." *Didache*, 1:1. For the text of the *Didache* with commentary see Aaron Milavec, *The Didache: Faith, Hope, & Life of the Earliest Christian Communities, 50–70 C.E.* (Malwah, NJ: The Newman Press, 2003).

21. In a very un-Roman way, converts from paganism are informed that they must not only love one another but love their enemies, fast for their persecutors, turn the other cheek, walk two miles when asked to walk one, and give to all who ask (although they are also warned, "Let the alms sweat in your hands,"—that is, charity must be done with discrimination); *Didache*, 1:2–6. The converts are then confronted with a list of commands. Some of these would have been quite familiar and reasonable to Romans, such as "You will not murder" and "You will not commit adultery" (although for pagan Romans, a husband having sex with slaves or prostitutes was not considered adulterous, whereas Christians were warned by Christ, "I say to you that every one who looks at a woman lustfully has already committed adultery with her in his heart," Mt 5:28). But then followed strange commands—at least to the Romans—"You will not corrupt boys," "You will not have illicit sex (*ou porneuseis*)" "You will not murder offspring by means of abortion [and] you will not kill one having been born." Against the norm in Rome, Christians were required to reject pedophilia, fornication and homosexuality, abortion, and infanticide. The list of prohibitions also includes "You will not make potions" (*ou pharmakeuseis*), a prohibition against wide-scale practices in the Roman Empire involving drugs, including mixtures that were supposed to stop conception or cause abortion. Such laws would have been familiar to Jews, but not to Roman pagans. For the connection to Judaism, see *The Didache: Its Jewish Sources and Its Place in Early Judaism and Christianity* (Minneapolis, MN: Fortress Press, 2002), pp. 117–18, 133–34. On the Christian prohibition of contraception see *Didache*, 2:2, and 5:1–2. For the prohibition in the context of Rome and the ancient world generally see John Noonan, *Contraception* (Harvard: Harvard University Press, 1965), p. 10 and John Riddle, *Contraception and Abortion from the Ancient World to the Renaissance*, p. 23, on the *pharmakos* (physician or potion-maker) giving *pharmakeia* (potions, poisons) as contraceptives and abortifacients. The ancient pagans (Greek, Roman, Egyptian) used a variety of concoctions, ingested or applied, as contraceptives and abortifacients—everything from pomegranate peels, giant fennel, acacia gum, crushed Juniper berries, cabbage flowers, date palm, rue, and myrrh to crocodile dung (our knowledge of this last one coming from an Egyptian papyrus, c. 1850 BC; see Riddle, p. 66). See also Riddle's *Eve's Herbs: a History of Contraception and Abortion in the West* (Cambridge, MA: Harvard University Press, 1997), Ch. 2 and Angus McLaren, *A History of Contraception, from Antiquity to the Present Day* (Oxford: Basil Blackwell, 1990), ch. 2.

22. There is a good map showing the expansion of Christianity in Jonathan Hill, *How a Tiny Sect from a Despised Religion Came to Dominate the Roman Empire* (Minneapolis, MN: Fortress, 2011), p. 28.

23. Hill, *How a Tiny Sect*, p. 82.

24. See the discussion of calculating the growth of Christianity, including a helpful table, by the historian-sociologist Rodney Stark in *The Triumph of Christianity: How the Jesus Movement Became the World's Largest Religion* (New York: HarperCollins, 2011), ch. 9.

25. Pliny, reporting to Trajan about 112 AD, described the seemingly humdrum bureaucratic procedure he had designed for judging those accused of being Christians:

> in the case of those who were denounced to me as Christians, I have observed the following procedure: I interrogated these as to whether they were Christians; those who confessed I interrogated a second and a third time, threatening them with punishment; those who persisted I ordered executed. For I had no doubt that, whatever the nature of their creed, stubbornness and inflexible obstinacy surely deserve to be punished. There were others possessed of the same folly; but because they were Roman citizens, I signed an order for them to be transferred to Rome.
>
> Soon accusations spread, as usually happens, because of the proceedings going on, and several incidents occurred. An anonymous document was published containing the names of many persons. Those who denied that they were or had been Christians, when they invoked the gods in words dictated by me, offered prayer with incense and wine to your image [i.e., a statue of the divine emperor Trajan], which I had ordered to be brought for this purpose together with statues of the gods [Jupiter, Juno, and Minerva], and moreover cursed Christ—none of which those who are really Christians, it is said, can be forced to do—these I thought should be discharged. Others named by the informer declared that they were Christians, but then denied it, asserting that they had been but had ceased to be, some three years before, others many years, some as much as twenty-five

years. They all worshipped your image and the statues of the
gods, and cursed Christ.

Pliny the Younger to Trajan, Letter X.96, available at the Georgetown University
website, http://www9.georgetown.edu/faculty/jod/texts/pliny.html.

26.   Stephen Benko, *Pagan Rome and the Early Christians*, p. 13, 21–24.

27.   Ibid., ch. 3.

28.   See the excellent overview by Peter Leithart, *Defending Constantine: The Twilight of an Empire and the Dawn of Christendom* (Downers Grove, IL: IVP Academic, 2010), ch. 2.

29.   Eusebius, *The History of the Church*, trans. G. A. Williamson (New York: Dorset Press, 1965), 8.2, p. 330.

30.   Christians were stripped and flogged with whips, scraped with iron combs used to card wool, and had salt and vinegar poured over their fresh wounds; they were put on the rack; they were slowly roasted to death over fires individually or thrown on great piles to be burned alive en masse (an entire town in Phrygia, men, women, and children, was set on fire by soldiers); they were strangled or run through with swords; they were tied hand and foot, put into boats, and drowned in the sea; they were jailed and then led into the arena to be torn to pieces by panthers, bears, boars, and bulls; they had their skin torn bit by bit with pottery shards, or they were decapitated ("So many were killed on a single day," Eusebius remarks, "that the axe, blunted and worn out by the slaughter, was broken in pieces, while the exhausted executioners had to be periodically relieved."); women were stripped and hung upside down for public humiliation, and sometimes believers were hung this way over a fire so as to be choked by the smoke; Christians had their limbs tied to trees that were bent down and then let snap, tearing their legs or arms from their bodies; sharp reeds were driven under fingernails, molten lead was poured down backs, genitals horribly mutilated, eyes gouged out and cauterized with a hot iron, and the list goes on. Eusebius, *The History of the Church*, 8.3–9, 11–12, pp. 330–44.

31.   Ramsay MacMullen, *Christianizing the Roman Empire*, pp. 29–30.

32.   Benko, *Pagan Rome*, pp. 39–40.

33.   Ramsay MacMullen, *Christianizing the Roman Empire*, p. 8, and his *Paganism in the Roman Empire* (New Haven, CT: Yale University Press, 1981), II.4.

34.   Robert Wilken, *The Christians as the Romans Saw Them*, p. 45; Benko, *Pagan Rome*, p 47.

35.   Wilken, The Christians, pp. 108–112. See also, Benko, *Pagan Rome*, pp. 147–58.
      There was not yet an official New Testament canon, but there were, by this time—
      c. 170 AD—generally recognized authoritative writings that would later be
      officially declared part of the canon. The polemic of the late second-century
      Greek philosopher Celsus against Christianity, *The True Word* (c. 170 AD), is the
      first sustained and comprehensive intellectual attack levied specifically against
      the beliefs of the church. One mode of attack Celsus used was to undermine the
      account of Jesus in the Gospels by asserting that Jesus was an impostor who
      himself fabricated the story about the virgin birth to cover up the fact that he
      was a child born out of wedlock, and who had learned magic when Joseph and
      Mary had taken him to Egypt and used it as an adult to fool people into thinking
      he was actually divine. Moreover, Jesus's divine birth, miracle-saturated life,
      death, and resurrection were simply imitations of existing legends about pagan
      gods and demi-gods, Celsus argued, and the Gospels were unreliable anyway,
      given that they were written so long after the events. Celsus's attacks should
      sound familiar. The "impostor" approach was revived in that most influential of
      clandestine radical Enlightenment works, *The Treatise of the Three Impostors*,
      which emerged from Benedict Spinoza's circle of skepticism and circulated
      widely in the eighteenth century. Another approach, championed by the third-
      century anti-Christian philosopher Porphyry as well as the apostate emperor
      Julian (sole emperor, 361–363 AD) was to credit Jesus with being a great moral
      man and very pious worshiper of the one true God, who was later made to be
      divine by his disciples. Wilken, *The Christians*, pp. 152–54, 178–79.

36.   J. H. W. G. Liebeschuetz, *Continuity and Change in Roman Religion* (Oxford:
      Oxford University Press, 1979), pp. 292–93. Quoted in Peter Leithart, *Defending
      Constantine: The Twilight of an Empire and the Dawn of Christendom* (Downers
      Grove, IL: IVP Academic, 2010), p. 153.

37.   See my discussions of Aristotle, Burke, and Tocqueville in *10 Books Every Con-
      servative Must Read*, chs. 1, 5, and 6.

38.   "Associations of this sort organized by members of the same trade or occupation
      did not restrict the activities to matters of 'professional' interest. The clubs were
      also social organizations, and the members met together regularly for food and
      drink, fun and relaxation, and support in times of trouble. As a consequence,
      they were a natural breeding ground for grumbling about the conduct of civic
      affairs and they often became involved in politics. Clubs would support candi-
      dates for local office, sponsor campaigns, and post campaign slogans on the walls

of local buildings." Wilken, *The Christians*, p. 13. There were a great number of such intermediate institutions, from those centering on common crafts—wool-workers, beekeepers, or weavers—to those centering on particular deities, for example the *Herakleistai* (dedicated to Hercules) and *Iobacchi* (dedicated to Bacchus).

39. See Rodney Stark, *The Triumph of Christianity*, pp. 21–22; Wilken, *The Christians*, pp. 10–15, and Ch. 2.

40. Benko, *Pagan Rome*, p. 59.

Chapter 3: How the Bible Kept the Church from Becoming a Department of the State

1. Quoted in Hugo Rahner, *Church and State in Early Christianity* (San Francisco, CA: Ignatius Press, 1992), p. 9.

2. From Justin's "First Apology," as quoted in Hugo Rahner, *Church and State in Early Christianity*, p. 23.

3. Theophilus of Antioch, "To Autolycus," as quoted in Hugo Rahner, *Church and State in Early Christianity*, p. 24.

4. See Hugo Rahner, *Church and State in Early Christianity*, pp. 28–38.

5. Origen, "Commentary on the Letter to the Romans," in Hugo Rahner, *Church and State in Early Christianity*, p. 32.

6. The literature on Constantine is vast and continually being updated, and there is a lot of scholarly disagreement, and even bickering. To get some notion of all this, read Noel Lenski, ed., *The Cambridge Companion to the Age of Constantine*, rev. ed. (Cambridge: Cambridge University Press, 2012), and then the review of Lenski's work by Timothy Barnes, "Constantine after Seventeen Hundred Years: The Cambridge Companion, the York Exhibition and a Recent Biography," *International Journal of the Classical Tradition*, Summer 2007, pp. 185–220. I am generally in agreement with the positive assessment of Constantine in Peter Leithart's *Defending Constantine: the Twilight of an Empire and the Dawn of Christendom* (Downers Grove, IL: InterVarsity Press, 2010). See also Rodney Stark, *The Triumph of Christianity: How the Jesus Movement Became the World's Largest Religion* (New York: HarperCollins, 2011), ch. 10.

7. See the prologue and epilogue of the *Code of Hammurabi*, available on Yale Law School's website at http://avalon.law.yale.edu/ancient/hamframe.asp.

8. This is the same *kosmos* that the glorious prologue to the Gospel of John declares that the Word came into. The Gospel further states that, although Jesus was "in the world (*kosmos*), and the world (*kosmos*) was made through him, yet the world (*kosmos*) knew him not" (John 1:10).

9. I have corrected the Revised Standard Version, which misleadingly translates *psuchē* [soul] as "life."

10. Christians are now divided over the nature and number of the sacraments. Both the Catholic and the Greek Orthodox Church have seven sacraments. Lutherans, Methodists, and Reformed Christians accept two. The Anglican Church has as few as two or as many as seven, depending on how one counts. Most of the other types of Christians—Baptists, Pentecostals, Evangelicals, and so on—do not recognize any sacraments, even while they do in one way or another baptize, and most celebrate something like the Lord's Supper, if only as a memorial.

Chapter 4: From the Conversion of Constantine to the Fall of Rome

1. Constantine continued to use the traditional title, but the imperial title would later be changed from *Pontifex Maximus to Pontifex Inclitus* (Renowned Pontiff), to describe an emperor with no claim to priestly power. For the intricacies of this transition see Alan Cameron, *The Last Pagans of Rome* (Oxford: Oxford University Press), 2.2.

2. Eusebius, *Life of Constantine*, trans. Averil Cameron and Stuart Hall (Oxford: Clarendon Press, 1999), IV.61.2. I have substituted "mystical" for this translation's "secret" in the last sentence. The Greek *aporrētos* means "forbidden" in the sense of words not to be spoken publicly, which can mean secret but also more appropriately here, too holy or sacred to be spoken publicly, and hence, mystical in the Catholic sense, as dealing directly with the divine mysteries present in a sacrament. Eusebius's *Life of Constantine* is also available on Fordham University's website at http://www.fordham.edu/halsall/basis/vita-constantine.asp.

3. Eusebius, *Life of Constantine*, IV.62.1–3.

4. Here again, the literature is vast. In addition to overview treatments in Leithart, *Defending Constantine*, ch. 8 and Henry Chadwick, *The Early Church* (New York: Penguin, 1990), ch. 8, one might consult Timothy Barnes's two important works, *Constantine and Eusebius* (Cambridge: Harvard University Press, 1981) and *Athanasius and Constantius: Theology and Politics in the Constantinian Empire* (Cambridge: Harvard University Press, 1993).

5. Another Eusebius, Eusebius of Caesarea, was an orthodox bishop and a confidant of Constantine. He wrote the first church history as well as the first biography of Constantine; both are invaluable resources.

6. Hugo Rahner, *Church and State in Early Christianity*, p. 64.

7. Owen Chadwick, *The Early Church* (New York: Penguin, 1990), p. 143.

8. As recorded in the *Justinian Code*, 11.44.1, available on the University of Wyoming website https://uwacadweb.uwyo.edu/blume&justinian/Book%2011PDF/Book11-44.pdf.

9. See Andrew Borkowski and Paul du Plessis, *Textbook on Roman Law*, 3rd ed. (Oxford: Oxford University Press, 2005), pp. 114–16; Lactantius, *Divine Institutes*, VI.20.

10. As recorded in the *Justinian Code*, 9.17.1, available on the University of Wyoming website https://uwacadweb.uwyo.edu/blume&justinian/Book%209PDF/Book9–17.pdf.

11. As quoted in Leithart, *Defending Constantine*, pp. 219–20.

12. Ibid., pp. 219–21.

13. See James Kennedy and Jerry Newcombe, *What If Jesus Had Never Been Born?* (Nashville, TN: Thomas Nelson, 2001), p. 13.

14. For the effect of Christianization on squeezing out Roman sexual license of all sorts see Amy Richlin, "Sexuality in the Roman Empire," in David S. Potter, ed., *A Companion to the Roman Empire* (Chichester, West Sussex (UK): Wiley-Blackwell, 2010), pp. 327–53.

15. For an overview of the difference in imperial legislation after the conversion of Constantine see Leithart's *Defending Constantine*, ch. 9–10.

16. *Justinian Code*, 1.1.1, available on the University of Wyoming website, https://uwacadweb.uwyo.edu/blume&justinian/Code%20Revisions/Book1rev%20copy/Book%201-1rev.pdf.

17. See Justinian, *The Digest of Justinian*, trans. Alan Watson (Philadelphia, PA: University of Pennsylvania Press, 1985), 2 vols.: I, p. xliii, pp. liii–liv.

18. Augustine, *Political Writings*, ed. Michael Tkacz and Douglas Kries (Indianapolis, IN: Hackett, 1994), *The City of God*, Book I, preface.

19. Augustine, *The City of God*, Book I, preface.

20. Ibid., Book IV.4.

21. Ibid., Books II–IV.

22. Ibid., Book II.21.

23. Ibid., Book I.8, V.11, V.19.

24. Ibid., Book XIV.28.

25. Ibid., Book V.16–17.

26. Augustine, *Confessions*, trans. Henry Chadwick (Oxford: Oxford University Press, 1998), I.1. Here I've altered the Chadwick translation to the more familiar plural.

27. Augustine, *The City of God*, Book V.24.

28. Ibid., Book V.26.

29. Ibid., Book V.25–26.

Chapter 5: The Middle Ages: Defining the Church-State Distinction

1.   To make a very long, complex story short, the fifth century witnessed an extremely divisive dispute about the incarnate Christ. The orthodox argued that the fullness of divine nature and human nature were both present in the union of God and man. The heterodox Monophysites argued that there was only a single, divine nature in Jesus Christ (in Greek, *monos* means alone or only, and *phusis* means nature). The Eastern emperor Zeno had come up with a compromise formula, the *Henoticon*, that was meant to please all parties in the dispute. Zeno (like Constantine in compromise-with-the-Arians mode) wanted to achieve political and ecclesial peace at the expense of theological truth. Emperor Anastasius, who took the imperial throne after Zeno and who was himself a Monophysite, pushed the *Henoticon* even harder.

2.   Pope Gelasius I, Letter to Anastasius I (494), quoted in Brian Tierney, *The Crisis of Church & State* (Englewood Cliffs, NJ: Prentice-Hall, 1980), pp. 13–14. See also Norman Cantor, *The Civilization of the Middle Ages* (New York: Harper, 1993), pp. 86–88, and Gerd Tellenbach, *Church, State and Christian Society at the Time of the Investiture Controversy*, trans. R. F. Bennett (New York: Harper, 1959), pp. 33–37.

3.   Tellenbach, *Church, State and Christian Society*, p. 35.

4.   Pope Gelasius I, *On the Bond of Anathema*, quoted in Tierney, *The Crisis of Church & State*, p. 14.

5.   Ibid., pp. 14–15.

6.   See Nomi Stolzenberg, "The Profanity of Law," in Austin Sarat, et al., eds., *Law and the Sacred* (Stanford, CA: Stanford University Press, 2007), pp. 29–90, and more generally, the excellent work by Steven Smith, *The Disenchantment of Secular Discourse* (Cambridge, MA: Harvard, 2010).

7.   Humbert, *Adversus Simoniacos*, as quoted in Tierney, *The Crisis of Church & State*, pp. 41–42.

8.   Hugh of St. Victor, *De Sacramentis Christianae Fidei*, quoted in Tierney, *The Crisis of Church & State*, pp. 94–95.

9.   Ibid., p. 95.

10.   Cantor, *The Civilization of the Middle Ages*, ch. 2–3.

11.   See the insightful Joseph Strayer, *On the Medieval Origins of the Modern State* (Princeton, NJ: Princeton University Press, 2005), ch. 1. This work was originally published in 1970, but it is still rightly considered a classic.

12.   Tellenbach, *Church, State and Christian Society*, ch. 3.

13.   For this and the next sections, see especially Tellenbach, *Church, State and Christian Society*, Cantor, *The Civilization of the Middle Ages*, ch. 2–11, and Uta-Renate

Blumenthal, *The Investiture Controversy: Church and Monarchy from the Ninth to the Twelfth Century* (Philadelphia, PA: University of Pennsylvania Press, 1988).

14. Quoted in Tierney, *The Crisis of Church & State*, p. 183.

15. Ibid., p. 24.

16. Quoted in ibid., pp. 29–30.

17. Quoted in ibid., p. 29.

18. On the Gregorian reform see especially Cantor, *The Civilization of the Middle Ages*, ch. 11 and Blumenthal, *The Investiture Controversy*, ch. 3.

19. Tierney, *The Crisis of Church & State*, p. 45.

20. Ibid., p. 45.

21. Quoted in ibid., p. 58.

22. Quoted in ibid., p. 60.

23. Quoted in ibid., p. 60.

24. Quoted in ibid., p. 61.

25. Quoted in ibid., pp. 58, 67.

26. Quoted in ibid., p. 63.

27. See ibid, pp. 66–73.

28. See ibid., pp. 133–134.

29. Quoted in ibid., pp. 135–136.

Chapter 6: Machiavelli Invents the Secular State (and Its Church)

1. Quentin Skinner, *The Foundations of Modern Political Thought* (Cambridge: Cambridge University Press, 1978), vol. I, p. xxiii.

2. "Before the sixteenth century, the term *status* was only used by political writers to refer to one of two things: either the state or condition in which a ruler finds himself (the *status principis*); or else the general 'state of the nation' or condition of the realm as a whole (the *status regni*)." Skinner, *The Foundations*, vol. II, p. 353.

3. See especially Harvey Mansfield, *Machiavelli's Virtue* (Chicago: University of Chicago Press, 1996), ch. 12.

4. Leo Strauss, *Thoughts on Machiavelli* (Chicago: University of Chicago Press, 1984 reprint), p. 9.

5. Niccolò Machiavelli, *The Prince*, trans. Harvey Mansfield (Chicago: University of Chicago Press, 1985), ch. 18, p. 70. For more examples, see Harvey Mansfield, *Machiavelli's Virtue*, pp. 288–91. As Skinner also notes, "when Machiavelli speaks of his desire to advise 'a prince wishing to maintain his state' (*uno principe volendo mantenere lo stato*), what he usually has in mind is the traditional [medieval] idea of the prince maintaining his existing position and range of powers."

Skinner, *The Foundations*, vol. II, p. 354. But the all-important innovation of Machiavelli's thought is the prince maintaining his existing position and range of powers *against Christianity and its morality.*

6. Machiavelli, *The Prince*, ch. 15, p. 61.

7. Ibid., ch. 18, p. 70.

8. The classic account of this esoteric way of writing is Leo Strauss's *Persecution and the Art of Writing* (Chicago: University of Chicago Press, 1988). Admittedly, some of Strauss's pupils have taken his insights too far and applied them where they are not, in fact, applicable.

9. See especially Niccolò Machiavelli, *Discourses on Livy*, trans. Harvey Mansfield and Nathan Tarcov (Chicago: University of Chicago Press, 1996), I.11.1–3 and I.12.1. See Livy himself, *History of Rome*, I, xix, 4–5, as well as Plutarch, *Parallel Lives*, Numa, iv.7–8 and Polybius, *Histories*, VI, 56.6–13.

10. On this see the immensely insightful account of the "invention of religion" by William Cavanaugh, *The Myth of Religious Violence: Secular Ideology and the Roots of Modern Conflict* (Oxford: Oxford University Press, 2009), ch. 2.

11. See Maurizio Viroli, *From Politics to Reason of State: The Acquisition of Transformation of the Language of Politics, 1250–1600* (Cambridge: Cambridge University Press, 1992).

12. See Peter Gay's classic *The Enlightenment: An Interpretation, The Rise of Modern Paganism* (New York: Norton, 1977).

13. Machiavelli, *Discourses on Livy*, II.2.2, pp. 131–32.

14. Ibid.

15. Ibid.

16. See Mansfield, *Machiavelli's Virtue.*

17. Machiavelli, *Discourses on Livy*, II.2.2, pp. 131–32.

18. See Jonah Goldberg, *Liberal Fascism: The Secret History of the American Left, from Mussolini to the Politics of Change* (New York: Broadway Books, 2008).

Chapter 7: From Henry VIII to Thomas Hobbes: the State Church, Leviathan, and the Sovereign Individual

1. For an overview of the case for Machiavelli's influence in Henry VIII's court and the attendant scholarly disputes see W. Gordon Zeeveld, *Foundations of Tudor Policy* (London: Methuen & Co., Ltd., 1969), Peter Donaldson, *Machiavelli and Mystery of State* (Cambridge: Cambridge University Press, 1988), Felix Raab, *The English Face of Machiavelli* (London: Routledge & Kegan Paul, 1964), and Victoria Kahn, *Machiavellian Rhetoric From the Counter-Reformation to Milton* (Princeton: Princeton University Press, 1994).

2. Gerald Bray, ed., *Documents of the English Reformation* (Minneapolis, MN: Fortress Press, 1994), pp. 113–14.

3. For an account of the Great Bible and the fate of Cromwell, who would later be "erased" from the frontispiece Soviet-style, see Benson Bobrick, *Wide as the Waters: the Story of the English Bible and the Revolution It Inspired* (New York: Simon & Schuster, 2001), pp. 150–57.

4. William Cavanaugh, *The Myth of Religious Violence: Secular Ideology and the Roots of Modern Conflict* (Oxford: Oxford University Press, 2009), p. 175.

5. John Bossy, *Christianity in the West, 1400–1700* (Oxford: Oxford University Press, 1985), ch. 8, and Cavanaugh, *The Myth of Religious Violence*, pp. 174–75.

6. Ioannis Evrigenis, *Fear of Enemies and Collective Action* (Cambridge: Cambridge University Press, 2007), p. 82.

7. On this tumultuous period see Christopher Hill's excellent *The World Turned Upside Down: Radical Ideas During the English Revolution* (London: Penguin Books, reprint 1991).

8. Thomas Hobbes, *Hobbes's Leviathan*, reprint of the 1651 edition of *Leviathan, or The Matter, Forme, & Power of a Common-Wealth Ecclesiasticall and Civill* (Oxford: Clarendon Press, 1965), IV.46, p. 524 [371]; and see also III.34, pp. 302–3 [207]. I've corrected Hobbes's interesting spelling to our standards. The numbers in brackets refer to the standard pagination, so that readers can find pages in other editions.

9. Thomas Hobbes, *Leviathan*, I.6, pp. 39–41 [23–24]. See also I.15, p. 122–23 [79–80].

10. Ibid., I.13, p. 97 [62].

11. Ibid., I.14, p. 99 [64].

12. Ibid., I.13, p. 98 [63].

13. Ibid., I.13, pp. 94–97 [60–62].

14. Ibid., II.29, p. 253 [171].

15. Ibid., II.17, p. 132 [87–88].

16. Ibid., I.11, pp. 80–81 [51].

17. Ibid., II.31, p. 283 [193].

18. Ibid., III.33, p. 291 [199].

19. Ibid., III.33, p. 291–92 [199].

20. Ibid., III.32, p. 288 [196–97].

21. Ibid., III.37, p. 339 [234].

22. Ibid., III.32, p. 289 [197].

23. Ibid., III.32, pp. 290–92 [197–98].

24. Ibid., III.37, p. 344 [237].

25. Ibid., III.39, p.361–62 [247–48].
26. Ibid., III.39, pp. 362–63 [248].
27. Ibid., III.42 pp. 421–27 [295–99].
28. With his characteristic bluntness, Hobbes informs the reader, "It is impossible a Common-wealth should stand, where any other than the Sovereign, has a power of giving greater rewards than Life; and of inflicting greater punishments, than Death. Now seeing *Eternal life* is a greater reward, than the *life present*; and *Eternal torment* a greater punishment than the *death of Nature*; It is a thing worthy to be well considered, of all men that desire (by obeying Authority) to avoid the calamities of Confusion, and Civill war, what is meant in holy Scripture, by *Life Eternal*, and *Torment Eternal*; and for what offences, and against whom committed, men are to be *Eternally tormented*; and for what actions, they are to obtain *Eternal life*." Ibid., III.38, p. 345 [238].
29. Ibid., III.35, pp. 318–19 [219].
30. Ibid., III.38, pp. 348–50 [240–41]. See also III.38, p. 355 [244–45] and IV.44, pp. 486–90 [343–46].
31. *Planned Parenthood v. Casey* (1992), 851.
32. See my *Moral Darwinism: How We Became Hedonists* (Downers Grove, IL: Inter-Varsity Press, 2002), chs. 7–8.

Chapter 8: Spinoza: the Liberal Elite and the Established Secular Church

1. For an account of Spinoza's life see Yirmiyahu Yovel, *Spinoza and Other Heretics: The Marrano of Reason* (Princeton, NJ: Princeton University Press, 1989); Margaret Gullan-Whur, *Within Reason: A Life of Spinoza* (New York: St. Martin's Press, 1998); and Steven Nadler, *Spinoza: A Life* (Cambridge: Cambridge University Press, 1999).
2. For the formal charge of excommunication see Yovel, *Spinoza and Other Heretics*, p. 3. For a more in-depth analysis see Asa Kasher and Shlomo Biderman, "Why was Baruch de Spinoza Excommunicated?" in David Katz and Jonathan Israel, *Sceptics, Millenarians and Jews* (Leiden: E. J. Brill, 1990), pp. 98–141.
3. On Machiavelli's influence see Steven Nadler, *Spinoza: A Life* (Cambridge: Cambridge University Press, 1999), especially pp. 111, 270; Steven Smith, *Spinoza, Liberalism, and the Question of Jewish Identity* (New Haven, CT: Yale, 1997), pp. 34–38; Eco Mulier, *The Myth of Venice and Dutch Republican Thought in the Seventeenth Century* (Assen, Netherlands: Van Gorcum, 1980), pp. 170–81; Edwin Curley, "Kissinger, Spinoza, and Ghengis Kahn," in Don Garrett, ed., *The Cambridge Companion to Spinoza* (Cambridge: Cambridge University Press, 1996), pp. 315–42.

4. Curley, "Kissinger, Spinoza, and Ghengis Kahn," p. 143. Curley bases this assessment in part upon the startling similarity between the opening two paragraphs of Spinoza's *Political Treatise* and chapter XV of Machiavelli's *Prince*, wherein both authors embrace the notion that politics should be based upon how men actually act rather than any notion of how they ought to act. Ibid., pp. 154–55.

5. Benedict Spinoza, *A Political Treatise*, V.7, included in Benedict de Spinoza, *A Theologico-Political Treatise and A Political Treatise*, trans. R. H. M. Elwes (New York: Dover, 1951).

6. For an account of this radical circle of friends and the influence of Hobbes among them, see Travis Frampton, *Spinoza and the Rise of Historical Criticism of the Bible* (London: Clark, 2006), ch. 6; Smith, *Spinoza, Liberalism, and the Question of Jewish Identity* (New Haven, CT: Yale, 1997), pp. 122–30; Edwin Curley, "The State of Nature and Its Law in Hobbes and Spinoza," *Philosophical Topics* 19 (1991):97–117, reprinted in Genevieve Lloyd, ed., *Spinoza: Critical Assessments*, vol. 3 (London and New York: Routledge, 2001), pp. 122–42; Curley, "Kissinger, Spinoza, and Ghengis Kahn"; and Robert McShea, *The Political Philosophy of Spinoza* (New York: Columbia University Press, 1968), ch. IX.

7. Benedict Spinoza, *Ethics*, I, Props. 7, 11, 14, from the translation by Samuel Shirley included in Baruch Spinoza, *Ethics; Treatise on the Emendation of the Intellect; and Selected Letters* (Indianapolis, IN: Hackett Publishing, 1992).

8. On the deification of human beings see Benedict Spinoza, *Ethics*, II, Prop. 10 and Corollary.

9. Benedict Spinoza, *Ethics*, II, Prop. 40, Scholium 2.

10. Yovel, *Spinoza and Other Heretics*, p. 130. For a detailed account of Spinoza's reformulation of Scripture see Scott Hahn and Benjamin Wiker, *Politicizing the Bible: The Roots of Historical Criticism and the Secularization of Scripture 1300–1700* (New York: Crossroad Publishing, 2013).

11. Benedict Spinoza, *Theologico-Political Treatise*, trans. Martin Yaffe (Newburyport, MA: R. Pullins & Company, 2004), Preface, 1.7. In the notes below, the numbers refer to the chapter, paragraph, and sentence number rather than the page number of this translation.

12. Ibid., 6.1.54.

13. Ibid., 6.1.64.

14. Ibid, Preface, 1.7 and 2.3.

15. Smith, *Spinoza, Liberalism, and the Question of Jewish Identity*, p. 56.

16. Spinoza, *Theologico-Political Treatise*, trans. Yaffe, 6.1.33–34.

17. Ibid., 6.1.17. Emphasis added.

18.   H. Richard Niebuhr, *The Kingdom of God in America* (Middleton, CT: Wesleyan University Press, 1989), p. 193.

19.   Spinoza, *Theologico-Political Treatise*, trans. Yaffe, 13.1.2–4.

20.   Ibid., 13.1.9–10.

21.   Ibid., 14.1.15.

22.   Ibid., 14.1.13.

23.   Ibid., 14.1.14.

24.   Ibid., 14.1.54.

25.   Ibid., 14.1.25.

26.   Ibid., 18.4.5, and all of 20.

27.   Ibid., 19.1.2.

28.   See ibid., 16.8.18.

29.   On the connection to Hobbes in this regard see Edwin Curley, "The State of Nature and Its Law in Hobbes and Spinoza," *Philosophical Topics* 19 (1991):97–117, reprinted in Genevieve Lloyd, ed., *Spinoza: Critical Assessments. Volume III*, pp. 122–42; Curley, "Kissinger, Spinoza, and Ghengis Kahn"; Robert McShea, *The Political Philosophy of Spinoza* (New York: Columbia University Press, 1968), ch. IX.

30.   Ibid., 16.1.3.

31.   Ibid., 16.8.2–5, 16.2.8. Spinoza points to Romans 5:13, where St. Paul maintains that "there is no sin before there is law."

Chapter 9: Rousseau's Radical Liberalism: Establishing Civil Religion

1.   Jean-Jacques Rousseau, *Discourse on the Origin and Foundations of Inequality among Men* in Roger Masters, trans. and ed., *The First and Second Discourses* (New York: St. Martin's Press, 1964).

2.   Ibid., p. 105.

3.   Ibid., pp. 203–213, n. j. Rousseau's account is obviously indebted to the evolutionary arguments in *De Rerum Natura* by the Roman Epicurean Lucretius in the first century BC.

4.   Rousseau, *Discourse on the Origin and Foundations of Inequality*, p. 110.

5.   Ibid., p. 117.

6.   Ibid., p. 115.

7.   Ibid., pp. 92–93.

8.   Ibid., pp. 105, 111–12, 118–19, 133.

9.   Ibid., p. 116.

10.   Ibid., pp. 120–21, 137.

11.   Ibid., pp. 126, 134–35, and especially 218–20.

12. Ibid., p. 126.

13. Ibid., p. 128.

14. Ibid., p. 193.

15. Ibid., pp. 138–39, 154–55.

16. Ibid., pp. 138–40, 146–47.

17. This is especially vivid in Rousseau's first important public piece, the *Discourse on the Sciences and Arts*, also in Roger Masters, trans. and ed., *The First and Second Discourses* (New York: St. Martin's Press, 1964). See especially pp. 36–38, 41–46, 54–58.

18. Jean-Jacques Rousseau, *On the Social Contract*, ed. Roger Masters, trans. Judith Masters (New York: St. Martin's Press, 1978), III.vi, p. 88.

19. Ibid., IV.viii, pp. 124–26.

20. Ibid., IV.viii, p. 126.

21. Ibid., IV.viii, p. 126.

22. Ibid., IV.viii, p. 127.

23. Ibid., IV.viii, p. 127, Rousseau's footnote.

24. Ibid., IV.viii, p. 127.

25. Ibid., IV.viii, pp. 128–30.

26. Ibid., IV.viii, pp. 130–31.

27. Ibid., I.vii, p. 55.

28. Ibid., IV.viii, p. 131, Rousseau's footnote.

29. Ibid., IV.viii, p. 132.

Chapter 10: Liberalism Triumphs in the Modern World

1. Isaiah Berlin, "Two Concepts of Liberty," *Four Essays on Liberty* (Oxford: Oxford University Press, 1958), p. 21, n. 47.

2. The atoms Hobbes postulated are not atoms as modern science has actually found them to be. For more on atoms in philosophy and science, including an argument that contemporary physics and chemistry actually provide evidence for God's existence, rather than for materialism, see my *A Meaningful World: How the Arts and Sciences Reveal the Genius of Nature* (Downers Grove, IL: IVP, 2006).

3. See my *Moral Darwinism: How We Became Hedonists* (Downers Grove, IL: IVP, 2002).

4. Plato, *The Republic of Plato*, trans. Allan Bloom, 2nd ed. (New York: Basic Books, 1991), 557b–563e.

5. See my *The Darwin Myth: The Life and Lies of Charles Darwin* (Washington, DC: Regnery, 2009).

6. Peter Gay, *The Enlightenment: An Interpretation, the Rise of Modern Paganism* (New York: Norton, 1977), p. 59.

7. See especially Simon Schama's *Citizens: A Chronicle of the French Revolution* (New York: Alfred A. Knopf, 1989), ch. 17–19, and Michael Burleigh, *Earthly Powers: The Clash of Religion and Politics in Europe from the French Revolution to the Great War* (HarperCollins, 2005), ch. 3.

8. On the actual numbers slaughtered, and the attempt by scholars to decrease them see Schama, *Citizens*, pp. 791–92.

9. Burleigh, *Earthly Powers*, p. 97.

10. As readers are unlikely to read through—or even to have access to—the volumes of Comte's ponderous *Cours de philosophie positive*, I will refer to the introductory chapters where Comte outlines everything for the reader. These are available in August Comte, *Introduction to Positive Philosophy* (Indianapolis, IN: Hackett, 1988). On Comte's stages or "states" (states of mind, not political states) see pp. 1–4.

11. Comte, *Introduction to Positive Philosophy*, pp. 12–13.

12. On the relationship between Comte's bizarre behavior and his philosophy, see Burleigh pp. 228–32.

13. See the insightful essay by Jeffrey Hadden, "Toward Desacralizing Secularization Theory," *Social Forces* 65:3 (March 1987), pp. 587–611.

Chapter 11: Sorting Out Some Confusions

1. See Hayek's famous essay, "Why I Am Not a Conservative" appended to his *Constitution of Liberty* (Chicago: University of Chicago Press, 1960).

2. Quoted in Chadwick, *The Secularization of the European Mind in the 19th Century* (Cambridge: Cambridge University Press, 2000), p. 10.

3. Quoted in Owen Chadwick, *The Secularization of the European Mind*, p. 104.

4. R. W. Scribner and C. Scott Dixon, *The German Reformation*, p. 36. This is also the conclusion of W. D. J. Cargill Thompson, *The Political Thought of Martin Luther*, p. 154.

5. Bob Scribner, Roy Porter, and Mikuláš Teich, *The Reformation in National Context*, p. 9.

6. See, for example, J. W. McKenna, "How God became an Englishman," *Tudor Rule and Revolution: Essays for G. R. Elton*, ed. D. J. Guth and J. W. McKenna (Cambridge, 1982), pp. 25–43; Joseph R. Strayer, "France: The Holy Land, the Chosen People, and the Most Christian King," in Joseph Strayer, *Medieval Statecraft and the Perspectives of History* (Princeton: Princeton University Press, 1971), pp. 300–311, W. Bradford Smith, "Germanic Pagan Antiquity in Lutheran Historical

Thought," *Journal of the Historical Society* IV (2004):3, pp. 351–374, and A. G. Dickens, *The German Nation and Martin Luther* (London: Edward Arnold, 1974).

7. G. W. Hegel, *The Philosophy of Right*, translated by T. M. Knox, section 272, p. 218.

8. Quoted in Burleigh, *Earthly Powers*, p. 160.

9. Quoted in ibid., p. 189.

10. Quoted in ibid., p. 189.

11. Ibid., p. 145. On nationalism as a religion see also the excellent discussion in William Cavanaugh, *The Myth of Religious Violence: Secular Ideology and the Roots of Modern Conflict* (Oxford: Oxford University Press, 2009).

12. Burleigh, *Earthly Powers*, p. 199.

13. Chadwick, *The Secularization of the European Mind*, p. 93.

14. Hugh McLeod, *Secularization in Western Europe, 1848–1914* (New York: St. Martin's Press, 2000), p. 61.

15. For this period in France see McLeod, *Secularization in Western Europe*, pp. 59–67.

Chapter 12: John Locke and the Two Faces of Liberalism

1. Must reading, in this regard, is Jonathan Israel, *Radical Enlightenment: Philosophy and the Making of Modernity 1650–1750* (Oxford: Oxford University Press, 2001).

2. On the ambiguity of Locke see Leo Strauss, *Natural Right and History* (Chicago: University of Chicago Press, 1953), Ch. V, and *What is Political Philosophy?* (Chicago: University of Chicago Press, 1988), chs. I, VII, VIII; Paul Rahe, *Republics Ancient & Modern*, vol. II, *New Modes and Orders in Early Modern Political Thought* (Chapel Hill, NC: University of North Carolina Press, 1994), esp. pp. 62–75; Thomas Pangle, *The Spirit of Modern Republicanism: The Moral Vision of the American Founders and the Philosophy of Locke* (Chicago: University of Chicago Press, 1988), chs. 13–21.

3. John Locke, *Second Treatise* in *Two Treatises of Government*, ed. Thomas Cook (New York: Hafner Press, 1947), II.4–8.

4. Ibid., II.4.

5. Ibid., II.4, 6–7.

6. Ibid., III.16–21.

7. Ibid., V.25–37.

8. Ibid., IX.123.

9. See the fine account of the radical mayhem in Christopher Hill, *The World Turned Upside Down: Radical Ideas During the English Revolution* (London: Penguin Books, reprint 1991).

10. On Locke as a member of England's revolutionary party against the king, see the insightful Richard Ashcraft, *Revolutionary Politics & Locke's Two Treatises of Government* (Princeton: Princeton University Press, 1986).

11. See the chapter on Locke in Hahn and Wiker, *Politicizing the Bible*.

12. John Locke, *The Reasonableness of Christianity as Delivered in the Scriptures*, ed. George Ewing (Washington, DC: Regnery, 1965), section 243. See also section 252.

13. John Locke, *The Reasonableness of Christianity*, section 243.

14. John Locke, *A Letter Concerning Toleration*, translated by William Popple (London, 1689), reprinted and edited by James Tully (Indianapolis, IN: Hackett Publishing Company, 1983), p. 23.

15. Ibid., pp. 23–24.

16. Ibid., pp. 26–27. Locke calls this "the *principal Consideration*…which absolutely determines this Controversie…." (p. 38).

17. Ibid., p. 27.

18. Ibid., p. 28.

19. Ibid., p. 47.

20. Jean-Jacques Rousseau, *Discourse on the Origin and Foundations of Inequality among Men*, pp. 154–60.

21. See the trenchant account by Owen Chadwick, *The Secularization of the European Mind in the 19th Century*, ch. 3, especially sections 5–6.

22. Owen Chadwick, *The Secularization of the European Mind in the Nineteenth Century*, pp. 81–82.

23. Ibid., pp. 90–91.

24. Michael Burleigh, *Earthly Powers*, p. 243.

25. Robert Owen, "A New View of Society," Preface. Owen's essay is helpfully available on Yale Law School's online Avalon Project, http://avalon.law.yale.edu/19th_century/owenpref.asp.

26. Ibid.

27. Michael Burleigh, *Earthly Powers*, pp. 239–40.

28. Quoted in Burleigh, *Earthly Powers*, p. 240.

29. Chadwick, *The Secularization of the European Mind*, p. 91.

30. Quoted in Michael Burleigh, *Earthly Powers*, p. 270.

31. Hugh McLeod, *Secularization in Western Europe, 1848–1914*, p. 46.

32. Ibid., *1848–1914*, p. 119.

33. Ibid., p. 119.

34. Again, readers interested in a very in-depth analysis of the rise of modern historical-critical scholarship, please see Hahn and Wiker, *Politicizing the Bible*.

35. David Friedrich Strauss, *The Life of Jesus Critically Examined*, 4th edition, Peter Hodgson, ed. (Philadelphia, PA: Fortress, 1972), section 16, introduction, pp. 87–88.
36. Ibid., section 151, p. 780.

Chapter 13: The First Wave: Locke, Deism, and the Founders

1. *Everson v. Board of Education* (1947): 330 US 16.
2. Daniel Dreisbach, *Thomas Jefferson and the Wall of Separation between Church and State* (New York: New York University Press, 2002), pp. 3–5.
3. When Justice Hugo Black repeats the famous phrase from Thomas Jefferson's 1802 letter to the Danbury Baptist Association in *Everson*, he cites *Reynolds v. United States*, as if *Reynolds* provided the needed precedent for Black's insistence that Jefferson's musings are the definitive interpretation of the First Amendment. *Everson v. Board of Education* (1947) 330 US 16; *Reynolds v. United States* (1878) 98 US 164. The focus of *Reynolds* is whether polygamy must be allowed for Mormons as a matter of religious liberty. The court quoted Jefferson to affirm that the federal government could not establish religion (and hence could not consider Mormons heretics), but "Congress...was left free to reach actions which were in violation of social duties or subversive of good order." Polygamy was a moral violation, not a religious right: "Polygamy has always been odious among the northern and western nations of Europe, and, until the establishment of the Mormon Church, was almost exclusively a feature of the life of Asiatic and of African people."
4. The actual words of the First Amendment mean exactly what they say and no more: the national Congress is not allowed to establish a national religion, nor can the national Congress prohibit the exercise of any religion. The secular and secularizing notion, pushed by Black using Jefferson—that it is the national government's job to actively secularize America by putting churches behind a wall to separate them from the public sphere—is not in the First Amendment.
5. The following, from Jefferson's private notebooks, was written sometime in the fall of 1776: "A heretic is an impugner of fundamentals. What are fundamental? The protestants will say those doctrines which are clearly & precisely delivered in the holy scriptures. Dr. Waterland would say the Trinity. But how far this character [of being clearly & precisely delivered] will suit the doctrine of the Trinity I leave others to determine. It is no where expressly declared by any of the earliest fathers, & was never affirmed or taught by the church before the council of Nice [i.e., Nicaea]." Thomas Jefferson, "Notes on Heresy" in Lenni

Brenner, ed., *Jefferson & Madison on Separation of Church and State: Writings on Religion and Secularism* (Fort Lee, NJ: Barricade Books, 2004), p. 36.

6. Jefferson's version of the Bible, unsurprisingly, ends with a verse patched together from bits of the Gospels of John and Matthew: "There laid they Jesus [John 19:42] and…rolled a great stone to the door of the sepulcher, and departed [Matthew 27:60]." There is no resurrection. Thomas Jefferson, *The Jefferson Bible: The Life and Morals of Jesus of Nazareth Extracted Textually from the Gospels in Greek, Latin, French & English* (Washington, DC: Smithsonian Books, 2011), p. 82.

7. Thomas Jefferson to Dr. Benjamin Rush, April 21, 1803, in Lenni Brenner, ed., *Jefferson & Madison on Separation of Church and State*, p. 168.

8. Thomas Jefferson, "Syllabus of an Estimate of the Merit of the Doctrines of Jesus, compared with those of others" (April 21, 1803), I.1–2, in Lenni Brenner, ed., *Jefferson & Madison on Separation of Church and State*, p. 169.

9. Ibid., II.1–2, p. 170.

10. Ibid., III.1–2, p. 170.

11. Ibid., III.4–5, p. 170.

12. Ibid., III.3, p. 170.

13. Ibid., III.5, p. 170.

14. Thomas Jefferson, Letter to William Short (August 4, 1820) included in Lenni Brenner, ed., *Jefferson & Madison on Separation of Church and State*, p. 339.

15. Thomas Jefferson, Letter to Jacob de la Motta (September 1, 1820) in Lenni Brenner, ed., *Jefferson & Madison on Separation of Church and State*, p. 342.

16. James Madison, Federalist X, in Alexander Hamilton, James Madison, and John Jay, *The Federalist* (Washington, DC: Regnery, 1998), p. 112.

17. Letter to John Adams, April 11, 1823, in Thomas Jefferson, *Letters and Addresses of Thomas Jefferson*, William Parker, ed. (New York: Wessels, 1907), p. 274.

18. Rousseau, *On the Social Contract*, p. 131.

19. Thomas Jefferson, *Notes on the State of Virginia*, Query XVII, excerpted in Lenni Brenner, ed., *Jefferson & Madison on Separation of Church and State*, p. 54.

20. Ibid., Query XVII, p. 56.

21. Ibid., Query XVII, p. 54.

22. Thomas Jefferson, First Inaugural Address, March 4, 1801, and Second Inaugural Address, March 4, 1805.

23. Thomas Jefferson, Letter to the Danbury Baptist Association, January 1, 1802.

24. See Wainwright's Introduction to John Locke, *A Paraphrase and Notes on the Epistles of St. Paul to the Galatians, I and 2 Corinthians, Romans, Ephesians*, ed. Arthur Wainwright (Oxford: Clarendon Press, 1987).

25. Locke, *Second Treatise*, V.37, 41–42, 49.

26. Ibid., V.32–34, 40, 43.
27. Ibid., VIII.95; IX.123.
28. Alexis de Tocqueville, *Democracy in America*, trans. and ed. with an introduction by Harvey Mansfield and Delba Winthrop (Chicago, IL: University of Chicago Press, 2000), Vol. II, Part 2, Ch. 11, pp. 506–8.
29. Ibid., vol. II, part 2, ch. 15, p. 519.
30. Ibid., vol. II, part 2, ch. 11, p. 509.
31. Ibid., vol. II, part 2, ch. 11, p. 509. The alternative translation is that of Henry Reeve (New York: Random, 1990), II.11, pp. 132–33.

Chapter 14: The Second Wave: Radicals at the Universities

1. George Marsden, *The Soul of the American University: From Protestant Establishment to Established Nonbelief* (Oxford: Oxford University Press, 1994), p. 104.
2. Ibid., p. 104.
3. Ibid., p. 106.
4. Quoted in ibid., pp. 114–15.
5. See Christian Smith, "Introduction: Rethinking the Secularization of American Public Life," in Christian Smith, ed., *The Secular Revolution: Power, Interests, and Conflict in the Secularization of American Public Life* (Berkeley, CA: University of California Press, 2003), pp. 36–37. I highly recommend Smith's book to anyone interested in the intentional secularization of American culture, and I acknowledge my indebtedness to his arguments and detailed analyses in this present chapter.
6. Smith, "Introduction," p. 37.
7. The words of the act are available on Cornell University Law School's website, "7 USC § 304—Investment of proceeds of sale of land or scrip," http://www.law.cornell.edu/uscode/text/7/304.
8. Quoted in Christian Smith, "Secularizing American Higher Education: the Case of Early American Sociology," in Smith, ed., *The Secular Revolution*, p. 107.
9. Hahn and Wiker, *Politicizing the Bible*.
10. On Kinsey, see my *Ten Books That Screwed Up the World, and Five Others That Didn't Help* (Washington, DC: Regnery, 2008).
11. On the connection between sociology and progressivism in politics see Gillis Harp, *Positivist Republic: Auguste Comte and the Reconstruction of American Liberalism, 1865–1920*.
12. Smith, "Secularizing American Higher Education," p. 106. See also Dorothy Ross, *The Origins of American Social Science* (Cambridge: Cambridge University Press, 1991), ch. 7.

13.   Ibid. p. 111.

14.   On Ward's early life see Harp, *Positivist Republic*, ch. 5.

15.   Ibid., p. 118.

16.   Ibid., pp. 120–21.

17.   Quoted in ibid., p. 141.

18.   See ibid., pp. 144–49.

19.   Ibid., p. 123.

20.   Ibid., pp. 123–27.

21.   Smith, "Secularizing American Higher Education," p. 112.

22.   Ibid., p. 119.

23.   Ibid., p. 122.

24.   Both quoted in ibid., p. 123.

25.   Quoted in ibid., p. 124.

26.   Quoted in ibid., p. 125.

27.   Both Ross's and Smith's words come from ibid., p. 147.

28.   Smith, "Introduction," p. 1.

29.   Ibid., p. 34.

30.   Ibid., p. 37.

31.   Ibid., p. 53.

32.   Ibid., pp. 32–33.

Chapter 15: Secularization, American Style

1.   *Everson v. Board of Education* (1947): 330 U.S. 16.

2.   Ibid., (1947): 330 U.S. 8–14.

3.   John Jeffries Jr., and James Ryan, "A Political History of the Establishment Clause," *Michigan Law Review*, November 2001, Vol. 100:279–370. Quote from 297.

4.   My analysis is indebted to the excellent article by John Jeffries Jr. and James Ryan, "A Political History of the Establishment Clause," noted above.

5.   Ibid., pp. 281–82.

6.   Ibid., p. 282.

7.   Ibid., pp. 300–2. A sign of this is that the "Blaine Amendment," proposed for the Constitution (and almost passed), in declaring that "No State shall make any law respecting an establishment of religion" actually meant that no state shall in any way fund a "sectarian" (i.e. Catholic) school.

8.   Ibid., p. 300, n. 105.

9.   Ibid., p. 298.

10. *School District of Abington Township, Pennsylvania v. Schempp* (1963), 374 U.S. 313.

11. See Michael Burleigh's excellent treatments of active and brutal secularization via the separation of church and state in the previously cited *Earthly Powers*, pp. 95–107, 314–15, 336–64, and *Sacred Causes: The Clash of Religion and Politics, from the Great War to the War on Terror* (New York: HarperCollins, 2007), pp. 46–54, 124–34.

Chapter 16: Disestablishing Secular Liberalism

1. For an excellent discussion of these approaches to defining religion, see William Cavanaugh, *The Myth of Religious Violence: Secular Ideology and the Roots of Modern Conflict* (Oxford: Oxford University Press, 2009), esp. pp. 43, 55, 102–22.

2. Alasdair MacIntyre, in his works, *After Virtue: A Study in Moral Theory*, 2nd ed. (Notre Dame, IN: University of Notre Dame Press, 1984); *Whose Justice? Which Rationality?* (Notre Dame, IN: University of Notre Dame Press, 1988); and *Three Rival Versions of Moral Inquiry: Encylopaedia, Genealogy, and Tradition* (Notre Dame, IN: University of Notre Dame Press, 1990).

3. Bob Unruh, "Tab For Refusing To Photograph Lesbians: $6,600," WorldNetDaily, December 17, 2009, http://www.wnd.com/2009/12/119282/.

4. For the secularization of legal education in America see David Sikkink, "From Christian Civilization to Individual Civil Liberties: Framing Religion in the Legal Field, 1880–1949," in Christian Smith, ed., *The Secular Revolution: Power, Interests, and Conflict in the Secularization of American Public Life* (Berkeley, CA: University of California Press, 2003), Ch. 7.

5. John Jeffries Jr., and James Ryan, "A Political History of the Establishment Clause," pp. 287–91.

6. Kraig Beyerlein, "Educational Elites and the Movement to Secularize Public Education: The Case of the National Education Association," in Christian Smith, ed., *The Secular Revolution: Power, Interests, and Conflict in the Secularization of American Public Life*, p. 193.

7. On the origin of the university in Medieval Christendom, see David Knowles, *The Evolution of Medieval Thought*, 2nd ed. (London: Longman, 1988), chs. 13–14, Edward Grant, *God and Reason in the Middle Ages* (Cambridge: Cambridge University Press, 2001); Olaf Pedersen, *The First Universities: Studium Generale and the Origins of University Education in Europe* (Cambridge: Cambridge University Press, 2009); Thomas Woods, *How the Catholic Church Built Western Civilization* (Washington, DC: Regnery, 2005), ch. 4.

8. On the debunking of the warfare thesis by current scholars see my *The Catholic Church & Science: Answering the Questions and Exposing the Myths* (Charlotte, NC: TAN, 2011), chs. 1–3; Ronald Numbers, ed., *Galileo Goes To Jail, and Other Myths about Science and Religion* (Cambridge, MA: Harvard University Press, 2009), Introduction and ch. 2; David Lindberg and Ronald Numbers, eds., *God and Nature: Historical Essays on the Encounter between Christianity and Science* (Berkeley, CA: University of California Press, 1986), Introduction; Dana Lindberg and Ronald Numbers, "Beyond War and Peace: A Reappraisal of the Encounter between Christianity and Science," *Perspectives on Science and Christian Faith* 39.3:140–49; James Hannam, *God's Philosophers: How the Medieval World Laid the Foundations of Modern Science* (London: Icon, 2009).

9. Michael Shank, "That the Medieval Christian Church Suppressed the Growth of Science," in Ronald Numbers, ed., *Galileo Goes to Jail, and Other Myths about Science and Religion*, ch. 2, pp. 21–22.

10. Ibid., pp. 26–27.

11. I am indebted to Matthew White's *The Great Big Book of Horrible Things: The Definitive Chronicle of History's 100 Worst Atrocities* (New York: Norton, 2012).

12. See the excellent study, and synopsis of the literature in William Cavanaugh, *The Myth of Religious Violence: Secular Ideology and the Roots of Modern Conflict* (Oxford: Oxford University Press, 2009), ch. 3.

13. Quoted in a Chuck Baldwin interview with David Horowitz, Chuck Baldwin Live Talk Radio, June 6, 1997, available on chuckbaldwinline.com, http://www.chuckbaldwinlive.com/horowitz.html.

14. Kathryn Jean Lopez, "This Denver Family Is Not Entitled to Religious Freedom, Obama's DOJ Argues," National Review Online, September 26, 2012, http://www.nationalreview.com/corner/328602/denver-family-not-entitled-religious-freedom-obamas-doj-argues-kathryn-jean-lopez.

INDEX